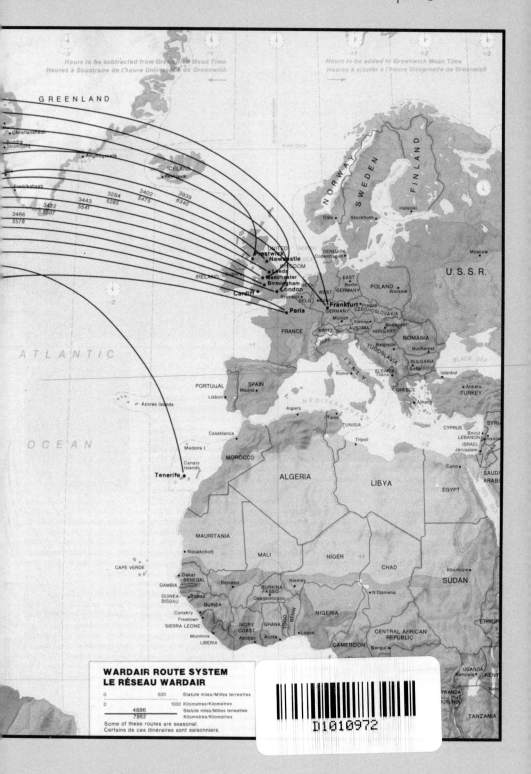

GREENLAND

Christianshaab
Sondre
Stromfjord

Angmagssalik

ICELAND
Reykjavik

Frederikshaab

3284   3402   3939
5285   5475   6340
3443
5541
3466   3422
5578   5507

NORWAY   SWEDEN   FINLAND

Oslo   Stockholm   Helsinki

Moscow

IRELAND   Dublin

UNITED
Prestwick
Newcastle   KINGDOM
Leeds
Manchester
Birmingham
London
Cardiff
Brussels
BELG

DENMARK
Copenhagen

EAST
Berlin   POLAND   Warsaw
WEST
GERMANY
Frankfurt   Prague
GERMANY   CZECHOSLOVAKIA
Munich   Vienna   Budapest
SWITZ   AUSTRIA   HUNGARY
ITALY   YUGOSLAVIA   ROMANIA
Bucharest
Belgrade
BULGARIA
Sofia
ALBANIA
Rome   Tirana   Istanbul
GREECE   Ankara
Athens   TURKEY

U.S.S.R.

Paris

FRANCE

BLACK SEA

Moscow

ATLANTIC

PORTUGAL   SPAIN
Lisbon   Madrid

MEDITERRANEAN SEA

Algiers
Tunis
TUNISIA
Tripoli

CYPRUS
Beirut
LEBANON   Damascus
ISRAEL
Jerusalem   JORDAN

SYRIA

Azores Islands

Casablanca

Madeira I.

Canary
Islands
Tenerife

MOROCCO

OCEAN

Cairo
SAUDI
ARABIA
EGYPT

ALGERIA   LIBYA

CAPE VERDE

MAURITANIA

Nouakchott

MALI   NIGER   CHAD

Khartoum
SUDAN

Dakar
GAMBIA   SENEGAL   Bamako
GUINEA-
BISSAU   Bissau
Conakry   GUINEA
Freetown
SIERRA LEONE   IVORY
Monrovia   COAST
LIBERIA   Abidjan   Accra   Lagos
GHANA

BURKINA
FASSO   Niamey
Ouagadougou
N'Djamena

BENIN
NIGERIA
TOGO

CENTRAL AFRICAN
REPUBLIC
CAMEROON   Bangui

ETHIOP

UGANDA
Kampala   KENY

RWANDA   Nai
BURUNDI

TANZANIA

WARDAIR ROUTE SYSTEM
LE RÉSEAU WARDAIR

0   500   Statute miles/Milles terrestres
0   1000 Kilometres/Kilomètres
    4886   Statute miles/Milles terrestres
    7863   Kilometres/Kilomètres
Some of these routes are seasonal.
Certains de ces itinéraires sont saisonniers.

−3   −2   −1   +1   +2   +3
Hours to be subtracted from Greenwich Mean Time
Heures à Soustraire de l'heure Universelle de Greenwich
Hours to be added to Greenwich Mean Time
Heures à ajouter à l'heure Universelle de Greenwich

THE
MAX WARD
STORY

T H E

MAX WARD

S T O R Y

A Bush Pilot in the
Bureaucratic Jungle

by MAX WARD

M&S

Canadian Cataloguing in Publication Data

Ward, Max, 1921-
The Max Ward story

Includes index.
ISBN 0-7710-8302-5

1. Ward, Max, 1921-   2. Wardair International Ltd. - History.   3. Businessmen - Canada - Biography.   4. Bush pilots - Canada - Biography. I. Title.

HE9815.W37W3 1991   387.7'06571'092   C91-094714-7

Every effort has been made to assign appropriate photo credits. Any corrections will be made in subsequent editions.

Printed and bound in Canada on acid-free paper.

McClelland & Stewart Inc.
The Canadian Publishers
481 University Avenue
Toronto, Ontario
M5G 2E9

DEDICATION

This book is dedicated to our Wardair people – that very rare and special breed. The achievements of Wardair were made possible because so many of you were willing to deliver that combination of dedication, loyalty, and excellence of performance that made us the very best in the aviation industry worldwide.

Throughout this book I have mentioned various names. There were, of course, a great many others, from every level of the company, whose contributions were equally valuable. I wish I could name every one of you. To *all* Wardair people, I want to acknowledge, with gratitude, respect, and affection, your wonderful devotion and comradeship over the years. What a team we had! The best in the world. And you were *all* a part of it.

CONTENTS

Pioneer Bush Pilots for Whom Wardair's Aircraft Fleet Were Named

It was with special pride that we at Wardair carried the names of some of Canada's outstanding adventurers on our aircraft – men who wrote the history of aviation in Canada, and followed in the footsteps of the Royal Navy explorers of the seventeenth, eighteenth, and nineteenth centuries. I am dismayed that they have received so little recognition for their contribution to Canada's history, considering the magnitude of their achievements in opening the vast areas of Canada's northlands.

Cy Becker
C. H. "Punch" Dickins
W. R. "Wop" May
Herbert Hollick-Kenyon
A. M. "Matt" Berry
S. R. "Stan" McMillan
Sheldon Luck
Z. Lewis "Lewie" Leigh
Don C. Braun
G. W. G. "Grant" McConachie
T. "Rusty" Blakey
C. C. Carl Aqar
H. W. "Harry" Hayter
Romeo Vachon
Jack Moar
H. A. "Doc" Oaks
Phil Garratt

ACKNOWLEDGEMENTS

A special word of thanks to Walter Stewart, who refers to himself as the "technician" on this book. It is true that no one needed a technician more than I did, but it is too modest a word for what Walter did. His expressive vocabulary, his turn of phrase, his ability to zero in on a thought, and his sense of timing, gave me new insight into, and respect for, those who are masters of communication. So, without his permission, I would substitute the words "technical communication artist," at the very least. (I can picture him rephrasing this if only he had the opportunity.)

At the beginning, I knew nothing about writing, and Walter knew nothing about airplanes, and inevitably, during the course of days of recorded interviews, we traded a bit of knowledge. He now knows that the jet engine is more correctly referred to as the jet power-plant, and I know the meaning and value of a "throw forward." And through it all, Walter's sly sense of humour survived intact.

Out of all this has come, at least, two wonderful new friends in Walter and Joan Stewart. Thank you, Walter, for this, and for your very major contribution to the completion of this book.

For Marjorie Morningstar, whose name flies on my latest aircraft, my love and gratitude. It was she who believed that I had a story that should be told – little as I wished to tell it – and encouraged, cajoled, and cheered me onward. Without her persuasion and her help, there would have been no book. It was she who, through forty-five years, compiled the forty and more books of records, stories, pictures, and lists that gave Walter and me a chronological history on which to build. She has read and reread every chapter, documenting changes, deletions, and additions, hunting for pictures and names. Best of all, she lived out this story beside me.

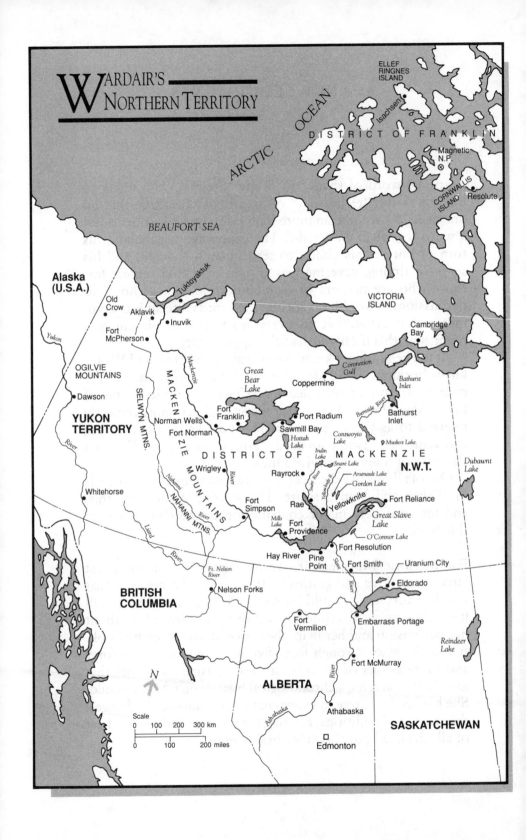

CHAPTER 1

▼

There Are Times When
I Wish I Had Been
Born an American

On the morning of January 18, 1989, I got up, shaved, dressed carefully, and ate breakfast with my wife, Marjorie, looking out the window of our condominium apartment on the Toronto waterfront at the early morning traffic pouring into the city along the Gardiner Expressway and Lakeshore Boulevard. This was all very normal, although I knew that this was not a normal day for me. Marjorie saw me to the door with a hug as she has done for more than forty-five years, and I picked up my briefcase and went out into the hall to the elevator. I went down to the basement garage and climbed into Marjorie's car, which I was borrowing for the day. My own car was in the shop. I drove out of the underground garage and onto the Lakeshore, but instead of turning north and west to the Wardair offices out by the Lester B. Pearson International Airport, as I would usually do, I turned east, and headed for the city's financial district.

I had a ten o'clock appointment with Rhys Eyton, the President of PWA Corporation, the holding company that controls, among other things, Canadian Airlines International Limited – CAIL. I would find out this morning if Rhys was serious about buying Wardair, and the question I kept turning over in my mind as I drove downtown was, "If so, should I sell?"

To me this was not simply a matter of bits of paper representing shares. I had founded Wardair thirty-six years earlier, with a single-engine de Havilland Otter aircraft, bought on time; I had nurtured the airline, worried over it, watched it grow to a fleet of modern, wide-bodied jets – McDonnell–Douglas DC-10s, Boeing 747s, and Airbus A-310s. From a bush-pilot operation, hauling trappers and miners through the Arctic wilderness, it had blossomed into the nation's third-largest airline, with an international reputation for class and efficiency. Wardair had given me a good life, and more adventure than I cared to think about; it had thrilled me and nearly killed me, and I loved it with a passion born of joy and rage, triumph and frustration, pleasure and despair.

If PWA Corporation took us over, I would walk away with some money, and that would be nice, for a change. Although my family and I owned almost a third of the common stock, there had never been a time, since this all began just after the Second World War, that Marjorie and I had not faced a mountain of debt. Marjorie had backed me all the way, on every move. Whenever the company produced any money, and there were many years when it did, I ploughed it straight back into new airplanes, and while our four children never went hungry, they didn't know much of luxury, either. Long after I became president, and had a successful business, I paid myself less than our pilots made, to keep every penny I could scrape up working to build Wardair. One result was that, for all the years we lived in Yellowknife, where the airline began, we owned only one house, which burned down. We lived mostly in rented houses, and they were in such short supply that we were constantly on the move. One summer, when I was frequently away, Marjorie and the children had to move so often that I lost track of them. Once, when I came back to Yellowknife from a trip to the High Arctic, I called Heidi, the telephone operator, and asked her if she knew where Marjorie was.

"Hold on," she said. "I'll track her down."

When Marjorie came on the line a few moments later, I said, "Hi. Where are we living today?"

Oh, yes, money would be nice. But this wasn't about money, had never been about money; it was about building something, accomplishing something, doing what you set out to do. What I had set out to do was to put together one of the largest and finest scheduled airlines in the world, and if I sold out now – there was no point in kidding myself about this – I would have failed.

What is more, I would have been defeated, not by fair and open competition, but by the constant, perverse, and ill-humoured activities of the regulators of Canadian aviation, by the politicians and bureaucrats. At least, I think I am justified in blaming them. Instead of putting all my energy into running an airline, I had spent much of my career trying to run interference against all the experts. These were the geniuses of the Air Transport Board and the Canadian Transport Commission, who knew almost nothing about how to conduct an airline, and everything about harassment.

And I had almost won. That was the galling part. I had come so close to pulling it off. All the years of hearings and re-hearings, all the threats and intimidation and suspensions and offers to close me down and shut me up – they were finally coming to an end. Canada had entered, about a decade late, into the era of airline deregulation. After waiting and begging and demanding for a third of a century, I had finally been given a licence to fly a scheduled airline. Just as I ran out of time.

By the time deregulation started in Canada, the U.S. carriers were a decade ahead in getting their industry in order. "There you go, Max," the regulators finally said. "Go out and play with the big boys." The big boys across the border, by this time, were all amalgamating into giants, and we Canadians were just entering that era.

If I didn't sell, the alternatives were unpalatable. Wardair was now carrying a heavy load of debt, taken on when we expanded so swiftly to meet the challenge of scheduled service, and if we didn't do something, we would run out of money within a year. I had stared at bankruptcy before, in 1982, a year of terror for Marjorie and me, and I had no wish to go through that again. Still, there were other options. Indeed, I had had an expression of interest from a source of private funding; but that would have involved losing control of my airline, and I was resolved not to do that if I could help it.

Alternatively, I could sell off airplanes; we had the finest, newest fleet in Canada, and the truth is, we had kept in business for years by trading aircraft. I could also sell part of the company, and keep the rest of it, with some sort of management contract. But that didn't appeal to me much either. I was sixty-eight, too set in my ways to be told by someone else how to run the airline I had built from nothing. Better, probably, to make a clean break. In the world of commerce, there's a time to buy and a time to sell. I knew instinctively that the time to sell had come.

There were a number of other issues that went into the mix, and they passed through my mind as I nosed into the downtown traffic, not the least of which were the 5,200 employees of Wardair. Some of them had been with us for many years; they were a proud and dedicated and enthusiastic group. Anyone who took over the company would recognize that these wonderful people, who had built a world-wide reputation for excellence, were indispensable to the airline, with or without me. Still, some jobs would be - had to be - lost.

I had made a speech the day before at the Sheraton Centre, which touched on some of the problems that had hit us hard in the past few months. Air Canada was the darling of the government, and the government still made the rules, I noted. I finished that speech by remarking ruefully, "I guess what we need most is for more Canadians to fly with us."

It was true, but it wasn't quite that simple. I couldn't blame Canadian travellers for following the line of least resistance, when the presence of a Crown-owned airline had, for so many years, determined travel habits. We were in a ballgame where the umpire owned the bat and ball - and the home team. Not many calls went the way of the Visitors, and we were always the Visitors. While the crazy regulations had disappeared (such as the ones that insisted that Canadians join a club if they wanted to get a flight at charter rates, and which led to the establishment of organizations like the North-West Section, American Vacuum Society), Wardair was still relegated to the least desirable positions in air terminals. We were still completely cut off from access to the huge market in government-funded travel, by which the shoals of bureaucrats move across the nation and the world. We were up against travel agents whose commissions went up as they increased their volume of sales from the major carriers, which meant that for their own economic well-being they pretty well had to steer the bulk of the business to Air Canada or CAIL. I had customers tell me, time and again, that they had specifically asked a travel agent to book them on Wardair, only to be told that they would have to go on Air Canada, because there was no Wardair flight to their destination – when there was. Ordinary travellers have no idea how complicated the business of airline travel is, or to what degree it is out of the hands of the airline itself. These complications made it mandatory for us to create an instant, scheduled airline, because we had to have a complete network of national and international flights to compete in the market of the times.

Well, we had been up against problems before, and we had licked them. I certainly wasn't sure if we could lick them this time, though, before economics pushed us over the brink and we lost everything. Nor was I sure that I wanted this challenge, with the odds stacked against us. And then there was another problem that I didn't want to face, which was that the Canadian market was just not big enough for three major carriers, and that it was now too late for Wardair.

If I were to sell, the price had to be right, because we had had a share offering a year before, and the shares went for $17.25 each. They had since fallen, with the news of our loss of $18 million in the first part of the year, to around $9.00. I now knew that the loss for the complete financial year of 1988, which would be toted up in a few weeks, would come in at close to $100 million, and that wouldn't do the shares any good. It wasn't like the old days, when the airline was mine alone, and the debts, and the decisions, affected only me and my family and employees. I would feel very badly if the friends and allies and perfect strangers who had backed us with their dollars couldn't at least get their money back.

That was why, when Rhys Eyton and I first started to talk about a share price, I had asked him for $25 a share.

"Hell, Max," he said, "for $25 a share, you can have Canadian!" I thought about it, but I knew the debt would be far in excess of what I could contemplate. Too bad; it would have been wonderful to see Rhys's face if I could have made him a serious offer. Well, if $25 was too rich for his blood, I would have to come up with something a little less, but still fair to my shareholders.

By the time I had wheeled Marjorie's car into the parking lot behind the King Edward Hotel on King Street, my mind was pretty clear. I would lay my cards on the table, and if the response seemed to be encouraging, I would work out the details within the next few weeks. However, I neither expected nor wanted to make the decision this morning. One postpones making such a difficult and final choice if one can.

I went into the hotel, where I was meeting first with Jim Ryan and W. C. Sharpstone, two vice-presidents from First Boston, our investment bankers, who had come up from New York, just in case this meeting with Rhys evolved into something they needed to take to the next stage. Then we walked along King Street to the corner of Bay, and went into one of those towering glass palaces where bankers and brokers spend their working days. We were meeting Rhys in the conference room of one of the nation's largest brokers.

However, when we got to the conference room, and the door swung open, I saw to my total surprise that the far side of the table was lined with the senior PWA Corporation and CAIL executives; not just Rhys, but also lawyers and accountants and brokerage people.

It threw me off balance momentarily, as I realized that possibly the moment of decision had arrived. The talk, plans, dreams, and schemes of months and years had come down to one crucial moment. Whatever I said now would affect thousands of lives for years to come.

After very little of the usual preliminaries, Rhys looked at me in that solemn, let's-get-down-to-it way he has and asked, "Well, Max, how much do you want for Wardair?"

I said, "The minimum price is the price we went out into the marketplace for a few months ago. Seventeen and a quarter."

In his usual fashion, Rhys was well-prepared, and you could practically see the numbers clicking over behind his eyes. With 14.4 million Wardair shares out, at $17.25 a share, I was asking for close to $250 million for the airline. Rhys asked for a little time to consider the offer, so the First Boston people and I left. We went to chat in an adjoining room.

Not long after, we were led back to the conference room, at which point Rhys agreed to the price, on the condition that our balance sheet on takeover was as it had been represented to him. Rhys is a chartered accountant, and he knew our financial position almost as well as I did.

We shook hands on the deal, and I got up and walked out.

So that was it; after all the years of struggle and uncertainty, and hanging on when there was nothing to hang on to, and building a company, and knowing moments of sheer wonder and sheer terror, Wardair was gone in a few minutes.

The First Boston people were quite elated, as we headed back to the King Eddy, but I was not. I barely remembered where I'd left the car; I no longer remember how I got home again. I had said to Marjorie, in our early days, that when you build something, you must be prepared to fight for it and protect it. And that we had done, together with all our Wardair people, over long, long years. No more.

There are times when I wish I had been born an American. Oh, not often; most of the time I am an enthusiastic Canadian – perhaps you might say a *Western* Canadian – and I beef about Ottawa because it is our favourite national pastime. But there is more to it than that. If I had been an American, or if, about thirty years ago, when I first began to realize what a strange and impossible game I had gotten into, I had moved to the United States, I am convinced I could have made it to the very top of this business. To put it at its baldest, no American who had attained the stature internationally that we attained with Wardair could have or would have been blocked from securing a scheduled service for a third of a century. Wardair had entered the international charter-airline business when it was in its infancy. Virtually every airline that competed with us over those years, foreign or domestic, had by this time been awarded scheduled rights somewhere, while, year after year, the Canadian authorities refused scheduled rights to us. We won awards, year after year, for our comfort, our service, and the helpfulness of our personnel. The British consumer magazine, *Holiday Which?*, gave us their top award for 1985, as the world's finest charter airline. This was based on a survey of opinion from United Kingdom travel agents, who were reacting in turn to what their customers, some of the world's most sophisticated travellers, reported to them.

Then, when we were finally admitted to the select circle of scheduled airlines late in 1985, we won the Golden Wings Award from *Holiday Which?* magazine as the world's finest scheduled carrier, two years in a row – the only two years, it turned out, that we were in the competition.

To me, the significance of the award was that Canadians had shown they were able to provide a service superior to that of such airline notables as Singapore Airlines, Cathay Pacific, and Thai International, and such giants as British Airways, Swissair, Lufthansa, Japan Airlines, and KLM. Possibly Wardair's greatest contribution was to demonstrate clearly to Canadians that they could be the world's best, and that the satisfaction of such an achievement was worth the effort.

There was one other matter that always gave me great pride: Wardair's record for safety is unparalleled. In our thirty-six years of operation, not one passenger was lost in an accident. Even if the rest of the world didn't know the details, they knew we were efficient, friendly, accommodating, and safe. The world had made its judgement about Wardair; the only people who didn't appreciate us, apparently, were those responsible for air-transport policy in Canada.

So, over the years when air transportation became more competitive elsewhere, particularly in the United States, Air Canada, and Canadian Pacific as well, operated under an umbrella of protection raised by government policy and regulatory action. These policies and regulations isolated Wardair from competitive access to mass markets that we and other charter carriers had originally developed through low-cost, affordable fares.

And I suppose that's what bothers me the most. I did what you are supposed to do, what all the economic texts and all the political speechifiers tell us they want business people to do. I invested my time and energy in trying to build something. I risked my money and my reputation and I spent a lifetime – from age twenty-five to age sixty-eight – to build up a company, provide employment, serve a need – and for what? My career, my business, did not depend only on what I did; it was shaped by politicians and bureaucrats.

This is a story of free enterprise that was not free. Wardair was strangled for too many years by government regulations and policies that brought charter carriers to their knees, that said to entrepreneurial companies like Wardair, "You are not wanted in the business, and we are going to do our best to get rid of you."

When the government finally tabled an epochal paper called *The Freedom to Move* in 1985, and thus launched the process of clearing away much of the proliferation of needless regulation after twenty-nine years of bitter battle, the reform came too late for Wardair.

In setting down my story here, I hope to put on the record a good deal that hasn't yet been told about the way in which the Canadian North was opened, about the life of a bush pilot, and about the fun, the danger, the adventures, and some of the positively bizarre episodes that were connected to those wonderful years. But my story is not one of adventure – although it certainly contains adventures – not a story of business – although it certainly contains a lot of what I learned about business. It is a personal story that demonstrates how Canada, a nation that, as early as 1929, moved more freight by air than any other country in the world, could, by the 1990s, be forced into the backwaters of aviation. How? By a fundamental federal government policy that consistently, for fifty years, denied private enterprise a free competitive position in a fledgling but flourishing industry.

I cannot help but reflect on how different Canada's role might have been today, in ever-widening, competitive aviation markets, had political and bureaucratic policies been different.

CHAPTER 2

▼

Born to Fly

If you were born and brought up in Edmonton during the 1920s and 1930s, the most exciting people around were the bush pilots, who were always in the news with stories of their exploits. My whole idea of adventure, of living, was tied up in the notion of joining their ranks some day in a magnificent flying machine. My boyhood was spent building toy airplanes out of boxwood, which I got from a butter-box factory near our home, or from the ingenious materials in a Meccano set. I made those airplanes as perfect as possible. If I was building something and it didn't come out right, I would do it over again. I wouldn't try to fix it; I wanted it right, and I would never be content until I knew I had done as good a job as could be done. I didn't lose my temper when things went wrong; I would just sigh and start again.

When I was still in public school, I used to go over to the Edmonton Municipal Airport, which was quite close by, and make a nuisance of myself around the hangar, catching an occasional long-distance glimpse of one of my bush-pilot heroes.

I have one older sister, Lillian, who lives in Edmonton. I suppose I was the usual younger-brother pest to her, but she put up with me with what I now see was great patience, if also with some considerable frustration at times.

My childhood was one of singular happiness and contentment; I didn't have any of the interesting but dreadful psychological scars that make for fascinating reading later on. I was happy and busy with all the usual things of childhood. I ran a lot; I would run all over the city and the surrounding countryside, and later, when I got a bike, I roamed all over the place. My parents gave me a great deal of freedom, and I used every bit of it, wandering around and exploring on my own. I went to public and high school in Edmonton, but I was not interested in school, and my later high-school years were spent marking time until I could join the air force, and fly.

I was quite easy-going – though I suppose everybody thinks that of himself – and about the only thing that really made me furious was to be told I couldn't do something. As soon as someone said, "Oh, you could never do that," I wanted to do it. You can make what you will of that and of its effect on my later career.

I was not much of an athlete in school, although I was well-enough coordinated, because I was too busy with my newspaper route and doing other things. I didn't watch sports, which is what everybody did in those days, because I wanted to be a participant, not a spectator.

I drifted along, I guess, enjoying myself thoroughly, but not doing anything much out of the ordinary, until after high school, when I came upon the second great fascination of my life, my wife-to-be.

I first saw Marjorie at a dance in the Masonic Temple in downtown Edmonton; the building is still there, although, for some reason, there is no plaque commemorating the night of our epochal encounter. Marjorie was wearing a red tartan outfit, and she was a skinny little thing, but the moment I saw her standing by the dance floor in that outfit, something happened in my inner workings, and I have never been the same since. I told Horace Dickie, the fellow I was with – he, like myself, was an elderly seventeen-year-old – "There's the girl I'm going to marry."

Horace thought I was crazy. Marjorie was sixteen at the time; she went to a different high school, at the other end of town, and I didn't know her name, or anything about her, except that I was going to marry her. I would like to be able to report on the witty conversation we had that night as we danced, but there was none, and we didn't. I gawked, and Marjorie looked down at the floor, but in those days, you did not just sashay up to a girl you didn't know and ask for a dance. I didn't, anyway. So, absolutely nothing happened that night, except that my life was changed forever.

Edmonton was not a large city in those days – the population was about seventy thousand – so it was not too difficult to ask around and find out who she was: Marjorie Doretha Skelton. And where she lived: which turned out to be on a street without any pavement in the south end of town. Her father, William Skelton, was working for a building-and-heating firm, so I persuaded Horace Dickie, who had access to his dad's car, to drive me over there one evening. I had a brilliant scheme. We would drive past her house and pretend to get stuck in the mud, and Marjorie would come out, and we would meet. The problem was, we really did get stuck. Horace stopped the car for a bit, let out the clutch, and the vehicle promptly sank into the mud and stalled. We had a tough time rocking it out of there, during which Marjorie's parents came to the window to see what all the noise was about in the street, and Marjorie snuck into her bedroom and peeked out through the bedroom curtains. I didn't see her, but she knew, right away, who was out there. So, we didn't get to meet then, either.

The next time I saw Marjorie, she was selling apples for the Kiwanis Club on a street corner, and I walked by – I did a lot of walking by in her neighbourhood in those days – and did some more gawking. But no talking. I backed all the way down the block, so I could stare at her, and nearly killed myself tripping over my own feet, but I could not speak. Perhaps it was just as well, because, when I finally did get up enough courage to telephone and ask her for a date, she announced firmly that there would be no date unless and until we were properly introduced. That was finally arranged, through a girl I knew at Victoria High who knew Marjorie from the Junior Choir at First Baptist Church, and we went to a movie – I have no idea what it was – one Friday night. I asked her to marry me on that first date, and, like Horace, she thought I was crazy. But I wasn't; I just happened to know what I wanted, and she was it. I had not done a lot of dating up until then, and hadn't really been all that dazzled by girls, but, once I met Marjorie, that was it. And, I may say, that remained it, from that day to this.

I realize that in describing our meeting and early courtship I am delineating a world that was far different from today, when life was both simpler and more complex. There can be few young men of seventeen today who are required to go through the ritual of an introduction to ask a girl for a date; our life was more complicated, in that way. On the other hand, we didn't have to worry about the other complications of social life today, did we?

Just about the time our courtship was progressing satisfactorily, the Second World War broke out, and I immediately went to join the air force. I knew what I wanted there, too: I wanted to be a pilot. However, when I showed up at the recruiting station in downtown Edmonton, I was told that, although they would take me as an air gunner, there was no guarantee that I would ever fly. I was dumb-founded; having spent so much time out at the airport admiring the planes and their pilots, I just assumed that when the war started I would join up and become a pilot. I had never been up in an airplane, because there was no way I could have afforded the five dollars it took for a flight with one of the many barnstorming pilots who roamed the country, but I knew I would love it, and be good at it. Not fly? I told the recruiter I would have to think it over, and went home.

By this time, I was working for the Canadian National Railways, the CNR – now just CN. My father was a ticket agent in Edmonton and managed to get me a job as a "call boy." My academic career not being brilliant, I needed to work. I didn't enjoy the job, which consisted of getting on my bicycle every day and riding around to advise train crews of when they would next be on duty. Not everyone had a telephone in those days – among the CNR workers, probably fewer were "on the phone," as it was called, than were off it – and the union contract provided that a call boy would be assigned to come around and personally inform the crews of their next trip. (I think it is a mark of the innocence of those days that no one ever made a joke to me about call boys.) I met a lot of nice people – cheerful even when you woke them up – and spent a lot of time on my bike, which suited me fine.

But, of course, it was not a career, so a few months later I was back down at the recruiting station, and this time I was more successful. I would be admitted to the air force, and, if I could make it, I would be put through for pilot training. I never had a moment's doubt that I would make it. I would like to say I joined to fight the wicked Hun, but what did I know about the wicked Hun? In the isolationist Western Canada of those days, we knew little of international affairs; what we knew, we got from the newspapers, and they didn't know much more than we did. I remember once hearing one of the teachers from Victoria High, Major Towerton, explain that most of what we read about the gallant Allies smiting the Germans hip and thigh was just nonsense. The newspapers spoke of the tremendous losses suffered by the Wermacht, but this teacher said that, in fact, the Wermacht was inflicting tremendous losses, not suffering them, and the Germans were storming through the Lowlands. I repeated what he said, and was told that I was totally misinformed, although, as I was to learn, he had it just about right.

In any event, I regret to say that it was not from any impulse to save my country from perdition that I joined the air force, but for the excitement of it, and the chance to fly.

Marjorie raised no objection; in those days, courtship was a rather different matter than it is today, and it seemed reasonable that I would join the air force, which would ensure food, clothing, and shelter, which were about the only things we really worried about.

I was admitted to the air force, given a uniform, put through all the medicals, and required to fill out all the endless forms. I also found myself living at the Edmonton Exhibition Grounds, which had been turned into a manning depot, and my first night there I was in a panic. I looked out towards the gate, with its armed guards; I looked at the fence, which was a high one; and I realized that, for the first time in my life, I was locked in. I had never been fenced in before, and I didn't like it one bit. However, there was nothing I could do but grin and bear it.

I have only foggy memories of the basic training course we went through at the manning depot – six weeks of marching, drilling, learning the rudiments of military discipline – but I have a very clear memory of what happened next. The air force lost me; lost me entirely. It was an early, and ominous, indication of what it is like to be in the control of bureaucracy.

After basic training, a group of a dozen of us were shipped out to Fort Macleod, in southern Alberta, to perform guard duty. This apparently came about because, in those early days, the air force was not really prepared for the massive influx of recruits it wanted to turn into aircrew, and the bureaucrats simply didn't know what to do with us until space could be found for us in training school. So they made us into guards – we couldn't do much harm – and shipped us off to Fort Macleod on the Oldman River, where the North-West Mounted Police had built a stronghold in the last century to control the whisky traders who operated from nearby Fort Whoop-Up.

There were no rampaging American traders in the district any more, so the air force set us to watch over the collection of Anson aircraft then flying out of the place. Then they lost us. Our papers went astray and remained astray for weeks, during which we had nothing to do but watch the Ansons – known as "flying greenhouses" because there was so much glass in them – and protect the area against any German U-boats that might happen by. This went on for several weeks, the Ansons flying, us guarding, the U-boats staying resolutely away (which showed what a good job we were doing), and then our papers rematerialized as suddenly and mysteriously as they had disappeared, and we were shipped back to Edmonton, to begin aircrew training.

We lived in the Athabasca residence at the University of Alberta, which had been taken over by the air force, and every morning we marched off to classes in a nearby training school. The residence and, indeed, the training school were always neat and clean, and the food was always well-prepared. The same caterers who had worked for the university worked for the air force and, while it was traditional to complain about the food and living conditions, the truth is, they were first class. I was very impressed with my new life, even though it now included all the logarithms and other educational horrors I had ignored at high school. For the first time in my life I really paid attention and worked diligently on the academic subjects, which were considerable in aircrew training. Courses that took a year in high school were absorbed in a month in the air force, with no excuses and no backchat. Fine, I said, and I did very well indeed.

Marjorie lived only a few blocks from the university, so when I had time off I used to dash over to her place. Quite often, I didn't get back until after Lights Out. I would get Marjorie to drive her father's car right up beside the fence, and I would use the car's running-board as a step to start me over the wire. It did not take enormous cunning to sneak in after hours, since the guard duties were shared among the recruits, and, by mutual consent, we always looked the other way when we saw a fellow sufferer sneaking in. The training centre itself was run by officers from the Royal Military College, and everything was very taut and disciplined, but the fences were another matter entirely.

I did well during initial training, and, when we were all paraded out to hear our names, and futures, read out by an officer one brisk morning, WARD, MAXWELL, was assigned to High River, Alberta, about eighty miles south of Calgary, to learn how to fly Tiger Moth (Tiger Schmitts) aircraft.

My first flight – the familiarization flight – turned out to be quite interesting. Very interesting, in fact. Or, if you want to be blunt about it, a lot more interesting than I cared for. The United States had not yet come into the war, and a number of American pilots had drifted up to Canada to build up their flying time. It was one of these whom Fate chose to give me my first flight. He had a friend teaching school in a little one-room schoolhouse some distance south of High River, so we took off and headed for there. We flew straight and level, and he let me have the controls for a bit; it was all very exciting and civilized. Then, as we got close to his friend's school, he growled into the Gosport, a sort of speaking tube through which the pilot, in the front seat, could communicate with the trainee in the back, that I should be sure I had my harness tightened right up. Well, why not? I got everything as tight as could be, and reported the same to the pilot, and he promptly proceeded to do loops and rolls right over his friend's school. In short order I lost, respectively, my poise, my courage, and my breakfast. It seemed quite likely to me, as we rolled and swooped around the prairie sky, that I was going to die – and it also seemed to me a very good idea. By the time we returned to High River, I was a basket-case; however, although I had trouble with airsickness for some time after that, it never affected my determination to go on flying.

I took naturally to the air – so much so that a number of my instructors insisted, quite wrongly, that I must have had previous flying training. I totally enjoyed flying, and I still do. There is no particular merit in this; I didn't have to work at it, it was just there. I knew how an aircraft would react, and what to do when things went wrong, as much by instinct as by training, and I was always conscious of the attitude of the aircraft, that is, where it was in relation to the ground – a handy attribute if you want to avoid bumping into things.

I was allowed to try a solo flight after only four or five hours of dual flying, and the squadron commander took on the task of supervising this final check-out. (You never flew your first solo with the instructor who had trained you, who might not be impartial.) After a few minutes of flying around, the squadron commander told me to do an approach to land, and, when I had the aircraft all lined up to set down, he suddenly wrenched the stick. He was trying to make sure that if something went wrong, I would react in the right way; but all that happened was that I got mad at him for ruining my approach, and I wouldn't fly the plane properly. As a result of my stubbornness, I flunked the test, and didn't pass my solo until after another four hours' flying time. Later, when I became an instructor myself, I realized that what he had done was quite correct, but at the time, I only felt rage.

Discipline was not my strong point. The High River station, like the initial training school, was run by Royal Military College officers, on very tight lines. They expected you to follow all the rules, especially on parade. One day, there was alleged to be something wrong with my uniform, so I was hauled out of line and dressed down and told to report back to the drill square after classes. When I did, the offended officer told me to put a pack on my back and march back and forth until I saw the error of my ways. It became a contest of wills; I refused to admit I had done anything wrong, and he refused to let me go. So I marched back and forth and back and forth until finally he got bored with the whole thing and dismissed me, unrevised and unrepentant.

When I had finished training on the Tiger Moths at High River, I was posted to Claresholm, a pleasant little town in the foothills of the Rockies, and the humming hub of one of the Commonwealth Training Centres. There, we flew Cessna Cranes. The Cessna Crane was a twin-engine aircraft, with wooden propellors and a Jacobs power-plant. It was a good, light plane and dandy for training, because it was very responsive and kept you on your toes. We got to be very good friends, that old Cessna and I. At Claresholm, there were a number of people in the course who only flew when they had to, but I flew every minute I could get, and put in more airtime than anyone else on the course. There was, literally, nothing I would rather do than fly, so, every time there was a plane available and I was free, away I went.

I would not have you believe that everything went smoothly. There was, for example, the time they woke us up in the middle of the night and told us to take off in our aircraft. I stumbled, half asleep, over to the Cessna, climbed aboard, and, when the engine wouldn't turn over, called over a mechanic and demanded to know why the plane wouldn't start.

He came up to the cockpit, peered in, and said, very sweetly, "Why don't you try it with the switches turned on?"

"Ah," I said, "switches."

Despite these occasional gaffes, I enjoyed night flying as much as flying in the daytime; there was something about flying alone, at night, across moonlit prairies, or up towards the looming foothills, with the engines roaring and the wind singing and the moon shining, that made you feel young, and free, and utterly unafraid.

I continued to have problems, however, with air-force discipline. One of the great thrills of daytime flying was to dash up into the foothills and fly low, where the sensation of speed was greatest – and the flying, of course, riskiest. It never occurred to me that I might bump into an unexpected hill, but it did occur to the air force, which disapproved of these flights, and forbade them. The obvious solution was not to tell the air force, but they found out anyway, sometimes, and I got into trouble this way more than once. On one occasion, Marjorie came down from Edmonton to meet me in Calgary, but I had been "gated" for the betterment of my soul and couldn't leave Claresholm. She, like the air force, was not amused.

While I found flying as easy as it was exciting, the unexpected exams sometimes caught one off guard. One day, after a late night out with a friend and fellow trainee, Greg Panassis, we came back to the station at the same time that our instructors were arriving for the day's work – and I was suddenly presented with a navigational exam.

For this exam, I would sit in the back of the aircraft and work out a plot for the pilot during a cross-country flight, and the great trick was to keep from getting lost. In part, this is a matter of mathematical calculation; you know how long you have been flying, and on what compass heading, and at what speed, and, making due allowance for the wind pushing your aircraft around, you ought to be able to calculate where you are at any given moment. You can check your estimate against reality – this is easier on the prairie than most places – by reference to identifiable points on the ground. They give you your "fixes" for the next legs of the flight. If you reckon that you ought to be over the water-tower at Lethbridge, and you look down and see a sign that says "Alberta Grain Pool, Nanton," you know something has gone wrong.

On this occasion, I gave the headings to the pilot, according to the briefing, but then I couldn't find any clear reference points as we flew along. There was only one thing to do, I figured, and that was to keep on as if I knew what I was doing, so I worked out the next legs by simply plotting where I should be, quite concerned that I might fail the exam because of not knowing my exact location. I was going to carry on with this plan until I finally hit something I recognized. Working backwards from that fix, I could recalculate the winds and drift, and go on from there. The instructor, beside me, asked me what I was doing, so, reluctantly, I told him.

"That's exactly right," he said. My relief was tremendous.

The time I put in flying made up for the lapses from discipline, and my marks on graduation from pilot training were very high indeed. Ironically, those high marks were my downfall. Out of a class of sixty-four trainees, two of us were pulled out and told, "You are now instructors. You will be posted for instructor training."

I was so disappointed that I went off by myself and cried and cried. Upon which I learned yet another lesson: namely, that tears don't change anything in the RCAF.

I received my pilot's wings on November 2, 1941, and, while there was a certain bitterness about the fact that I was not going overseas and not going to fly those wonderful Hawker Hurricanes, there was some satisfaction in the fact that I was gainfully employed, an officer, and in a position to put through my other major project, which was to become engaged to Marjorie. I went out – with my wings still pinned, and not yet sewn to my uniform – to Birk's jewellery store in downtown Edmonton, and bought the largest diamond ring I could afford. Or, as it turned out, couldn't afford, since I had to put 10 per cent down and make monthly payments out of my air-force salary for a year. (The diamond from that ring was lost, years later, when we were living in Yellowknife. With the insurance money for it, we bought ourselves an entire winter's supply of soft drinks, bottled locally in beer bottles by Sammy Peterson. Improvident? But typically young.)

There I was, just about to turn twenty, and already, although of course I hadn't the brains to appreciate how rare this was at the time, I had found two of the three great passions of my life.

It was with a comparatively cheerful heart that I kissed Marjorie goodbye and got on the train for an exciting, frustrating, and demanding new life as a flying instructor, a life that would begin with my learning *how* to instruct, in the far-away, and probably God-forsaken, city of Trenton, Ontario.

CHAPTER 3

▼

A Dangerous War
at Home

Trenton wasn't God-forsaken, as it turned out; it was a modest, pleasant little city on the banks of the Trent River in southern Ontario, not far from Kingston. The airbase there was – and continues to be – the major industry in town, and it was here that I was taught the trade of flying instructor. It was clear to me, soon after I arrived, that I could handle an aircraft with much more skill and precision than the instructor who was teaching me. But, after all, he wasn't there to teach me to fly, he was there to teach me to teach. I was still bitter about the fact that, instead of flying the new Hawker Hurricane, the hottest plane of the day, in defence of Britain, I would be tooling around on training craft, in defence of Trenton.

After instruction training, I was transferred to Moncton, New Brunswick, the other end of the earth as far as I was concerned. I was checked out on the Anson, which was the training aircraft, and then put to work producing pilots. Many of my pupils proved to be English – one of Canada's more important tasks during the war was to train British and other Commonwealth pilots – and it always seemed to me the English pilots were either very good or very bad, never mediocre. There were a great number of them; we had large classes and we worked hard. This was the first time I had been subjected to the regular, long-term routine of armed forces' life. Before this, I had been moving quickly from place to place and had largely escaped the drudgery of routine. Not that the flying was routine, but certainly much of what went on on the ground was, and, as usual, I did not cope very well with the surly bonds of discipline.

Soon after I arrived in Moncton, we were given a little chat by the chief flying instructor, a permanent air-force officer who frankly resented the ease with which we had obtained our commissions, a task that had taken him years in the peacetime air force. He wanted us to know that he regarded us as trash, beneath contempt and utterly incompetent. We didn't like him much, either.

The work itself was hard, challenging, and sometimes dangerous. There was a desperate need for the pilots we were turning out. I knew enough about the war, now, to know how key a role they would play in the conflict; the Battle of Britain had been decisively won, but the struggle to control the skies over Europe was still being played out, and these men would help to determine the outcome. So, while we were anxious to see them do well, and graduate quickly, we knew that they had to be properly prepared. I became, accordingly, a very strict and demanding instructor, and I would make my students go through their paces time and time again before I was satisfied. But then, when I was preparing a pilot-to-be for his flight examination – you will remember that this exam is always given by an instructor other than the student's regular teacher – I would compliment the student on just about everything he did, until he thought he was a real winner. If they were ready, I wanted them to go with confidence; if not, I wouldn't let them go. That was the only secret I had as a teacher, and it seemed to work. In all the time I worked as a flight instructor, I never had a student fail his final flight examinations.

Most of the time I was at Moncton, we used Ansons, although towards the end we began to use the single-engine Harvard. The Anson was an easy aircraft to fly, a twin-engine training-and-communications aircraft, designed in Britain and named for Baron Anson, the British admiral who inflicted such heavy damage on Spanish shipping during his voyage around the world from 1740 to 1744. He was a tempestuous fire-eater, raised to the peerage after his bloody victory against the French off Cape Finisterre, but the aircraft named for him – the military mind is not noted for its sense of humour – was really nothing more than a peaceable old wooden glider that happened to have a couple of engines installed. The version used by the RCAF was built by the National Steel Car Company, Limited, at Malton, Ontario, and I grew quite fond of the old thing. However, it did have some drawbacks as a training aircraft, since it liked a pilot who was in charge and knew what he wanted to do. Sometimes, we would get a student who was afraid of the airplane and who couldn't take control. This would show up on approach, because the aircraft would get its nose up and sort of drag in to the strip. This could be very dangerous because of the risk of stalling. If it stalled, the Anson would flip right over. Not a happy result. To get around this, when I had a student who showed a tendency to let the aircraft drag, I would take him up very high over a bank of puffy clouds.

"Now," I would say, "those clouds ahead are the landing strip, and you are going to set this aircraft down just as if you were landing her on the clouds."

If the student let the nose go up too far, all hell would break loose; the Anson would go into a power stall, flip over, and head for the ground. I would pull it out of the stall, while the student screamed and clutched his seat, but no student who had been through that experience ever let the airplane drag on landing again.

It was at Moncton that I learned the difference between the kind of precision flying I favoured and the kind of flying that was really useful in a dogfight. George Beurling, the Canadian air ace who had downed twenty-eight enemy aircraft during a four-month stint over Malta in early 1942, showed up in Moncton. He had first joined the RAF, and it was as an RAF pilot that he flew in Malta, but after he was wounded, he got a promotion and a transfer to the RCAF, which brought him home to Canada, for two reasons. The first was to keep him alive, since nothing could keep him out of the air, and he had long since used up his share of luck; the second was to promote recruiting by travelling across Canada. The government also hoped to get a little publicity out of him for their own purposes; the most famous picture taken of "Buzz" Beurling shows him shaking hands with Prime Minister Mackenzie King on the steps of the House of Commons during this trip.

He stayed with us at Moncton for a few weeks. We were very much in awe of the man and his reputation, but he was a most amiable person, with no airs whatsoever, and he desperately wanted to return to the overseas war theatre. He clearly identified the fighter aircraft for what it was – a platform for guns – and the object was to point those guns precisely to achieve their purpose. He was a master of the art, certainly Canada's best deflection marksman in that war. He knew exactly where to point his guns ahead of an enemy aircraft so that it would fly into a deadly stream of bullets.

The kind of flying I enjoyed, but didn't teach, was dashing under bridges, formation flying, that sort of thing. One of the tricks we used to do to perfect control over the aircraft was to put the tread of an Anson's tail wheel on the nose of the following aircraft, and keep it there. It took both nerve and skill.

"Let's learn to judge distance," I would say, and take the student down to fly through the smoke of a train puffing across the countryside. I'm sure we gave a few engineers fits. Besides pilot training, I taught bombing and gunnery, and as I became familiar with the tactics involved, I came to understand the kind of flying required. A bombing formation might be several miles long, a few miles deep, and a couple of miles wide, and the trick was to keep somewhere in that mass and drop your bombs on the target and get home alive. It took tremendous courage and coolness under fire, rather than the capacity to put the aircraft down on a dime. If you could get it home, and somewhere onto the tarmac after several hours of hell in the air, that was all that was asked of you.

It was quite a shock to find out that really skilled flying was not what the air force was looking for; what they wanted were bomber pilots who could keep in a formation and fighters who could shoot. If anything, my role as instructor would keep me from being posted overseas. There was another problem, too. The chief flying instructor who had given us such a harsh welcome to Moncton became even more contemptuous as time went by, and I couldn't resist replying in kind. I thought my insolence (which is what I guess it was) would persuade him to get me shipped overseas, but, of course, when he learned that that was what I wanted, he determined that that was what I would never get. My cause was not aided by the fact that I continued to run afoul of the strict discipline imposed by the air force.

My roommate in Moncton was a cheerful, outgoing man named Jacques Amyot, who was the station dentist. He came from a well-to-do Quebec City family, and had an incredible collection of classical records. It was through Jacques that I developed a taste for classical music, but that was not what got me into trouble; what got me into trouble was his out-going nature. We were charged, one day, with fraternizing with members of the women's auxiliary. We were out of uniform at the seaside when this offence took place, and we were not doing anything that would have got me into trouble with Marjorie, but the local customs were determined by officers' wives, who did not approve of us fraternizing with the great unwashed – the auxiliary were not officers, but "other ranks" – and this silly charge became another small black mark on my record. What with one thing and an-other, I was stuck in Moncton for two years, until late 1943.

During that time, I got to see Marjorie twice. Once a year I would get two weeks' leave, so I would get on the train in Moncton and head for Edmonton, where Marjorie was at university. I would spend about five days there, and then it was time to get on the train again and head back east. The visit was always worth the trip, but it was a long-distance sort of wooing. However, I was always conscious of the fact that a lot of my fellows were undergoing real deprivation overseas – and I wanted nothing more than to join them.

Once I had resigned myself to the fact that I was not going to get overseas, Moncton was not such a bad place to be. I was flying, and it was exciting, and one's early twenties are a wonderful time of life, although the work was demanding and the hours long, and there was always the chance that I would either kill myself or be killed by a careless student.

My closest brush with death as an instructor came not at Moncton, but at Hagersville, Ontario, where I was transferred after two years at Moncton. At the end of each training course on the Anson – we were back to using the twin-engine Anson at Hagersville – it was customary to take the students up in a small group, so that each could have some time at the controls, and each could learn from the others. In this particular case, I was taking up two students to fill in the formation-flying times necessary for their graduation under the RCAF training requirements. I had arranged for two other aircraft to formate – the word we used to describe the process of forming up in flight – with our own Anson. Each aircraft had two students, and their instructions were to formate on our right- and left-hand sides and to hold their positions in that formation. While we were getting into position, a sudden movement to our right and behind us caught my eye. I looked again, and saw an Anson coming up on us, moving far too quickly.

I told the trainee who was flying, as calmly and quietly as I could, "Okay, I'll take her," and grabbed the controls to hold the machine straight and level, just seconds before there was a tremendous crash and the Anson rocked and staggered in the air. The other aircraft had smashed into us, just behind the main cabin; its wing struck our fuselage and, as I glanced quickly out the window, I saw the stricken aircraft, with one wing torn away, flip over and plunge towards the earth. I was horrified, but there was nothing I could do, except try to get the aircraft back under control. The cabin was full of dust and debris from the crash and the aircraft was lunging all over the sky, but it resisted the temptation to go into a spin. The controls were sloppy under my hands – it was a bit like trying to fly through mud – but they did respond, and I was able to get the aircraft turned around and slowed down, and we limped back to Hagersville airport. Although it was not more than a score of miles away, it felt as if we had been flying forever; and when we finally got back to earth I discovered that the crash had torn fabric off the side of my plane, and it had wrapped around the elevators on the tail assembly, which explained why I found the aircraft so sluggish. The two students in the other aircraft were killed, and the rest of us survived mainly by a fluke. The Anson was built of metal tubes, wood, and fabric, not a very sturdy craft by today's standards, but the original design had a gun turret just behind the cabin. In the training craft, the weight represented by this gun turret was replaced by a large block of concrete, and it was into this concrete that the out-of-control aircraft had crashed. A few feet forward, and none of us would have survived.

There was an official inquiry, but it was unable to discover exactly what had gone wrong, or even which of the two students had been at the controls when the accident occurred.

Not long after this, I was transferred once more, to St. Catharines, Ontario, to work as a check pilot, rather than as an instructor. Air-force regulations, quite properly, require every officer who wants to collect flying pay to put in a certain number of hours in the air every month, and the check pilot goes along, just in case. St. Catharines was primarily a radio-operator training station, and most of my work consisted of giving check rides to the various pilots there.

Soon, however, I was given the extraordinary task of trying to rehabilitate returned pilots who had completed one or more tours overseas, and then, for one reason or another, had lost their nerve. "Battle fatigue," they called it. These were extraordinary, brave men who had simply been pushed over the limit by their experiences. Many of them had a chestful of decorations, and nearly all of them far outranked me, but it was my job to persuade them to get back in an airplane and fly again, to rebuild their confidence. This was not mere caprice on the part of the air force; the notion was that many of these men had had their confidence destroyed, their nerves shattered, but if they could conquer their fear and fly once more, they might be well on the way to recovery. We didn't even make them solo; it was enough that they took control of the aircraft one more time.

It didn't always work, of course, but when it did, it was enormously satisfying. It was a time when we didn't understand much about battle fatigue, and many people, including many of its victims, thought that what was involved was simple cowardice. Then, slowly, gradually, they would get their nerve back, and take control of the aircraft, and the smile on a man's face when he had won that battle made up for many of the other things we had to put up with.

One of the successes was a man named Maclean, who had flown with George Beurling in Malta and had many a hair-raising story about Beurling's escapades to tell. No one wanted to fly with the Canadian air ace, despite his tremendous reputation, because you couldn't count on him, apparently. He would break formation and go off on his own, hunting Germans, and leave his mates to fend for themselves. (I later read a piece about Buzz Beurling that quoted him as saying that he felt lost in a world without air combat. "It's the only thing I can do well; it's the only thing I ever did I really liked," he said. He was ushered out of the RCAF in October, 1944 – after he had shot down four more German planes – because of disciplinary problems, and when the Arab–Israeli conflict broke out, he joined up with the fledgling Israeli air force. Ironically, he was killed on a peaceful flight, when an aircraft he was ferrying crashed. That was in 1948, and he was twenty-seven years old. Somebody ought to write a book about his brief, tragic life.)

Maclean had been shot down and badly burned in his Spitfire; he was somewhat disfigured, and his confidence in flying and in himself was at a very low ebb. You will have to imagine what it was like for me to fly with someone like this, a man who had been through so much, who clearly outranked me and made me feel very much a greenhorn. You couldn't order such people about, you could only cajole and persuade and reassure, and hope that you didn't get flown into the side of a barn in the process. Maclean and I flew and talked and flew and talked some more, and slowly, gradually, you could see his confidence in himself return until he was, if not his old self again, at least someone he could be proud of and respect. I felt that, working with men like Maclean, I was doing something worth while, even if I couldn't be a fighter pilot myself.

We flew Yale trainers, a two-cockpit aircraft with a fixed undercarriage – a steady enough flyer, but it had a few tricks. I spent many an hour with sweaty palms taking these rehabilitating pilots through such routine but dangerous manoeuvres as the forced landing, in which you assumed that you couldn't get back to the base and had to set the aircraft down safely anywhere you could. More than once, as we came in towards the ground, the trainee would panic, or simply let the stick go, and sit there, frozen. I had tremendous sympathy for these men, but it took all the restraint I could muster to keep from screaming, "For God's sake, you're going to kill us both!"

We had a rough but level field set aside for these forced-landing sessions, and once, just as we came over the fence and started to set down, the trainee-officer kicked rudder and pulled back the stick, which started the aircraft into a flick roll. I had to react instantly and instinctively, grabbing my controls and shoving the plane's nose down, so that the wing struck the ground. This stopped the rotation his actions had begun, which certainly would have plunged us upside down into the ground, and I was able to get the aircraft under control again.

When we got back to the station, the commanding officer chewed me out for bending the wing-tip on the aircraft. I don't believe he had any idea of the kinds of problems we faced out there.

We were now well into 1944, and as the war in Europe progressed, two things became clear to me. The first was that we were going to win the war; the second, that I was never, ever, going to get any closer to it than I now was. Until this was absolutely clear, I had hesitated about getting married.

Marjorie and I were married on June 28, 1944, in Regina, where Marjorie's parents were living at the time. Her dad moved about quite a bit, in the building business, and this would later turn out to be a great blessing to us. We had our honeymoon in Banff. One of the things I remember about that honeymoon was that it was hot as a firecracker in the train going from Regina to Banff. It didn't matter.

After that, life was very much happier and easier in St. Catharines. Marjorie moved east and spent a good deal of her time at the beach on Lake Ontario, between the airbase and the town. I had my flying, and a new married life, and things were going very well indeed. But it was time to think about the future. I did not intend to make a life in the air force, so, with the war winding down, it seemed smart to consider what came next. We bought a second-hand Mercury, which we called "the Blue Hornet," and saved our money for the journey home.

When the war in Europe appeared to be coming to an end in 1945, a notice went up on the bulletin board in the officers' mess to the effect that anyone who wanted to get out of the service could do so, simply by applying. Up until then, everyone had talked about getting out, but when that notice came, and a lot of people began to think about the uncertainties of civilian life without a job, many changed their minds. In the end, only three of us applied to be demobbed: the commanding officer of the St. Catharines station, an Argentinian who wanted to go home, and me.

I came out of the air force with a tremendous flying background: I had 2,800 hours of flying time, and I knew a good deal about flying, although I didn't know anything about anything else.

When my papers came through, allowing me leave to return to the West to be demobbed, Marjorie and I took off in the Blue Hornet. We drove to Regina, then on to Calgary, where I was demobbed, and then back to Edmonton.

I knew, had known for years, what I was going to do next. I was going to be a bush pilot, or bust.

CHAPTER 4

▼

Into the North

I have already explained something of my fascination for the North, even though I had never been there, and for the men who were opening the area with their courage – and their planes. Men like C. H. "Punch" Dickins, "Wop" May, and Grant McConachie, who had become legends in their own time. I wanted to be like them; I also wanted to fly – had to fly – and wouldn't be heartbroken if I could run a burgeoning business too. The air force had given me the expertise I needed, and I was in a fever of impatience to get into the air again. The hope of being one of those first on the ground in the North after the war was one of the reasons I jumped out of the air force so quickly.

Of course, nothing ever works out as easily as we hope. When we got back to Edmonton, I went to see Jimmy Bell, the manager of Edmonton Municipal Airport, an old-timer who knew just about everybody in the flying business out there. He put me in touch with another old-timer, Jack Moar, who had flown in the Arctic and was anxious to start an air-freight business to take advantage of the boom that was bound to come in the post-war North. There was a good deal of prospecting for gold around Yellowknife in the Northwest Territories at that time, which was bound to lead to a demand for airplanes to fly in the freight and the prospectors and, in due course, the miners to wrench out the gold. Jack Moar was a very personable man, with a thousand fabulous stories and a gift for telling them. He is gone now, but his wife, Kitty, is still alive. Years later, we named one of our Airbuses for him.

The war had suspended the northern build-up that had begun in the 1920s, so there was an enormous potential just waiting to be tapped. One of the first to recognize this was Cy Becker, a First World War ace who had gone to work for Canadian Pacific Air Lines, and who would later become a lawyer for the firm I used. CP Air had been put together out of a dozen small regional lines in the West and North by James Richardson, a Winnipeg broker, in 1942. Becker, as general manager, was in charge of the expansion that would transform northern Canada, and his company ran the only regular air service between Edmonton and Yellowknife. But there was far more work than could be handled by a scheduled airline, just waiting for anyone with the gumption and the financial backing to go and get it. My meagre savings wouldn't be enough, but I would fly for Jack Moar; I didn't know how to run an airline, but he did, presumably. What could be more straightforward than that? Jack was a great person, and he needed pilots, so we shook hands on a deal. He planned to buy a couple of airplanes, and we would take it from there.

I presented myself to the Department of Transport examiners and obtained a transport licence, the highest standard of pilot's licence, and then I sat around Edmonton for the best part of a year, waiting for Jack Moar to get into gear. He was not a quick-starter.

Marjorie and I were staying with my sister, Lillian, and her husband, Alan Nicholls, who had lost an eye in combat while in the army overseas. None of us had any money, but the Nichollses owned an elderly house, and I renovated that while I waited, even doing the electrical work, since electricians were both hard to come by and expensive after the war. Lillian and Alan were a constant source of encouragement to us. In fact, we were in all ways most fortunate in the caring support of our families in the situations with which we found ourselves constantly coping.

To keep body and soul together, I also went to work selling war-surplus supplies for a man named Aitken, who was primarily in the tailoring business, but who would turn his hand to anything. Aitken had bought all kinds of war-surplus material from the services – rubber sheeting, tubing, fuel pumps – which had been in short supply for years. I would make the rounds of the farmers, hospitals, garages, lumber yards, whatever, around Edmonton and write up orders for this stuff. The work was interesting enough, I met a lot of fine people, and I managed to hold onto most of my savings, a couple of thousand dollars in war bonds that I had accumulated in the air force. Still, it was not the work I wanted to do.

Finally, Marjorie and I found a small place of our own, since we were expecting our first child – which turned out to be a daughter, Gai. We lived very simply, in a basement apartment on the south side of Edmonton, and used furniture I built myself. Marjorie and I didn't drink or smoke, so it didn't take much to support us, but I thought I would go crazy waiting for Jack to get going.

One happy break came during the summer when Marjorie and I took off with another couple, Toby and Genice Wood, who owned a convertible with a rumble seat, for a holiday trip to Vancouver via Banff. Toby was a student dentist who had been a dental technician in the army, and he was taking this chance for a break before settling down to his career. The Woods were a fine, fun couple, but their car, which had mechanical rather than hydraulic brakes, was very nearly the death of us.

The car didn't actually die on us until we were on the last lap home, not far from Edmonton; then the gear-shift gave up, just outside a small town, and we were brought to a rude halt. We pushed the stricken vehicle to the town's lone service station and, while the mechanic went to work on it, we held a council of war. How much money did we have left? Purses, pockets, and odd corners were searched and emptied, and we came up with a grand total of seventy-five cents. I thought I'd better talk to the mechanic before he discovered we didn't have any money.

"Ah, um," I said to him, "about how much do you think it's going to cost to, ah, get her going again?"

He had obviously overheard our cash pool going on; he looked steadily back at me and said, "Oh, seventy-five cents."

Thus it came about that we returned to Edmonton triumphant, exhausted, and absolutely out of cash.

I still remember that trip, for all its trials and tribulations, as one of the finest times of my life. Which is just as well, because it was the last holiday I would get for twelve years.

Jack Moar finally got hold of two aircraft in the spring of 1946. They were not new, of course; he bought them second-hand from the air force, a Cessna T-50 Crane and a Tiger Moth biplane. By this time, there was another pilot waiting along with me, Dick Cull, also ex-air-force, and the arrangement was that Dick would fly the Tiger Moth, and I would handle the Cessna, another training aircraft with which I was thoroughly familiar. Dick took the Tiger Moth up to Yellowknife to start commercial operations. Most of our business, we figured, would be from Edmonton to Yellowknife, carrying in people and supplies, or out of Yellowknife to the various survey camps.

In late April, I kissed my wife and new baby goodbye and took off from Edmonton airport, headed for a new world of adventure with Jack Moar. Who promptly stranded me in Fort McMurray in northern Alberta.

I'll never forget Jack's instructions on how to fly to Yellowknife: "Oh, we just go to Fort McMurray, and follow the Slave River north." This crude advice made perfect sense, and the fort made a natural stopping-off place before continuing the trip to Yellowknife. But, when we got there, Jack ran into another bush pilot, Matt Berry, and then suddenly announced to me that he and Matt and the Cessna were going back to Edmonton.

"We'll be back tomorrow," Jack said. "Wait here."

So I cooled my heels at Mrs. Coffee's hotel in Fort McMurray, while a day went by and then another, and then another, and still no sign of Jack. When I checked at the airport, there was no flight plan filed, and no word from my errant boss. I later learned that, on the flight back to Edmonton, Jack, at the controls, had landed with his wheels up, and bent the props of the Cessna T-50. He was lucky the damage wasn't worse. We kidded him a lot, because he claimed there was something wrong with the plane, that when he put the wheels down, nothing happened, but the crew at the airport jacked up the aircraft, hit the switch, and down came the landing-gear.

When Jack finally showed up at Fort McMurray, he didn't say anything much to explain the delay, just informed me that we would take off the next day for Fort Smith, on the

Slave River south of Yellowknife. There we stayed in the Hudson's Bay Hotel, run by a German fellow named Paul Kaiser, who made us sleep out on the veranda behind a screen but charged us the full rate for a room anyway. Fort Smith was really humming with miners, prospectors, and just plain adventurers following the call of the North. It was an exciting and vibrant time.

From Fort Smith, we hopped over to Yellowknife, which then was not much more than a tangle of shacks strung along Back Bay, an extension of the North Arm of Great Slave Lake, and around The Rock, which forms the spiritual centre of town, with dirt streets, wooden buildings, and a background of rock, lake, and bush. The town, I learned later, was named for the Yellowknife Indians, who had inhabited the area in the late 1700s. It sits on an outcropping of the Laurentian Shield near where the Yellowknife River empties into Great Slave Lake. The first permanent settlement was established here by Alexander Mackenzie, as a fur-trading fort, but it was never very prosperous. In the 1890s, prospectors found traces of gold in the area, but nobody got serious about it until a big strike in 1934, which set off a boom. By 1940, the population had hit one thousand – huge for a town in the territories at that time – but the onset of war ended the excitement, and Yellowknife was virtually deserted until 1944, when Giant Yellowknife Mines moved in and made a strike even bigger than the one in 1934. When the war ended, people poured north. The town at the time of this visit consisted largely of the old mining shacks, hastily thrown together from planks. The New Town, with its skyscrapers and apartment blocks, was not even a dream.

When I arrived, the town was still a virtual fiefdom of the Ottawa bureaucrats; it was run by the Commissioner of the Northwest Territories, in the national capital three thousand miles away, and by a group of mandarins, under an administrator, in the town itself. Yellowknife didn't elect a mayor until 1953. It was to become the territorial capital in 1967, and the Commissioner would move north then. In the immediate post-war period, it was a place of ferment, chaos, dirt, and discomfort. I loved it. Still do.

However, my enthusiasm was somewhat dampened by the fact that I couldn't figure out what Jack Moar was up to. We didn't seem to be doing much flying. Then one day Jack said that we were going to go over to Mills Lake, a tiny settlement across Great Slave Lake from Yellowknife, not far from where the Mackenzie River begins its journey north to the Arctic Ocean. Here, it turned out, Jack had bought a lot of war-surplus equipment, which had been stored by the American engineers for the building of the Canol pipeline from Norman Wells to Alaska as part of that mammoth engineering feat, the Alaska Highway. The Canol pipeline was built to supply fuel for the trucks and other equipment working on the highway. Mills Lake was a staging point on the Mackenzie River, from which materials were lifted north to Norman Wells, and Jack had bought a lot of the pumps, piping, and other supplies that had been left there.

I was not in the airline business, it seemed; I was back in the war-surplus game.

I flew over to Mills Lake, about an hour by air from Yellowknife by Cessna Crane, to have a look at the airstrip, with Jack Moar in the right-hand seat. The "airstrip" was just a dirt trough bulldozed across the landscape on the flatlands above the banks of the Mackenzie, and the spring rains had turned it into a sea of mud. I figured we couldn't land.

Jack was disgusted with me. "Hell, if you won't take her in there, I will," he said.

And he did, more or less. As we made our approach in the gathering evening gloom, Jack claimed that what looked like impassable gumbo was "just a couple of inches of mud; it's fine underneath," so he lined her up, set her down, and all hell broke loose. The moment we touched down, the wheels grabbed, mud splattered all over the windshield, the aircraft skidded, veered, and came to a sickening halt, after a very short landing run.

"Well," I told Jack, "you got her down. I'd like to see you get her up again."

Jack didn't say anything. He'd heard enough from this lippy kid.

There was a watchman on duty – he turned out to be the total population of Mills Lake at the time – who had seen us land from his perch on the river bank. He said he would be pleased and proud to have company, and it looked as if we were going to be there for a while, so we bunked down in one of the huts that had been abandoned by the Americans, to wait until morning – to see how bad the damage was.

When day dawned, the Cessna looked pretty woebegone, and so did Jack, but I surprised him by announcing that I thought we could plank the plane out. First, we had to jack each wheel up onto a length of plank, then taxi the plane forward, lay down more plank, taxi, lay planks, and so on, until we got the aircraft out onto higher, harder ground along the river bank. So far, so good, but when I looked over the proposed takeoff route, stretching along the Mackenzie, there was a ravine right smack-dab in my path. There was nothing for it but to haul out more planking – fortunately, the engineers had left lots of it around – and build a temporary bridge over the ravine.

This took several days. Then there was another problem. Taxiing the Cessna down the planks kicked up stones, which eventually shattered the propellor tips. One propellor was damaged more than the other, and out of balance, so I cut off both tips to about the same length to minimize vibration. The next problem was to draw sufficient power from the engine with the now-smaller props for takeoff, without exceeding the maximum RPMs.

Finally, I was ready to go. Jack and I decided it would be safer if I took the Cessna off by myself, so he stayed behind while I taxied her down the shore, gave her the gun – I ended up with one throttle pushed forward and the other way back, to try to get the two engines generating their maximum thrust – and wobbled into the air. I got back to Yellowknife all right, managed to get my hands on one used propellor to replace the most severely damaged one, and went back to get Jack. By my return, two days later, the strip was dry at Mills Lake, and we took off again with no trouble at all.

That was an indication to me that flying in the North was going to be somewhat different than flying out of air-force stations in southern Canada.

I got another taste of the same sort of thing soon after. In early June, about two months after I arrived in Yellowknife, Dick Cull, the Tiger Moth pilot, had an accident. He had taken Vic Ingraham out to locate a winter "Cat-train" – made up of a line of Caterpillar tractors – on Great Slave Lake for Vic's brother, Harry. Vic had lost his legs in a fire on a boat on Great Bear Lake. He owned Yellowknife's only hotel at the time, and he had helped to finance Harry's sawmill at the mouth of the Slave River, where it pours into the south side of Great Slave Lake, across the lake from Yellowknife. Lumber was in great demand in Yellowknife, and the sawmill was a profitable venture. Dick flew Vic over to the sawmill a few times, and on one of these trips, Dick, who was a bit of a daredevil in the air, did a series of rolls and loops, and poor old Vic, who had only artificial limbs to brace himself with, was thrown all over the cockpit; he was mad as hell. Dick came a cropper landing on an ice strip at Yellowknife Bay, smashing the lower wing of his biplane on a forty-five-gallon oil drum used to mark out the runway. So Jack bought a replacement lower wing for the Tiger Moth and flew it into Yellowknife. Aircraft engineers being in very short supply, I was given the job of installing the wing on the Moth.

Of course, I had only a dim notion of how to do it. I had seen pictures of the rigging of a biplane in a manual somewhere, so, with nothing more than these vague memories to guide me, I set about the task. I put the aircraft into a flying position, with the tail up, took off the old wing, marking all the bolts and wire, and jiggled the new one into position. The Tiger Moth was rigged by flying wires, and these had to be adjusted to get the wing to the right angle and tension. It took me three days to get the wing and aircraft rigged, and I had no idea whether the plane would fly or not. Before the aircraft could be certified to fly again, a proper engineer would have to sign it out, so Jack Moar got hold of one of his buddies from the Consolidated Mining company, and he and the engineer descended on my makeshift aircraft factory that was sitting on the shoreline, to check things out. The engineer looked at the Tiger Moth, walked around it, plucked a wire or two, and pronounced it fit to fly. He even signed the logbook to that effect.

I said, "You're crazy! Haven't you got some sort of rigging tools so we can check this thing?"

He just looked at me.

Dick Cull had more faith in my work than I did; like the engineer, he, too, walked around the aircraft and pronounced it fit to fly; then he climbed in, took off, and proceeded to loop and roll around the sky. I couldn't bear to look, but the wing stayed on, and he came in whistling.

Jack then asked me to fly the Tiger Moth back to Edmonton for a service check, and, since I would get to see Marjorie and Gai again, I was happy to comply. I might not have been so happy had I known what a tricky trip it would turn out to be.

The Tiger Moth had a flying range of about 130 miles at the best of times, so the six-hundred-mile trip to Edmonton would have to be done by stages. I flew to Fort Resolution, where there was a cache of fuel, then on to Fort Smith, and then to Embarrass Portage, refuelling each time. The next stage took me straight down the Athabasca River to Fort McMurray. To get out of the heavy headwinds – the Tiger Moth would only do about 85 mph at the best of times, and when the wind got too heavy, you might just as well get out and walk – I slipped down into the river valley and flew below the banks, just over the tops of a couple of steamboats, and landed at the fort in a starlit sky, with my fuel tank barely damp. I might well have gone down in the dark; however, my clearest recollection of that trip had nothing to do with worrying about running out of fuel, but of walking into the little radio shack and hearing the Grand Canyon Suite playing on the radio. The people in the shack didn't even know I had landed.

After a pleasant night at Mrs. Coffee's hotel, I started out again. This time, I took a ten-gallon keg of gasoline with me in the front seat; I figured on landing on the ballfield at Athabasca, filling up again, and that would get me to Edmonton. The only trouble was that, when I got to Athabasca in mid-afternoon, there was a ballgame in progress. I circled the field to let them know I was coming in, and the players, very reluctantly and with much shaking of fists, moved out of the way and let me land. I refuelled, and they were even more disgusted when I asked them to break up the game again so I could take off. More than three decades later, when I was receiving an honorary degree at Athabasca

University, a man who had been playing in that game came up to me; he still remembered the crazy pilot who had come in carrying his own gas tank with him and had broken up the ballgame.

While I was in Edmonton, I gave a lot of thought to what I ought to do next. It did not seem that any long-term connection with Jack Moar was going to work for me. At the same time, Toronto mining people were active in the area, and penny stocks were booming, to finance exploration and development in the north. Yellowknife was going to get only a tiny bit of this money, but even that would be enough to make it a thriving town.

Also, it was a town I had taken to instantly. It was not much to look at, God knows, and the conditions there were primitive: I was living in Vic Ingraham's hotel, which had, in the bathroom, a big can with a toilet seat on top of it. But you could go across to Sleepy Jim's restaurant and see the butter sitting on the counter in big tubs – rationing applied elsewhere in Canada, but not here. The people were friendly – crazy, but friendly – the countryside was magnificent, and for a young man in his twenties, looking for adventure and a chance to make his mark, it was the best possible place in the world.

I knew CP Air was doing a good job of serving the bush, but there was far more work than they could handle. I talked it over with Marjorie and decided that I would buy my own aircraft, fly it up to Yellowknife, and get all the business I wanted.

I put together a pool of $6,000: $2,000 left from my own savings, $2,000 from Marjorie's dad, and $2,000 from a family friend. The bush pilots in Yellowknife told me that the best aircraft I could get for the money was a de Havilland Fox Moth, a larger version of the Tiger Moth. The price was $10,000, with wheels, skis, and floats, and I would have to go to Toronto to pick it up. I could put down $4,000, finance the rest, and save a little for operating capital.

That's how it came about that, in July 1946, I boarded a Trans-Canada Airlines Lodestar in Edmonton and headed for Toronto with a bank draft in my pocket and a song in my heart. I was going to have my own aircraft at last.

Little did I know that just about the first thing I would do with it would be to crash it.

CHAPTER 5

Disaster Strikes . . . and Strikes

To begin with, everything went well. I went out to the de Havilland plant at Malton, outside Toronto, and walked through a whole hangar full of Fox Moths, and parts of Fox Moths, that the company had stockpiled for sale. George Mickleborough, the de Havilland representative who took me around, explained that the Fox Moth had been adapted from an earlier model built in the 1930s. The new version had three seats up front between the wings, and the pilot sat in the rear. Like the Tiger Moth, it was a biplane, which meant that it had lots of lift, and it could carry about five hundred pounds of freight, or three passengers, or a combination of the two. (That was what the designers said; I never found it wise to carry more than two passengers.) I arranged financing with Industrial Acceptance Corporation: they put up $6,500, while I put up my $4,000; I was to pay the loan off, I remember, at $415.46 a month.

Years later, I would be lashing out $50 million (U.S.) or more for an aircraft, and a lot of that would be borrowed, too – but no purchase ever thrilled me more than this first one.

The details were all cleared up by the end of the week, so I decided to head back at once, which meant leaving Toronto early on Sunday morning. George Mickleborough said that this would be okay; he would arrange for the watchman to let me into the hangar to pick up the aircraft – or, at least, to pick up most of it. The arrangement was that I would pick up the floats, which cost $2,500, at McDonald Brothers in Winnipeg. George advised me that I wouldn't have anybody to help me with the takeoff, but such is the confidence of youth that I said I didn't need any help.

When I got out to the airport, I walked around my beautiful new aircraft, registration number CF-DJC, and then, with the help of the watchman, pushed her out of the hangar. I hadn't flown this kind of aircraft since my first training days in High River, but that didn't concern me a bit. What did concern me was that starting her up was a bit complicated. You had to swing the prop by hand to get her going, so the design was such that one person could, in theory, perform the job from outside the aircraft.

First, I climbed into the cockpit and set the brakes, which were mechanical brakes, rather than hydraulics, and not very effective. Then, I clambered back out and set a little throttle just behind the engine, at the leading edge of the lower wing; in addition, a small, spring-loaded cable with a ring on the end, called a tickler, led from this to the engine, and primed the carburettor. Once I had this set, I threw the switches, and dashed around and swung the prop. Outside of giving me a pretty good workout, this produced no results whatever. I opened the throttle a little wider – no result; still wider – still no result. Finally, she caught, and I had to reach the throttle to reduce the power quickly. I dashed around the whirling prop to grab the wing and leaned against it, but because the brakes weren't very good, the plane began to swing around me. I managed to grab the wing-tip and hold on for dear life, so there we were, for a while, like those scenes you used to see in old westerns, where the greenhorn is trying to get into the saddle and the horse keeps spinning away from him. Still holding on desperately, I managed to inch my way up to the external throttle with my legs braced against the wing, and cut the engine down to an idle. Finally, I scrambled aboard, somewhat sweaty and considerably wiser.

"You're not supposed to leave without me," I told the aircraft, as I taxied her down and lifted into the Toronto sky.

I had had an auxiliary gas tank fitted, so I was able to get all the way to the Lakehead that night, even though I picked up some carburettor icing along the way and had to remember to turn on the carburettor heat. With luck, I thought, I could make it all the way to Winnipeg in two days. However, the weather turned against me, and I had to land, in the dark and in fog, at Kenora, about 140 miles east of Winnipeg. No sweat, I thought, I could easily hop over to Winnipeg the next morning. First, however, I had to get down at Kenora, which turned out to be more complicated than I thought, because there were no lights on at the airstrip when I got there after dark. Still, I could vaguely make out the runway, so I lined her up for the centre of the strip and set her down. One of the tricks to the Fox Moth was that, with the pilot's cockpit so far back, you couldn't see ahead of the aircraft, just out one side or the other; when landing, you set her on a straight path, and let her go.

I touched down, rolled a very short distance, and came to an abrupt halt, so abrupt that I was thrown into the dash and broke my nose. It turned out that they had been grading the gravel runway that day and had piled a ridge right down the centre. If I'd gone to either side, I'd have been all right; as it was, my beautiful new aircraft was wrecked.

I got out to the airport shack and fetched help, but there was nothing they could do for the Fox Moth; it would require major reconstruction. The next day, I phoned McDonald Brothers, and they sent out a trailer truck to haul us to Winnipeg. Thank God I had the aircraft insured. When the insurance agent called on me in Winnipeg, he asked me the cause of the crash. Because I had landed at night, in fog, with no landing aids available, I told him there was, unfortunately, no doubt about that. It was "pilot error."

He nearly dropped his notebook. "My God," he said, "you're the first pilot I ever ran into who ever made an error."

McDonald Brothers rebuilt my poor, stricken craft and put her on floats. Five weeks after I arrived in Winnipeg, she was ready to fly again, sitting by a dock on the Red River not far from downtown. Then I went over to the Department of Transport office to get my aircraft cleared for use again. The District Inspector of Air Regulations in the city at that time was a tough, gloomy-looking old bird named Fred Bone, who wasn't at all impressed by this stupid young whipper-snapper who had smashed up his aircraft on her maiden flight. He took my licence from me and grunted, "Well, I guess you need a float endorsement, that right?"

"Right," I said.

"Uh," he grunted. He looked at me, and looked at the licence again, and then he signed it and handed it back to me.

Just as I turned to leave the office, he said, "I suppose you've flown a float plane before?"

Well, no, as a matter of fact, I hadn't.

Fred looked shocked, and gloomier than ever. "Hell," he said. "I've already endorsed your licence. Well, come on, we'll have to do something about this. Meet me down at the dock in about an hour."

And he shook his head in total disgust.

An hour later, I was waiting down beside the plane on the river, with a railway round-house in the takeoff path, when Fred drove up in a great big Hudson car – I remember how impressed I was with it – and he scrambled down the river bank to the dock.

"Now, watch me," he said, when he got there. "I'm going to take her up for a circuit or two and show you how to handle her. Just do what I do, and you can't go wrong." He didn't look as if he believed it.

When he said to watch him, he didn't mean from inside the aircraft, since the pilot's cockpit held only one person; he meant that I should stand on the shore and observe. He revved her up, taxied out into the middle of the river, went through a warm-up, pulled up the water rudders, and took off. He did a couple of circuits, obviously enjoying himself thoroughly, landed, and taxied back to where I was standing on the dock.

"Now," he said, "come with me." And I walked up the high river bank to his car with him. He got in the car, lowered the window, and ordered, "You stand right here until I have gone completely out of sight and the dust has settled. Then," he said, "go back down and practise some landings. Got that?"

Then he grunted goodbye and drove off.

I waited until the sound of his vehicle had faded and then clambered into the plane. I did everything exactly the way Fred Bone had done it, and it went smooth as silk. After a couple of circuits, landings, and takeoffs, I refuelled and headed for The Pas. I was now checked out on floats.

From The Pas, I made it to Cooking Lake outside Edmonton in one hop. I was more than a month and a half late by the time I got to Yellowknife.

I had registered an Alberta company, Polaris Charter Company Limited, to fly material into the mining camps around Yellowknife, and as soon as I had finished up the paperwork in Edmonton, I took off for Fort McMurray. Then I pushed on up to Fort Smith. As in the Cessna, it was a one-day flight from Edmonton to Yellowknife if I left in the morning, and the North enjoyed fairly long hours of daylight at this time of year.

At Fort Smith, I landed below Pelican Rapids, where, unbeknownst to me, there was a mud-bank undercut by the swirling rapids just where you docked. I taxied up to the edge, as close as I could get to the bank, and when I got out on the float, I realized I would have to step into the water to get to shore. Well, I'll get one foot wet, I thought, and stepped off the float into about ten feet of water. I went right over my head, came up spluttering, scrambled ashore, and pulled myself onto the float. Actually, there was no danger of anything happening to the Fox Moth; it was sitting calmly in a back eddy. The only thing that could have gone wrong was for me to drown. I was beginning to learn that, in the North, things are not always what they seem, not even an innocent-looking little band of water.

I landed in Yellowknife the next day, taxied over to the government dock, and immediately started looking for work. It was now early September of 1946; I had debts to pay and a business to build and, so far, all I had managed to accomplish was to wreck my aircraft and nearly drown myself.

I arranged to park the plane at the protected end of Back Bay, the stretch of water Yellowknife had wrapped itself around, at a dock owned by Jim McAvoy, a mining man who turned out to be a wonderful friend to this green kid. He did a lot of work staking mining claims in the Arctic, and had a Fox Moth of his own. He helped me get my very first paying charter, which was to take two prospectors and their equipment in to a lake about seventy miles straight east of Yellowknife. I was very nervous about that first flight, although I hope I didn't show it, and when we got to the lake, I ran the aircraft right up onto the sandy shore, because I was afraid of denting the floats on a rock. They were very impressed with the service.

The charge for that flight was calculated at forty-five cents a mile, both ways, for a grand total of sixty-three dollars. I was in business at last.

Pretty soon, I had as much work as I could handle. Everybody was going to make his fortune by striking gold, and a few did, although far more spent their money in vain. I once talked to John McDonagh, a mining man who was on the board of de Havilland, who told me that if he managed to get twenty-five cents out of every dollar raised in stock sales actually invested in the property, he considered that he had done well. I was shocked. I thought when you bought mining stocks, they took your money and put it to work in the ground; but most of it went on promotion, legal fees, advertising, overhead, and heaven knows what all. In Yellowknife itself, there were two large mining companies, Consolidated Mining and Smelting and Giant Yellowknife Mines, both conglomerates. Out in the bush, in the two-hundred-or-so-mile circle where I had most of my business, there were a number of smaller outfits, some of which made money and some of which did not. The truth is that mining is a pretty tough business, although, in those heady days, it seemed that everybody was going to wind up rich. It was a time of great activity and excitement, and for a twenty-five-year-old, it was heaven.

Most of my customers were prospectors; not the old, grizzled ones you see in the movies, but middle-aged men. I would fly them and their equipment in to some tiny lakes about which they had heard a rumour or picked up a bit of inside information, drop them off, and retrieve them later when they were either rich or fed up. I never did have a customer who really struck it rich, although other pilots did. One of the lucky ones was a man named Spud Arsenault, a prospector who was offered $100,000 in cash for a property he had staked on Spud Arsenault Lake. The mining company held a big promotion in Edmonton and flew Spud in to show him off. At the promotion, the publicity boys turned up with a briefcase with $100,000 in U.S. bills in it, to illustrate how much money Spud was going to be getting. He took one look at it, said "Thank you very much," counted it, closed up the suitcase, picked it up, and walked out. He knew that most prospectors get more promises than cash for their properties, and when he saw the money, he decided to take no chances on getting paid later.

I lived in Vic Ingraham's hotel in Old Town Yellowknife until I could bring Marjorie and Gai up from the south. It was a busy, exhausting time; I worked long, long hours, and I was a very happy man, until the next disaster struck.

In late October, my friend Jim McAvoy asked me to fly him in to a small mining operation at a spot just west of Gordon Lake, an hour out of Yellowknife. The dock at this place was long and narrow, only about two feet wide, and perched on top of poles stuck down into the mud, a pretty tricky proposition for tying up an aircraft with a low wing. When we came in to land, there was ice forming on the lake and a strong wind, but I set the plane down easily enough and taxied up to the dock. When I saw how rickety the structure was, I decided to stay by the plane while Jim went to look at the drill cores, which were the reason for his trip. When we were ready to leave, I asked a couple of the men working there to help hold her against the wind, which was now quite stiff.

"I want one of you to hold the front of the wing strut, and the other to hold the back," I said. "When I get the engine going, and I am back in the cockpit, the one at the front can come across the wing-root [the straight piece that spans the cabin] and cast me off."

That's what we did, and everything seemed to be going well as I headed for my next job, which was to drop a fellow off at Spud Arsenault Lake. As we came over the lake, I noticed it had even more ice on it than the lake we had just left behind, so I was flying around looking for a patch of open water close to the property, when suddenly the engine went very rough. I switched off all power and glided down onto the lake, with the heel of the floats just skimming the ice, until I touched down on a stretch of open water and plopped her down. When we got the plane paddled into shore, I checked the oil tank, and it was bone-dry. The Fox Moth had a spring-loaded oil drain on the outside; clearly what had happened is that the parka of one of the men helping me had caught on this and opened the valve, and the tank had drained. With trembling hands, I opened the plate on the side of the engine and stuck in my finger. It came out covered in little bits of warm metal that used to be the bearings that protected the engine.

My engine was shot; I could not take off, and I was stranded in the wilderness miles from any signs of civilization, much less a mechanic. I had a pretty gloomy, thoughtful walk over to a mining camp, four miles from the lake shore, where my passenger and I would have to spend the night. During all the time I had spent in the air force, I had never pranged an aircraft through any fault of my own. Now, I had done it twice, in short order.

However, when I got to the mining camp, the other side of the North, the friendly side, came to the fore. Everyone realized what trouble I was in, and I was offered a hot meal and a space in the one large sleeping tent for as long as I wanted, with no questions asked and no bill, of course, ever to pay. That night, I sat up for a long time – I was far too distraught to sleep – with the fire-minder for the camp, a delightful old boy who had been educated at Oxford and had served in the diplomatic corps in Moscow on behalf of his native England. Like a number of the people in the North, he had a drinking problem, and the only way he could lick it was to get away from any place where alcohol was served, so he took whatever jobs he could get in the bush. One such chore was to service the airtight stoves that kept the tents from freezing. We sat up most of the night, and he took my mind off my troubles by reciting Shakespeare and Omar Khayyam and telling me stories of Russia. I have often wondered whatever became of him.

The North had many people like that in those early days, who had been quite prominent on the "outside," and were simply swallowed up in the wilderness.

The next morning, a group of the miners walked back to the lake with me, and we pulled the Fox Moth out of the water – where it soon would have been frozen in for the winter – and tied it safely down on shore. Now all I had to do was to get it fixed, if possible, get the skis I had bought with the aircraft up from Edmonton to fly it out on, get it certified to fly (which I couldn't do, since I wasn't an engineer), learn how to fly on skis (which I had never done), and my problems were solved. No, they weren't; first, I had to get out of there.

I knew there was a drilling camp on a lake several miles north and west of us, because CP Air were flying in there on a fairly regular basis, so I asked the miners if they would lend me a good bush man to help me find it. With luck, there might be a CP plane there, and I could hitch a lift back to Yellowknife. I had a sleeping bag, a compass, and a Very pistol, and I felt I couldn't get into too much trouble. So we started out, but it soon developed that the so-called bush man hadn't a clue as to how to proceed. A couple of hours out, I thanked him for his efforts and sent him back.

I went on, using the compass to keep a heading. There was nothing very difficult about this, although the bush man seemed to think there was. I would simply pick out some readily visible object in the desired direction, line it up with the compass, and head for it. When I got there, I would repeat the procedure; I always knew I was heading north-west, and I didn't see how I could go wrong, provided I didn't overshoot the lake I was headed for.

Just the same, I was considerably relieved when I topped the last ridge and looked down and beheld a beautiful Norseman aircraft on the water beside a camp, just as advertised. This was a deep lake, and the water was still open, so I knew all I had to do was get down the hill and I would be on my way. Then, to my horror, the Norseman started to warm up, turned into the wind, and went into her takeoff run. She was going back to Yellowknife without me! I began to run down the hillside, and, just as the Norseman was about to pass over me – luckily, his takeoff run went right over my patch of bush – I pulled out the Very pistol and fired a flare. The pilot, who turned out to be a man named Ernie Boffa, immediately tipped her wing and set the Norseman back down again on the lake to wait for me. I thought he would be pretty astonished to see me way out here, but I later learned that, in the bush, nothing is ever surprising.

I flew back to Yellowknife with Ernie and went about the sad business of straightening up my affairs. I was going to have to buy another engine – with fifteen hundred dollars I didn't have – and, somehow, get it out there and onto the aircraft. When I went to see Vic Ingraham about my bill at the hotel, it came to about six hundred dollars, most of the ready cash I had left. Vic knew of my troubles –

hell, everybody knew of my troubles – and he said, "That's a lot of money; let's cut it in half."

This he proceeded to do, so I still had a little operating money. It was the kind of gesture common to that country, and something I cherish and will never forget.

I sent off a wire to de Havilland, and took the CP Air plane back down to Edmonton. When I got there, there was a telegram waiting from George Mickleborough of de Havilland, informing me that a new engine was being shipped out to me; they would trust me for the fifteen hundred dollars. I gathered up my set of airplane tools and my skis and waited until solid freeze-up before heading north again. I couldn't afford the CP Air ticket this time, and I couldn't afford to air-freight my skis and motor. Truth be told, I couldn't afford anything, so it was with relief and gratitude that I accepted an offer from Garth Horricks, an ex-air-force pilot flying for Uscan Engineering Company, out of Yellowknife, to take me back with him in the company Norseman. He took me and my skis, my brand-new box of tools, and my engine, not just to Yellowknife, but right out to Arsenault Lake, where my poor old airplane was still tied up, covered with snow and waiting. What a cold-looking sight!

I knew I could fix the aircraft, if I didn't freeze to death first, because I had done so much work on her. Soon after I had landed in Yellowknife in September, the plane had come up for a regular check, so I had asked an engineer named Ernie Mills if he would do the job for me on a regular basis.

"No," he said, "I haven't got time to take on the maintenance of your aircraft. What I will do, though, is to take you through it once. You watch me and remember everything I do, and after that, you can do it yourself. If you tell anybody about this, or get me into trouble by not doing the maintenance correctly, I'll have your head."

After that, I looked after my own maintenance. I knew the airplane, and I could make her go again. I hoped. Whether I could change an engine at forty to fifty below, remove the floats, and install the skis, might turn out to be something else. Garth dropped me off on Arsenault Lake, along with all my equipment, and headed off back to Yellowknife – a lonely sight as he disappeared in the distance, I may tell you. I walked over to the Arsenault mining camp and told them I was going to be with them for a while, but once again, my offer to pay for room and board was refused, and the hospitality was wonderful.

Every morning, I would rise from a bed of pine boughs, eat breakfast, and trudge the four miles over to the lake to work on the Fox Moth. With the help of a couple of the miners, I had rigged a block and tackle to lift the aircraft and remove the floats and fit the skis. I had an engine tent and two blow-pots to keep at least a fraction of the cold out. As I took her apart, I set every bolt and nut down carefully; if I lost a single thing, I would be here until spring. I first changed from floats to skis, then got the engine out and the new engine mounted. It took me a little more than a week to change engines – I had to transfer all the accessories and fittings from the old engine to the new one – probably the coldest week of work I ever put in in my life to that point. Then, with some more help from my camping companions, I got the plane out onto the flat surface of the lake.

"Well, here goes nothing," I said, and set the switches and gave the propellor a vigorous tug. It caught on about the third or fourth try. If I didn't kill myself taking off, I was back in business.

I said a hasty goodbye to all the men who had been so friendly and supportive, and who kept to themselves their personal opinion of anyone who would get into that kind of fix, ran the aircraft down the lake, and took off. Flying on skis was even easier than flying on floats.

I knew I could do it. Now I had to find a way to pay off my debts and avoid any more calamities.

Later that year, Ernie Boffa, my rescuer, and one of the most famous bush pilots, flew my floats out to Yellowknife for me. Boffa was one of the top pilots in the North. He had flown everywhere, mostly as a barnstormer, earning a pittance by taking up customers for a brief spin; his wife, Nettie, collected the money, and he did the flying. Then he got into the bush-pilot business and flew all over the North with CP Air. He's retired now, and living in Los Angeles, and I hope the sun always shines on him, because I will always be in his debt for the feat – the considerable flying feat – of strapping my floats to the side of his ski-equipped Norseman and bringing them back to Yellowknife for me. Free.

It was the kind of gesture that made the toughness and the cold and the inconvenience and all the other hardships most worth while.

When I looked around, after I got back to Yellowknife, I wondered, briefly, if I had made a gigantic mistake. Bad luck – or was it bad management? – seemed to dog my footsteps. I was deep in debt, isolated from my family, and I seemed to be getting nowhere fast.

Should I chuck it all and try to find a sensible job? No, I decided; the things that had brought me here were still in place – the chance to fly, the people, the opportunity. I simply had to take my lumps, grin and bear it, and get back to work.

When I did that, my luck immediately took a turn for the better again.

CHAPTER 6

▼

Bush Pilot

That first winter in the North was busy, even as the days grew shorter and shorter (we had only about five hours of daylight in December and early January, from about 10:00 A.M. to about 3:00 P.M.) and the nights got colder and colder. You adjusted for the cold, expected and revelled in it, and kept on going.

I lived in the Yellowknife Hotel part of that first winter. It was a landmark in the Old Town, and had seen many strange sights and many strange characters since the early 1940s, when it was built. It was built on top of the area known as The Rock, just above the government dock on the bay, and, as the town's principal source of liquid refreshment, it was always popular.

Drink has always been a ferocious problem in the North. In Yellowknife, I came to count it a blessing when, late each winter, the town would run out of beer, and we got a bit of a break from excessive drinking until spring brought a beer-laden barge across the lake; then there was a worse blow-out than ever. The first barge in in the spring was always the beer barge, and it often had to push ice to get across the lake. There used to be a lottery on when it would arrive, and a lot of money changed hands – thousands of dollars.

While I lived in the hotel, I was fortunate to share a room – a single room was an unaffordable luxury in the crowded town – with Archie McEachren, a manager for Northern Construction and the Mannix engineering company. His companies were building a power dam at Snare River, about ninety miles out of Yellowknife, and, since my charges for the aircraft were fair and I was dependable, I soon got a lot of work flying Archie back and forth between Yellowknife and Snare River, to communicate between the two places. Through this, I met a man named Bun Russell, who was associated with the hydro development; he used to measure the river flows in various streams around the North, and gave me a lot of work hoisting him out to various sites. So did Jim McAvoy, the mining man. Bun and his wife, Margaret, became two of our best friends in the North.

I was in the air most of the daylight hours and often flew at night as well. Some of my fondest memories of those early days were of swooping through a clear, crisp, unbelievably beautiful moonlit sky, down towards the warm and waiting lights below. The air was very still in that cold; it was so smooth, it was like flying through water. The stars were crystal, the land was blue in the moonlight; it was absolutely gorgeous, although, of course, in that tricky light there was always the danger that you would misjudge the distance and try to land about twenty feet above the lake surface.

Marjorie, with Gai, was staying in Lethbridge, with her parents; I couldn't afford a place for them. In fact, I couldn't really afford my own place at the hotel, so, after Christmas, I went to see Bert Anderson, who ran the bakery and had some rooms above it. I asked him what his rooms were like, and his wife replied, "Oh, you'll love it." I soon found out what she meant.

I wondered what I was letting myself in for, but the room was a good deal cheaper than the hotel, so I moved. The room itself was tiny, and when I had my files, my records, a battered old typewriter, my little bit of clothing, and other odds and sods moved in, there was scarcely room to turn around. One advantage was that the aroma of freshly baked bread and buns greeted me daily.

However, the biggest advantage of Bert Anderson's place was that it was also the Yellowknife home of four young women who worked for CP Air, and of a group of waitresses, and their presence made me an incredibly popular fellow. People were always dropping in, ostensibly to see me, and then wandering off down the hall to see the girls.

I ate in the town restaurants. Sleepy Jim's, my first choice, burned down soon after I moved into Bert's – fire was a constant danger throughout the North, and remains so to this day – so I divided my custom between a Chinese restaurant, actually called The Wildcat Cafe, but always known as "the Chinaman's," the Busy Bee, and Ruth's Roving Hornet. Ruth was a rather sultry gal, but she had a sting like the hornet for which she named her restaurant and ran a very tight ship. Meals were served at set times, and if you turned up late, you caught a blast. I once saw her chew out a couple of old-timers for their bad manners, so, when I ate at Ruth's, I was always on my best behaviour. Still, she served the best food in town, in generous proportions, so it was worth risking the edge of her tongue to eat there.

A good deal of our time was given to combating cold, a task that began in the fall, when we flew up to Old Fort

Rae, about forty-five miles west of Yellowknife, to get outfitted. We bought caribou-skin parkas with deep hoods, mukluks, and duffles for our mukluks, along with mitts – not gloves – made out of moose hide. The Hudson's Bay store charged about twenty-five dollars for a caribou parka lined with flannelette, and about ten dollars for a pair of mukluks or mitts. With these, we were set for the winter. Caribou hide is very light but extremely warm, and you needed all the warmth you could get; the only heat inside the cockpit of the Fox Moth was what came off the exhaust manifold, and, when the windscreen frosted up, as it always did in cold weather, you had to slide back the coop-top to see out the sides when landing. These caribou parkas smelled to high heaven once they warmed up inside a room, so they had to be kept in an outer porch – if you had the good fortune to have an outer porch. They also shed like mad, so, if you kept them indoors, most of your food was served up complete with a hair or two.

The Indians lined the parkas with flannelette, so the inside was usually decorated with bunnies and Teddy bears, an incongrous sight on some of the rough types around there.

In those days, I never bought anything I didn't absolutely have to have. If I went anywhere where I couldn't wear my full warm gear, mittens and all, such as to a movie, I had to keep my hands in my pockets, because I didn't have any gloves. My first Christmas in Yellowknife brought a welcome pair as a gift from my buddy Toby Wood.

The old Moth was a sweetheart to fly, and although we tried not to take her out when it was colder than fifty degrees below zero Fahrenheit, I have flown at sixty and even sixty-five below on emergency flights. This aircraft had a four-cylinder, inverted, inline engine, for those who care about such things, and, when it got really cold, we used to put a strip of tin on the intake where air came in to cool the cylinders. The depth of the temperature determined how large a piece of tin we put over the intake – the colder, the larger the strip, and thus the less air that got in. Not exactly in line with today's computer-driven technology, but it worked.

On a typical day that winter, I would get up in the dark, eat breakfast, and walk down The Rock to Back Bay, where the Fox Moth was parked with its nose thrust into a fourteen-by-ten-foot tent. I'd open the cowlings and start an airtight wood heater I had in the tent with kindling set by for the purpose; I often had to goose the fire up a little with a splash of gasoline, because it was so cold. Then I would get the blow-pot moved right under the engine, pump it up, and start the engine heating while I went to cook the engine oil. No kidding. The oil was drained out into a five-gallon pail each night, and of course by morning it was solid as tar; you could hold the pail upside down and the oil wouldn't move. It had to be heated on the airtight stove until it was steaming. Then I would pour the hot oil into the engine, push the aircraft on her skis out of the tent, and fire her up. I always filled up with gas each night, so that task was already done. The Fox Moth burned about twelve gallons of gas an hour, and I could carry forty-five gallons in a main and an auxiliary tank, which gave a maximum range of just under four hours' flying time – about 350 miles, which made the safe range for the aircraft about 280 miles, or 300 if you wanted to take a chance. Trouble was, as the engine built up hours, the oil consumption increased considerably, and one had to carry extra supplies along on the flight. You could run out of oil before you ran out of gas.

If there was hoar-frost, which there often was in the winter, when there was more moisture in the air, it had to be brushed off the wings, unless I had foreseen it coming and had put wing covers on.

If I had passengers to fly that day, and if they were on time, we'd take off. If they hadn't turned up yet, I'd shut the engine down and rewrap it in the engine tent, but at no time, in the really cold weather, could you leave the aircraft for more than an hour without firing up. By really cold weather I mean below forty below; when it was a mere twenty below on the Farenheit scale, we'd think, "Boy, this is a great day; we can push back our parka hoods."

If the air was moist, you would soon get hoar-frost on the wings again, so I always carried along a corn broom with a sawed-off handle. When the hoar-frost started to build up and slow me down, I'd set the aircraft down on a frozen lake, haul out the broom, and sweep her off, wings and all. Some of my passengers wondered about my strange housekeeping habits when I would suddenly interrupt a flight to land and sweep the wings.

Flying over the Barren Lands was tricky. The compass on the Fox Moth was small and not too steady; it would fluctuate thirty or forty degrees in each direction as one approached the magnetic Pole, so I learned to average it out, figuring my heading by guessing how far the needle swung on each side of the dial. The land below was not much help in this country, as it was a sea of snow, as featureless as any other ocean. About the only way you could pick out a lake, if it was light enough to see a lake, was to look for shadows on the terrain. On a typical trip, I could carry two passengers and their baggage, and they were pretty crowded at that. If they were prospectors, they would usually have a tent, a small airtight stove, a supply of staples, rifles, a pick, and an axe – that was about it.

One of my great early-winter trips was with Bun Russell, the man who measured streams for the Hydrographic Survey. The first day of that trip, we flew out to Fort Reliance, 165 miles east of Yellowknife. There we bunked in with Herb

Humphries and Ed Lysyk, the two RCMP officers who patrolled the area. They had a spotlessly clean cabin, and when we came in the back door, we were told firmly to take off our footgear. We slept in the living room that first night; as the newcomer, I got to sleep on the floor, while Bun slept on the couch, which was just as hard, but warmer. The cabin was heated by a stove made out of a forty-five-gallon oil drum. The trees in that part of the territory were large enough to provide logs that would last all night, which was a blessing. Years later, Ed Lysyk, who went on to a distinguished career in the RCMP, became head of security for Wardair. He has been a long-time friend.

The next morning, I warmed up the Moth and we hopped over to the Lockhart River, about thirty miles away, where Bun got out his measuring gear. Then we had to chop holes in the ice, lower the equipment, and read off the results. We chopped a hole every ten feet straight across the river, through ice several feet thick, and by the time we were through late that afternoon, we were thoroughly cold, very tired, and totally famished. I still remember walking into the RCMP cabin, when we got back to Fort Reliance, to be greeted by a welcome blast of warm air and the aroma of cooking – although I have forgotten exactly what we got to eat. Typical fare was caribou. Ed and Herb took turns with the cooking, and they were both excellent chefs. They had a lot of goodies shipped in once a year from Fort Smith, including hardtack, which usually went to the dogs.

After that, Bun and I went back to Reliance about once every two months, and I could always sleep, even when I lost the toss and had to sleep on the floor. We always had a wonderful visit.

The work was hard but exciting, and I was able to cover the plane's expenses, pay rent, keep my loans up to date, and even begin to salt a little away. In its first three months, Polaris Charter earned a few dollars, and I was pretty proud of myself. Of course, if I were to succeed, it meant working right through Christmas, which I had to spend hundreds of miles from my family, but I couldn't afford to take that busy season off. Marjorie and I wrote many, many letters back and forth, but to tell the truth, I wasn't really lonely at this time. Of course, I always missed Marjorie and Gai, but there just wasn't time to think about being lonely. I didn't get to see my family until the spring break-up in 1947, when we changed from skis to floats and overhauled the aircraft. This was always done "outside" then – "outside" being Edmonton.

After the disastrous start I had had, I seemed to be living a charmed life, but of course, in the North, danger is never far away. On one long trip during that first winter, hauling freight by myself, I ran into a heavy blizzard and decided to set down before I got myself totally lost. This was something I had worried about, almost every day, since that first forced landing with the Fox Moth. What would I do, I would think as I peered out over the edge of the wing, down to the featureless, blank, frozen landscape, if I had to land right now? When it happened, it turned out to be almost an anti-climax. I spotted a small lake through the drifting snow, set down, and taxied over to the shoreline, where I saw a large group of trees. Then I wrapped my engine, built a fire, and made a pot of tea while I waited for the weather to clear. When it did, in a couple of hours, I simply packed up and went on my way. I always carried a full blow-pot and pail for oil, so if I had to overnight in the bush, I could.

Before that experience, I had always wondered and worried about my capacity to survive in this challenging land. Now I knew that, if I kept my head, I'd come out all right, and I stopped fretting. Or, rather, I confined my fretting to wondering if I could make it financially.

*

Making it financially looked increasingly dubious – despite the fact that I was getting as much work as I could possibly handle – after a brief encounter I had with the forces of authority not long after break-up the next spring, when the plane was off her skis and back onto floats. I was working on my dock on Back Bay, loading up passengers and freight for a flight, while, behind me on the dock, there were packages and equipment waiting for my next trips. As I moved back and forth, I noticed a couple of stern-looking, well-dressed gentlemen standing there watching my every move. After a bit, one of them came up and asked me, in a friendly tone of inquiry, whether I was flying these goods for myself or for somebody else. I explained that I was hired to carry the prospectors who were already aboard out to a camp.

"That's very interesting," the gent said. "And do you have a licence to fly a commercial air service?"

"A licence? Do I need a licence?"

The other man came up. "You do, son, you surely do," he said.

"Well, okay, where do I get one?"

The two men looked at each other. "Well," said the first, "it's a little more complicated than that."

And so it proved. I was about to be strangled in red tape that stretched thousands of miles. At first, I paid little attention. I mean, they were just a couple of guys hanging around the dock, weren't they? Well, no, they weren't. The two men were Romeo Vachon and Dan McLean, members of the Air Transport Board out of Ottawa, and they turned up on the dock again a few days later, when I was once more bustling around arranging a flight.

This time they introduced themselves properly and told me, in no uncertain terms, that I couldn't operate an air service without a proper licence, I wasn't going to get a licence until a lot of paperwork had been done and a lot of time had passed, and, if I tried to go on working on my own,

I would be charged. However, they had a solution. There was an old-timer in town named George Pigeon, who had flown in the eastern Arctic in the 1930s and had been in Ferry Command during the war. He had a commercial licence to run an air service, but he needed some help with it. George wasn't as vigorous as he used to be. So why not, the gents from Ottawa suggested, join up with George? He owned a Stinson Station Wagon and a Piper Supercruiser. If we were to form a company together, the gents happened to know, George would put in his Stinson, keeping the Piper for non-commercial use, I could put in my Fox Moth, and we would be in business. Legitimately.

This did not strike me as the ideal solution. It seemed to me a better way out would be to get a licence for myself.

Well, that might not be so easy, they said. As it turned out, the thing about George, who was a very fine fellow, was that he had a wife named Theresa, and she was very fine, too. Theresa's family had been good friends with Lionel Chevrier back in Montreal, and Lionel Chevrier was at this time Minister of Transport. What I was learning was that it was a lot easier for someone who had connections to get a licence than for me to get one.

I was young enough, and naive enough, to find this a little hard to take, so I told the gents from Ottawa that I appreciated their concern, but I wasn't sure they knew exactly what was the best way for me to run my own business – later, of course, I learned that the gents from Ottawa always know how to run everybody's business – and I would have to think it over. They departed, and I went back to work.

A few days later, an RCMP officer came to see me; he obviously felt bad about what he had to do, but he told me I was operating without the proper licence, and I'd better stop. Then I got a letter from the Air Transport Board telling me exactly the same thing. It was impressive, in a way. Here

was a government in Ottawa that, to the casual, outside
observer, didn't seem to know what it was doing anywhere,
and that had screwed up almost everything it touched in
the North. However, in a sudden burst of efficiency, they
were able to track down one tiny independent operator in
far-off Yellowknife, and nail him to the wall.

I could see the handwriting on that wall, so I went to
call on George Pigeon, who turned out to be a voluble,
excitable, and thoroughly likeable French-Canadian from
Montreal. We worked out a deal just about on the lines
the Ottawa gents had suggested, in a partnership corporation
called Yellowknife Airways Limited, and that was the end
of Polaris Charter Company. George put his Stinson into
the deal, I put in my Fox Moth, and we each owned 50
per cent of the venture. George made it clear that he was
no longer interested in the arduous life of a bush pilot, but
he had another friend, Hank Kohnen, who would fly under
George's licence.

I can't say I was thrilled with the new arrangement, but,
at least at first, it went well. We had enough business for
two pilots, and built an office. Not much more than a wooden
hut with a few crude furnishings, it was still a big step up
from standing on the dock and writing bills of lading on
my knee. I did most of the building, and most of the flying,
and we got along very well. As the business began to expand,
we were able to hire another pilot, George Fletcher. He flew
the Fox Moth or the Stinson, which was a four-passenger
aircraft that would travel a good deal faster than the Moth.

I was in a pretty good mood all that summer, not so
much because the business was booming, but because the
CP Air passenger list on August 8, 1947, named among its
Edmonton passengers "Mrs. Marjorie Ward and child."

I moved out of the room over the bakery and back into
Vic Ingraham's hotel. However, it was not the same building
that I had stayed in earlier; that one had burned down during

the winter in a fire that took the life of Carl Peterson, an old-time prospector who had spent most of his life in the area. By one of those tragic ironies, Carl had finally saved up enough money to retire in the South, and he was killed the very night before he was about to fly out of the North. Vic Ingraham built his new hotel up the hill in New Town, where there were trees and other scenic wonders, and which was rapidly becoming the locus of business and housing for Yellowknife.

Of course, we couldn't afford to live in a hotel for long; we were there about six weeks, and Gai learned to walk during that time. Curly-haired and smiling, she charmed the rugged frontier types who haunted the building. So many of these men with rough, tough exteriors badly missed having their own homes and wives and children. They treated Gai with great gentleness and longing as she navigated the stairs down to the lobby, or trotted happily from one to another of them. Vic Ingraham was a favourite with her, and he had a parrot in a cage that completely enchanted her. She was a wonderfully happy baby, which was fortunate for us, as we were confined to one room at the hotel.

Finally, I managed to buy an old, one-room house. It was about fourteen by sixteen feet, not a palace, but in housing-hungry Yellowknife, I was lucky to get it, and for one thousand dollars. I moved this old house down to the end of Back Bay, put it up on cement pads on the sand, and added another room to it, making it about ten feet longer. This is where we spent the winter of 1947–48, and a sprightly winter it was, too. I installed an oil heater, which worked quite well; at least the air from about knee-level up was warm. But if you didn't get all the water dried after you scrubbed the floor, it froze solid.

We had had a builder add another section to our tiny house in the fall, and it would have given Marjorie and me a bedroom, and created two other small rooms for Gai and our second baby, expected in June 1948. But the furnace that would have heated these rooms failed to make the last boat across Great Slave Lake before freeze-up. Consequently, the addition was useless to us until the next May, and we continued to cook, eat, sleep, do the washing and everything else in one fourteen-by-sixteen-foot room. We also had a tiny shower-room, fed by a gravity system, and this was pure luxury. Our guests often betook themselves into it at some point during an afternoon or evening visit. Drinking-water was delivered weekly to our 250-gallon tank, and it was a precious commodity.

It was Marjorie who had to do most of the coping with the exigencies of life in a wooden hut in the North, and she coped cheerfully and well, while I got on with the business.

She later wrote about her first Christmas in Yellowknife in a way that deserves inclusion here:

> I remember the first Christmas I spent in the North as one of the loneliest of my entire life. The day before Christmas, the doctor from Fort Rae called to book an emergency flight to Rat River, a small Indian community, leaving Christmas morning. Max was up and gone long before daylight. In the corner stood our little Christmas tree, with home-made popcorn strings and red and green paper streamers. All of us thought it quite beautiful, and there were a few presents under it – most of them for Gai, of course. As the day progressed, I let her open the parcels – mine as well as hers, because, naturally, opening them is part of the wonder for someone not yet two years old. . . .
>
> We had a large window in our one-room house, so that I could watch the aircraft activity on Back Bay, directly in front of the house. But in the winter, this window was always covered with hoar-frost half an inch thick. . . . I scraped a little hole low down, for Gai to peek through,

and a bigger one for me, higher up, and we kept checking all day to see if Daddy was back. The hours weren't enhanced by the fact that I was "expecting," and never felt truly well all day.

It was dark again before Max brushed the snow from his moccasins at the door. He came bearing some wonderful white embroidered leather gloves for me, trimmed with white fur. They were so beautiful that I could never bring myself to wear them, and I still have them, although they got soiled later from smoke damage during a fire.

The rest of the day was better. A dozen of us got together at Caroline and Walter England's home in the New Town, for turkey dinner. Each of us brought some good, edible thing, plus our own plates, knives, forks, and glasses. No one ever had enough china or cutlery for more than six people. But even now I remember how difficult it was for me to recover from the aching loneliness of spirit. Max and I had not been together the Christmas before, either, since we could not afford for him to leave the business in the North and go "outside," where I was, and that added to the disappointment.

I learned in time not to have great expectations of certain days or certain events. It was a small death of a childish piece of my personality, but I missed it.

By this time, Leigh Brintnell had begun to build Bellanca Skyrockets in the former Northwest Industry facilities at the edge of the Edmonton Municipal Airport. (When Charles Lindbergh was going to fly the ocean, he tried to get a Bellanca Pacemaker, but couldn't. It was an old design by Guiseppe Bellanca, a noted aircraft designer. Lindbergh ended up with an Orion.) The Bellanca was larger than the Moth, and would carry sixteen hundred pounds of freight – more than three times the Moth's capacity – or ten passengers. It was powered by a Pratt and Whitney engine, and would cruise at 110 mph. It had large front windows, but no door for the pilot – he just climbed in and out of the window – and a large freight door along each side. Tubular and fabric-covered, with wooden wings, it was a beautiful aircraft, and I drooled over the prospects of getting one, but the partnership couldn't possibly afford it. Each one cost something like twenty-five thousand dollars and I couldn't even put up my half of the down payment. However, the fact that a thing was impossible didn't dissuade me, and in the end, I decided we had to have this aircraft. I flew down to Edmonton and borrowed five thousand dollars from my brother-in-law's mother, Mrs. Anne Nicholls. I signed this note personally, and that turned up to haunt us later. Now we really had a debt-load to pay off. On the other hand, we had an aircraft that could range farther – up to about five hundred miles – fly faster, and carry more.

I flew all over the territories that summer, hauling prospectors and their equipment, helping Bun Russell with his river checks, carrying men and supplies into the mines, and carrying out ore samples and information – as well as a lot of played-out miners. It came to me that what I had read about the role of the bush plane was true; up here at the top of the world, there were no roads worth speaking of, and no railways at all. There were only the boats, which were confined to whatever course the river chose during the summer months, and the tractor trains, made up of sledges pulled by tractors across the frozen lakes in the winter. Thus, the bush planes and pilots, which could operate in all seasons, were more than a part of the transportation system; we were the lifeline of the Arctic. Without us, the area could never have been opened as it was. I was proud of my role. Now, if I could only make some money at it.

*

Early in June, when Marjorie was expecting our second child, was the worst time for such an event, because it was right in the middle of "break-up." In those days, the aircraft had to go out to Edmonton to change over from skis to wheels or floats and to complete a heavy maintenance check. Our friends Bun and Marg Russell at Snare River were also expecting a baby, possibly a week after Marjorie was due, and Marg could not remain isolated at Snare over the "break-up" period. So, it was arranged that I would fly down to Edmonton to do the float change-over, pick up Marjorie's mother, and Marg would come to stay in Yellowknife with Marjorie for the "break-up" period. She would then be there to look after Gai in case I wasn't back from Edmonton in time for the event.

Well, it was a good plan. The women joined forces as arranged, and they had some fun with their mutual predicament. Although neither Bun nor I could be around, our two RCMP friends from Fort Reliance, Herb Humphries and Ed Lysyk, were in Yellowknife, and kept an eye on them. Herb and Ed arrived for several meals, carrying quarts of ice cream as a treat, and achieved favourite-guest status by always doing the dishes afterwards.

Although our friends cooperated, Nature did not. On June 2, well ahead of her time, Marg was escorted to hospital by Marjorie, instead of vice versa, and the nurses were a little puzzled as to which one they should keep, as both appeared about to give birth. Later that day, the first plane of the float season got out to Snare River, and Bun Russell and Alan Selby, another friend, were able to get a lift into town. Of course, Bun was overjoyed to find he had become a father early. Fortunately, he and Alan bunked that night at the Ward residence, and so it came to pass that Bun was on hand to take Marjorie to the hospital in the middle of the night, accompanied by Maurice McCleery, a friend from down the way, who had a truck at hand for the transportation. Marjorie's reappearance at the hospital, with two men, neither of whom was her husband, didn't concern the nurses one bit. They were accustomed to friends looking after friends. Maurice and his wife, Pat, had a daughter only two days old, and Bun thought it appropriate that he, too, should be present for the arrival of our baby – our second daughter, Blythe.

Bun and Alan Selby stayed on for several days to tend Gai until I could fly the Bellanca back from Edmonton, bringing Grandmother with me.

Bun's telegram to me in Edmonton, alerting me to these momentous events, read, "Mine a boy, yours a girl. Bring planeload of flowers."

And I did.

I ought to have known, I guess, with life moving along on a fairly even keel – at least Marjorie and the children were with me, and the business was booming, even if it wasn't my own – that Fate would be waiting around the corner with a club, but I didn't.

CHAPTER 7

▼

Defeat, Retreat – and Return

In the fall of 1948, I was chartered by the Hudson's Bay Company for a trip to Nelson Forks, on the Nelson River, in British Columbia. (The Nelson is a tributary of the Liard, which in turn spills into the Mackenzie at Fort Simpson.) My job was to pick up a trapper, Hugo Brodelle, and his wife, and fly them in to his winter trapline in rugged terrain near the headwaters of the Nahanni. Just picking them up was no simple task; to get to Nelson Forks, you landed on the Nelson River in one of the few reaches of that stream broad enough for the purpose, and hiked three miles to the post. We had dinner there, and, later that night, I was overcome by a feeling of depression and tension. I thought I was going to be sick, but I wasn't physically ill. It was a strange and unfathomable feeling, but I shrugged it off.

The next morning, we took off and headed for the mountains. Hugo had to direct me, because the maps of this area consisted of dotted lines and the statement "unmapped," and I had no adequate directions. Hugo knew he could get there by following a chain of lakes and rivers, so away we went, with me memorizing the route backwards so that I would be able to find my way out again.

We were going to have to make two trips, because we couldn't take Hugo, his wife, his dog-team, and all his necessary supplies for the winter, at one go. On the first run, we would drop the dogs and supplies, then come back for Hugo's wife and for the rest of his gear. The Bellanca was not a happy mountain-climber, so we wound our way between the peaks, which we couldn't possibly fly over. After a couple of hours or so of winding our way past the soaring cliffs – while the six-dog team yowled its displeasure in the background – Hugo pointed me down a long, narrow valley between two mountains, and, because of the roar of the engine, made a sign with his hand; at the end of the valley, we would make a sharp right turn and find the lake.

I nodded once, gulped twice, and sure enough, he was right. There was his lake, a little jewel in the mountains. The operative word here was "little." Because we were high in the mountains, the air was thinner, which made the takeoff run longer. Hugo had assured me earlier that there was always a strong wind blowing down the valley and at his lake, which helped, because wind provides lift for an aircraft. The lake was ringed with snow and was beautiful, in a savage sort of way. There was, as he had promised, a strong wind blowing. We landed, unloaded the excited, yapping dogs, tied them up, and took off again into rapidly deteriorating weather. I had the route in my head by now – a happy trick I always seem to have had – but I was worried, because the route always looks different when you are going the other way. It was with a sigh of relief that I circled and landed near Nelson Forks late that day. The next morning, thank heaven, the wind was blowing just as strongly, although the sky was clear, and I was able, once more, to set down on that tiny lake in a sea of snow, with Hugo, his wife, and the rest of their supplies.

The trip back was fantastic, past the Nahanni Mountains and Nahanni Butte, with the hills taking on their autumn colours, the clouds white, the rivers and lakes a flashing blue, and the sun a gorgeous gold. There were the long, graceful arrows of geese piercing the sky, honking their way south, and, along one river bank, I saw moose watching me gravely, wondering why I was intruding on their paradise.

After a brief stopover at Fort Simpson for fuel, I flew back to Yellowknife. As I started my descent onto Back Bay, right over my own house, I could see there was something wrong, but I was concentrating on my approach and couldn't work out what it was. When I taxied up to the dock, George Pigeon was standing there, waving his arms, and yelling, "It's okay! They're all right! They all got out!"

I looked over to our house and saw a blackened shell.

Later, when we reconstructed the events of the previous two days, I realized that the sudden fit of illness and depression that overwhelmed me at Nelson Forks had come at the exact time the fire broke out at home. I don't know if it was mere coincidence, and I can't pretend to explain it if it wasn't; I merely note the fact that it happened.

The fire had apparently started in a stove-pipe above the water heater, and Marjorie spotted it quickly enough to get herself and the two children out. Fred Frazer, the local administrator for the Department of Northern Affairs, very kindly let us move into one of the government apartments built in the New Town for their employees, even though it was against the rules. However, it could be no permanent solution; we would have to do something about housing.

*

Work went on, and indeed, the pace stepped up. One day during the winter, when I went down to the dock, I counted twenty-one aircraft scattered around Back Bay. There were Ansons – looking very strange on skis.– Cessna T-50s, Fairchild 81s and 82s, Fox Moths, Stinsons, Piper Cubs, even a Dragon Fly and a de Havilland Rapide. Not all of these were suitable for bush-flying, which required a combination of stability, quickness at takeoff and landing, and the capacity to carry a decent payload (the Ansons and T-50s were war-surplus aircraft, and couldn't be fitted with floats, so they were not really "bush" planes). A number of ventures failed, but there was no lack of work for anyone who wanted to take it on. Incidentally, a lot of these operators never had a licence, although they were doing commercial work, but the bureaucrats, by and large, didn't come near the place in the winter. I was in the air every possible hour in the Bellanca, and we were hiring other pilots to help out. One of these trips turned into a tragedy.

On the morning of January 22, 1949, Grant Ford, flying for us in my Fox Moth, started out on a routine charter to take Henry Denis, an exploration engineer at Consolidated Mining and Smelting, and Thomas Lee, a prospector, out to a developed lead-zinc site on O'Connor Lake, south and east of Yellowknife. Grant hadn't been with us long, but he was a solid, experienced pilot with air-force training. I remember standing outside Lil's Cafe, where I had taken a brief coffee-break, and watching him go overhead to the east.

That was the last we saw of any of them, alive. The Fox Moth did not have a radio, so there was no report on their progress, and I wasn't worried at first. But when Grant didn't show up that night – the flight there and back would not have taken all day – I decided he might have had engine trouble either along the way or at O'Connor Lake, so I took off in the Stinson and followed the route they ought to have taken, across the eastern end of Great Slave. The lake was frozen solid, of course, so I kept a watch out for a downed plane, but saw nothing. At the O'Connor Lake site, I was told they had never arrived. (These days, all this would be done on the radio, but we had very crude equipment back then.) On the way back, I scoured the landscape again, and again without result, and when I got to Yellowknife, I put out a call for help from any pilots in the area.

Grant's flight had been on Sunday; I flew all day Monday, along with Herb Gratius, another pilot then working for Yellowknife Airways, and, by Tuesday, we had established a base at O'Connor Lake to work from, searching the rugged terrain all around, in case, as seemed most likely, Grant had either overshot or wandered off course. By Wednesday, two aircraft from Associated Airways, an Edmonton firm, had joined in, flown by Doug Ireland and Vern Simmonds, along with two more from CP Air, flown by Ernie Boffa and Al Finsand.

At a strategy session on Wednesday, after a long day of fruitless flying, we decided we were more likely to find the missing men at night, so we set flares on O'Connor Lake, creating a takeoff area. We figured that if the trio were still alive, they would have a fire burning, which would be much easier to spot against the blackness than would a few shadows against the day's landscape of dazzling white.

In the end, we were flying day and night, snatching a few hours of sleep − or trying to − in bedrolls on the frozen floor of the cookhouse at the O'Connor Lake site. I flew the Bellanca now, so another pilot could have the Stinson, and I still carry a vivid memory in my mind of taxiing down O'Connor Lake in the middle of the night, with a blue flame shooting out of the short, squat exhaust stack of the Bellanca engine and reflecting a blue light on the snow.

I always had a spotter with me on these flights, but it was still a little spooky trying to read a map and keep yourself from getting lost while searching for someone else. We ranged far and wide over country I had never seen before. The RCAF eventually joined in the search, which became one of the biggest ever in the North, but, while we were grateful for their help, and more than grateful for the fuel they dispensed with a generous hand, they weren't accustomed to bush-flying – the development of search-and-rescue teams came much later – and we didn't have much confidence that they would find anything.

While the men were searching day and night through weather that ranged from –30° to –50° F, the home front was caring for Grant's young wife, Merle. As always, the Northern people helped wherever they could, keeping her for meals or overnight, watching each other's children so that someone could be with her. Jim Fitzpatrick, a local ham-radio operator, had been able to reach Merle's parents and her brother Bruce "outside" – there were no long-distance phone lines – and it helped a little for Merle to be able to talk to them. Particularly wonderful to her was Dixie Stevens, the wife of the engineer at Snare River. Dixie stayed with Merle much of the time.

The plane was finally spotted ten days after takeoff, by Fred Riley, who, as an experienced fire warden, was a trained spotter. Fred was flying with Vern Simmonds, once more going over the route between O'Connor Lake and Yellow-knife. About twenty miles south of Yellowknife, Fred's eye was caught by something out of place, and he told Vern to go down and circle the spot. There it was, a burned-out wreck, with no sign of life. The subsequent inquiry concluded that Grant had missed O'Connor Lake entirely, because of fog and bad weather conditions, and had turned back for Yellowknife. Then he ran out of oil and the engine

Left: Pilot Officer Max Ward at your service. This was taken in Belleville, Ontario, when I received instructor training at Trenton. I was green as grass. (Photo by McCormick)

Below: When this picture was taken in 1950, I was loading Gus D'Aoust's dogteam into the Bellanca, to take him to the Barren Lands from Fort Reliance.

Oh, to be young again! Here I am in my lovely Fox Moth, at Snare River, NWT, in 1947. (Photo by Don Braun)

Above: This is the Beaver on the ice near Yellowknife in 1956. That's Eva Ledger-wood in charge of the dog-team, and Hank Hicks in charge of the Beaver. (Photo by Reg Corlett, de Havilland)

Opposite: Of course we smiled a lot; what did we know? Marjorie and I are at the Snare River camp in 1948; she's clutching magazines and a precious cargo of fruit. (Photo by Bun Russell)

Below: Those were the good old days – except this day. This is a picture of our survival camp after the plane crash on the Burnside River in November 1951. That's me hiding from the camera by the cockpit.

This is something I did a lot – loading my friend Norm Byrne for a trip in the single-engine Otter. The picture was taken in 1953, but I'm still wearing my school sweater from Victoria High. (Photo courtesy Henry Busse/NWT Archives)

Our pre-flight arrangements were not exactly high-tech. That's Don Braun with the pipe, looking on as Johnny Dapp, with the ruler, and Jack Wainwright plot a trip for him in our Yellowknife office in 1956. (Photo by Reg Corlett, de Havilland)

Our large and efficient – and good-natured – staff gather on the Back Bay ice in Yellowknife in 1956. From left are myself, Don Braun, Hank Fulgrabe, John Langdon, Dick Huisson, unidentified, and Janet Lamb (later, Mrs. George Curley). Our office building is at the right, and Old Town, Yellowknife, behind. (Photo by de Havilland)

The Wardair fleet in 1956, lined up below The Rock in Yellowknife. There are three single-engine Otters and a Beaver. That's Vic Ingraham's Yellowknife Hotel at right (before it burnt down). (Photo by Reg Corlett, de Havilland)

Our four children in 1956. You can see why we were so proud! Gai, left, was ten, Blythe eight, Kim three-and-a-half, and Blake eight months. Blake will love this picture.

Johnny Dapp is overseeing the loading of an Otter, with a Herman Nelson heater going full blast to thaw out the engine. This was on Back Bay in Yellowknife. (Photo by Reg Corlett, de Havilland)

My specialist hangar – it worked like a charm. Frank Grumman designed it so we could work on the Bristol Freighter in shirtsleeves in −40° F. weather. (Photo by Guenther Moellenbeck)

When the town of Yellowknife bought a fire-engine, it was trucked to the end-of-the-road at Hay River, Alberta, and then we air-lifted it to Yellowknife. Here it is about to disappear into the capacious maw of the Bristol Freighter. (Photo by Henry Busse, NWT Archives)

In Toronto, we loaded an entire Beaver aircraft into the Freighter for the flight to England. Jack Ford, my co-pilot, is at the right talking to the model who joined us, to my surprise, for the voyage. The de Havilland workers at left seem impressed. (Photo by de Havilland)

quit. That should have been inconvenient, but not fatal. However, for some reason, Grant must have panicked and tried to land on totally unsuitable terrain. The plane crashed, burst into flames, and all three men perished.

One of the toughest things I ever had to do was to go and tell Merle – Grant was only twenty-six, and she was younger – that we had found her husband, but not alive. I took Ollie Stanton, Yellowknife's outstanding doctor, along with me for moral support, but it was still a moment I would prefer to forget.

Accidents happened in the early days of flying, although, considering the amount of flying done, they were quite rare. As a matter of fact, sixteen of the men I knew in those early days lost their lives in air accidents, part of the price that was paid in developing the Arctic.

The tragedy seemed to bring to a head my dissatisfaction with the partnership I had formed – actually, it was more of a shotgun wedding than a partnership – with George Pigeon. I was working night and day, but not getting anywhere, and, while I liked George well enough, I had no faith that any business that depended on his cooperation would ever amount to anything much. An added complication was that George had always wanted to add his Supercruiser to the partnership, but I had objected because, with more assets in the company, he would have a bigger stake than I. However, we had an accountant by this time, to keep track of our growing business, and he persuaded me that this was the proper way to go. With three planes in the business, he thought, we would soon be able to pay off the still-massive debt on the Bellanca. But by the middle of 1949, I could see the partnership wasn't working. Among other things, George and I didn't agree on how the business should be run.

I concluded that I would have to get out of the arrangement, but it wasn't going to be simple. I still had assets in the partnership, but they didn't pay me anything. At the same time, I owed Mrs. Nicholls the five thousand dollars I had borrowed to put down on the Bellanca, an aircraft that stayed in the partnership, of course, under George's control. The insurance money from the Fox Moth had gone to Yellowknife Airways, and I couldn't use it to clear off the debt. So, I left Yellowknife Airways at a large personal financial loss; but the pressures of the partnership had seemed a higher price to pay.

To cover my debts, as well as to live, I went to work that spring as a pilot for Tommy Fox, the owner of Associated Airways. The company was centred in Edmonton, where Tommy lived, but it had an operation in Yellowknife. I thought I would let somebody else worry about the administrative end of things for a while, since I was wondering if perhaps I wasn't cut out for this business after all. If I could ever get enough money saved up to pay off my mountain of debts, I thought, I might just chuck the Arctic and go to work with Marjorie's father in the building business in Lethbridge.

For Associated, I flew a Bellanca Skyrocket and a Beaver, the new plane de Havilland came out with in 1947. It was the finest bush plane of the time, the first Canadian example of what is now called a STOL (Short Takeoff and Landing) aircraft. The U.S. armed forces, although they had never before purchased a foreign aircraft, agreed to purchase Beavers after a demonstration in which a Beaver took off faster than a helicopter while carrying twice the helicopter's load.

Until the fall of 1949, I worked for Associated Airways, following my now-familiar pattern of rising early, readying the aircraft, loading up, flying off somewhere in the bush, unloading, turning around, and flying back again. On some jobs, I had to do more than the mere tasks of loading, navigating, and flying; I turned my hand to whatever needed to be done, whether it was helping a prospector set up his tent or assisting my friend Bun Russell as he took river measurements.

It was on a trip with Bun in June of 1949 that I encountered tragedy again. We were out checking the flow on the Indian River, about 120 miles north of Yellowknife, and Bun had brought along a mining geologist, Dr. Mike Feniak, to help. The way we measured a river when there was no ice was to string a metal cable across the water from bank to bank, and to sling the devices that measured the water flow from this cable. It took two men to handle and read the measuring instruments, and a third to hold the canoe steady for them in the rushing spring water. My job was to handle the canoe from the front, while Mike, in the middle, wrote down the measurements, and Bun, in the back, handled the measuring equipment and called out the figures. We had just begun to work our way across the stream, when a sudden swirl of current caught us by surprise, and the boat capsized. I was able to hold on to the cable, and Bun's end swung in towards the shore, so that he simply scrambled out onto the bank, but Mike had been pitched out on the mainstream side and he was gone from us in a second. In that icy water, he could not have lasted more than a few minutes. Bun ran down the shore, trying to spot him in the swirling stream, but he had disappeared. It was not until I flew in some men from the RCMP to help with the search that we were able to locate his body, far downstream, and bring it back to Yellowknife for burial. Mike and his wife, Betty, had a small daughter, Barbara, and Betty was in hospital with a new son, Peter. Later in my life, a similar tragedy struck one of my own daughters, in an accident that cost her husband his life.

By the time of the tragedy, I had made up my mind. I was leaving the North.

I hadn't made it as a bush pilot. Luck, or bad judgement, or something, had dogged my footsteps, and this latest disaster seemed just another sign that I wasn't cut out for the business. Probably, gauging by the way small operators were going under, the aircraft industry wasn't going to prosper in the long run, anyway. Or, at least, so I told myself.

Late in the fall of 1949, Marjorie and I and the two girls packed up and moved to Lethbridge. What followed was, in many ways, a difficult time in our lives, but it had its compensations. It was the only time we lived near Marjorie's parents as a family. Consequently, our little girls grew to know and love their grandparents, two cousins, and my brother-in-law, Bill, and his wife, Eleanor. Marjorie's mother was to die suddenly in 1953, so Marjorie's memories of our time with her in Lethbridge are particularly treasured.

I left the North with a good deal of anguish, but Marjorie walked away without a backward glance. We had taken such a bruising, for so long. Gai was in hospital with one of her almost-continuous chest conditions, which always threatened to turn into pneumonia, when I came home to say that we should leave, the next day. I was to ferry a Fairchild Husky to Edmonton, and there would be room for the whole family, so we would save the considerable amount required for commercial airline tickets. Because of the fire, we didn't have much furniture to move – a crib for Blythe, which we set up in the Husky with her asleep in it, a high chair, an old washing machine, and a record player were all we had, besides a few personal belongings. We took along with us some friends, Janet and Darrell Hayes and their two children, who were also moving out and were glad of the free ride. It was a lovely flight.

The first thing Marjorie did when we got to Lethbridge was to haul me around to the flower shop, where she had worked just before going North. Back then, she had kept mentioning a husband who was flying up north, but he never appeared, and she got the distinct feeling that perhaps they thought she had made me up. It was my duty to turn out on parade and be inspected.

I went into the building business. We got a basement apartment in Lethbridge, an attractive little city just north of the Canada–United States border, and I went to work for a builder who did a lot of contracting for my father-in-law. I shifted lumber and sawed and hammered by day, and, in the evenings, I worked all-out at a correspondence course in architectural drawing. If I was going to be a builder, I was going to know something more than how to put up a wall.

I still owed five thousand dollars, a lot of money in those days, on the Bellanca I didn't own, and in the autumn of 1950 I started a lawsuit to get rid of this debt. I sued Yellowknife Airways, my old partnership, on the grounds that since they had the aircraft, they also could have the debt. I wanted them to give me five thousand dollars so I could pay it off. In the meantime, George Pigeon had sold out to another Yellowknife operator, Matt Berry, and I got a letter back from an Edmonton law firm that was like a slap in the face with a wet fish. The lawyer was Cy Becker, the man who had been so instrumental in putting together CP Air, and his letter was a straightforward brush-off. His clients knew nothing of me, nothing of any debt against the aircraft, and, in short, nothing of anything, and I could go peddle my papers. I would later come to recognize this kind of legal bullying for what it was, but at the time I was devastated. How could they say they didn't know me?

However, I didn't have any money to fight with, so I gave it up. I would pay the debt back from the building business.

I decided that I knew enough, now, to build a house on my own and sell it. Marjorie's father, Will Skelton, agreed to bankroll the venture, and sure enough, the first one worked out so well that it was sold even before it was finished. I built another, and then a third. We did everything, in those days; I even made the window frames, because I couldn't afford to buy them. We lived in the second one while I built the third, and then moved into the third when the second was sold.

I was making money, enough to pay off the debt, enough to move Marjorie and the kids into one of my houses until it was sold, enough to think about making real money in the future.

"Hey," I would tell myself every day as I went to work, "This is really fine. I guess."

But it wasn't. I kidded myself for quite a while that I didn't miss flying. Who needed the hassle, and the long hours, and the slow-payers, and the endless headaches, and the danger? Well, as a matter of fact, I did.

One evening, I was shingling one of my houses, and I was up on the roof and I looked west, out to the foothills of the Rockies, with the mountains rising behind them, and the blue light of twilight. Out there, past that hill, I knew there was another hill, and another, and another, and here, up on a roof, I was never going to be able to go chasing after them. I stood there on the roof, looking west, with my hammer dangling in my hand, and then I climbed down the ladder and went home and told Marjorie that there was an aching in my heart that would not stop.

I was going North again.

CHAPTER 8

▼

The Birth of Wardair

When I arrived back in Edmonton in early 1951, Tommy Fox immediately took me back on as a pilot for Associated Airways, based in Yellowknife, and I was soon flying the same long hours I had flown before. But this time I knew that nothing was going to drive me out of the North again, so, whatever hardships came my way, I rolled right over them. Much of the time, I found myself at the controls of a twin-engine Barkley-Grow, a sluggish sort of beast that had been designed in 1936–37 for passengers and air-freight. It had a pair of Pratt and Whitney engines, which you greased by slapping the stuff directly into open rocker-boxes. Never mind, it was an airplane, and I was back in the air.

For a few months, I flew the Barkley out of Edmonton, and then moved back North. I always knew there were risks, but I never became inured to death, even though it was so much a part of life in the bush. If people weren't killed by the elements, it seemed, they would kill themselves; at least, suicide was fairly common at that time, the product, usually, of a combination of loneliness and booze. Camp cooks, for some reason, were often suicidal, probably because they had easier access to alcohol than most. One of the least pleasant chores I had was to take a green Mountie – we often got them straight from training in Regina – into some remote bush camp to haul out the body of someone who had done himself in by shooting himself, or by some other equally unpleasant technique, and who had been left for several days before we could get out to pick him up. On a number of occasions, the new Mountie's stomach wasn't up to the task, and I added body-bagging to the list of the jobs a bush pilot had to perform. I would be pretty upset, too, but I'd do the chore and go over the hill to retch.

Then came the trip when I thought they were going to need a body-bag for me. It started on my birthday in late November, 1951. I was going to Bathurst Inlet, to deliver a Mr. Learmouth from the Hudson's Bay Company to their post there. The flight was a dead-reckoning operation during the worst time of the year to fly in the High Arctic. The ocean isn't frozen, so the haze builds up over the water and blows inland for quite a distance. Coupled to that was the fact that the radio station at Bathurst Inlet was only activated twice a week, at seven o'clock at night, and this was not one of its working days.

We left Yellowknife before daylight, because there were so few hours of light during that time of year. The farther North, of course, the less daylight in the wintertime, until around noon hour in late November the only light is refractory, as the sun is below the horizon. I was flying a Bellanca Skyrocket, a handy enough craft for this kind of trip, and one I knew well.

My mechanic on this flight was Neil Murphy, an experienced trapper. Neil's father, Matt, had a trapline at Muskox

Lake, and Neil was anxious to check on him and deliver his Christmas mail. Matt had been at Muskox Lake since late summer, and nobody had been in communication with him during that time.

When we stopped at Muskox, he wasn't there. He was out on his trapline. But he would have seen or heard the aircraft, and we knew he'd show up at the camp if we waited. So we waited and waited while the light grew dimmer and dimmer. Neil wanted to stay, just the same, and I didn't blame him. He hadn't seen his father for a long time. At last Matt turned up, with his dog-team and a huge bundle of furs, which he asked us to take back to Yellowknife. They were fine furs, fox and wolf, very light.

What we should have done was to stop right there and spend the night; the weather wasn't very good, anyhow. But time was money, and I had to get back to Yellowknife, so, when Matt finally showed up, I decided to push on, though, by this time, we had stayed too long visiting.

There was just enough fuel in the tanks to get us to Bathurst Inlet, with maybe three-quarters of an hour to spare.

The fuel-tank set-up in the Bellanca provided a bit of a hazard, anyway. The aircraft had two big, flat fuel tanks in the wings and the fuel level was measured by a glass tube on each side of the cabin. The tanks contained baffles, and the fuel outlet to the engine was inboard of the tanks, so if you were sloppy with your turns, there was always the danger that the gas would be trapped on the wrong side of the baffle, and the engine would suddenly quit. In a tight situation, it was an added thing to keep in mind.

We lost our gyro heading when we stopped at Murphy's camp, and as we headed off north into the haze, I was flying by dead-reckoning, and trying as best I could to coordinate the gyro with a wildly swinging compass. If we had flown from Yellowknife directly to Bathurst Inlet and not stopped, we would have been able to keep setting up the directional gyro. As it was, we were in a bit of a mess. The further north we went, of course, the less reliable the compass became, and when we approached the coast of the Arctic Ocean, it was swinging ninety degrees one way and then ninety degrees the other. All we had for direction, besides a questionable gyro, was instinct, which at this stage was also questionable.

Then, inevitably, we ran out of daylight. We couldn't see well enough to land and we were flying with little forward visibility – no sun, no stars, no astroshots, nothing. We just had to stay with the course we had; there was nothing else to go on. We were really in a jam. About the time the full realization of this came to me, hoar-frost plugged the Venturi tubes on the gyro, which promptly began to wobble. Now we didn't even have that to help us.

I knew that as we reached the coast the land would rise to around three thousand feet, with high hills and cliffs. It's very rugged country, and very pretty – in the right conditions – but now we were just about at the end of our tether, and I was beginning to do some serious worrying about our fuel supply. I knew by the terrain that we must be off the west side of Bathurst Inlet. I had to go with what I sensed and what I could see through the haze; there were no maps, and even if we'd had a map, we couldn't have seen well enough to pick out where we were.

Finally, I started to make out the shapes of hills below, and I knew the Burnside River must be there somewhere. I also knew that this river led into Bathurst Inlet. I figured we must be pretty well on the left-hand side of the river. But then, as the ice-particle fog from the ocean became worse, I realized I had to get down, fast, and I knew it was going to be a hairy business.

When we could see the dim outline of rock outcroppings below us, I began to search the terrain for something to focus on. Seeing what looked like a cliff ahead, I figured, knowing this country, that there must be a lake at the bottom where we could land. I knew the black wall of the cliff would give me a reference point, so I swung the aircraft around in a big circle. We opened the large side windows and, when we came around, I said, "Neil, you watch out that side and, if you see anything, yell. I'll watch out my side."

So, I went around, keeping my eye on the cliff and watching to see where my fuel was, and just as I straightened up, Neil yelled, "Pull up! Pull up!"

I yanked the controls and, all of a sudden, everything in the aircraft went "Zap!" and it began to shake and jump. We'd hit the top of a hill. We actually flew into a hill we didn't know was there.

I used power to try, in vain, to get us clear – but there was no way the aircraft was going to stay in the air. I knew that with a bang like that something had to be damaged somewhere.

I pulled the throttle off and just followed down the contour of the hill – I could see a hazy outline – until I reached the bottom. It was a trip that seemed to take forever. We glided down, nice and easy, and stopped in the snow just short of the lake we had been heading for.

The left side of the undercarriage had been broken and it sort of folded up on one side, so when I stepped out the window of the aircraft my foot landed right on the ground. Steam was coming up around the engine, and Mr. Learmouth in the back was saying, "Don't leave me in here! Don't leave me!"

I answered him as calmly as possible, "It's okay; it's not going to burn."

And, well, there we were.

It was dark by then. We all three stood outside the aircraft and looked around as best we could. We found we were in a big valley, and the snow was blowing off the cliff with a plume you wouldn't believe. We must have run into a seventy-knot-plus wind.

Fortunately, the airplane wasn't too badly damaged; besides the collapsed undercarriage, we'd bent the prop and wings, but the radio, in the belly of the aircraft, hadn't been hurt.

Our next concern was to make a camp before we froze. We had a tent on board, and we always carried caribou hides to put underneath our sleeping bags because they provide such excellent insulation. We were lucky, too, because we had picked up Matt Murphy's furs. They sure came in handy! All in all, we made ourselves pretty comfortable. We had a supply of food on board; we always carried that along, just in case. We rigged the tent under the aircraft wing – we had to, in the Barren Lands there are no trees to string it to – and spent the night in the tent.

But, before we settled down, we had to contact someone for help. We'd arrived about three o'clock in the afternoon, but we had to wait for the Heaviside layer to lower, around 7:00 P.M., to get our best radio signal out. (The Heaviside layer is named for an English physicist, Oliver Heaviside, who had established the existence of a layer in the upper atmosphere which helps to bounce radio signals, and which moves up and down.) Sun spots are active during some periods in the year, and you'll find sometimes that you can't get a signal through for days. We were lucky, too, because we were carrying a twenty-foot pole up to Bathurst with us. There's no wood in the High Arctic, of course, and because every piece is precious, we always took some with us if we were headed in that direction. We took the pole from the cabin and attached one end of the radio's trailing antenna to it. The compass had settled down by this time, the aircraft being static – very static – and I lined the antenna up in the direction of where I thought Yellowknife should be. We'd taken the battery into the tent with us while we waited, to keep it warm, so we could get a full charge out of it, and I'd isolated all the aircraft circuits except the one for the radio.

With Neil holding the pole vertical, I hit the button and called Yellowknife Radio, "EQR . . . EQR."

I had just called two or three times when darned if I didn't hear, "EQR . . . Yellowknife. Go ahead."

Just like that! It was a wonderful sound to hear.

We told Yellowknife we were close to Bathurst Inlet, probably just about thirty miles to the west of the Burnside River, and asked them to send somebody out to pick us up.

The next morning, we got up at first light, got the oil out of the engine, stamped a lot of large Xs in the snow, and got a small fire going to serve as a signal. Then I walked away from the aircraft, up into the rocks, where I could be by myself and take stock. I was thirty years old; I had a wife and two children, a pile of debts, and I had messed up my business, this flight, and very nearly three lives. I couldn't believe I had broken up that wonderful flying machine. I'd let myself make a beginner's mistake – I'd run out of time. For the second time in my adult life, I broke down and wept. Then I went back to see what else I could do to help get us out of there.

There was only one other aircraft operating out of Yellowknife at that particular time, a de Havilland Beaver, flown by Abe Dyke. (There was another Bellanca in the North, but it had been condemned by a Ministry of Transport inspector as unfit for service.) Abe got the Beaver organized, put three forty-five-gallon drums of fuel in it, and loaded the fuel tanks. Then he got an experienced Barren Lands trapper to travel with him, and the two of them headed north after us.

Would you believe it, they got lost! They spent two nights in the Barrens trying to get to Bathurst, and when they finally got there, they didn't have enough fuel left to come and pick us up – the only airplane in the North that could come to our rescue!

Well, not quite the only airplane in the North. The RCAF sent out a Dakota to look for us; they were then flying Dakotas out of Yellowknife, with very long-range fuel tanks installed. They knew we were all right, but I think they came just to see if Max Ward was where he said he was. The three of us were sitting in the tent in the twilight about midday on our fourth day, when the Dakota flew right over us. Of course, he was high; he had to be, because we were in a valley, with high ridges. When we heard him come over, I ran out and got the battery hitched to the radio, and Neil got the antenna strung out, and I called Yellowknife, since we didn't have the Dakota's frequency. I yelled, "The Dakota's right over us!"

Yellowknife heard us and contacted the Dakota. They kept repeating, "You're right over them," but the Dakota circled and circled without spotting the downed Bellanca, while we could see them clearly. We watched them get lower and lower; they had to come right down to about a thousand feet before they finally picked us out.

People don't realize how difficult it is to see a little aircraft in that vast land. Even though the Bellanca was painted orange and yellow, and the wings were clear of snow, we were hard to spot. You'd think the colours would stand out, but in the Arctic, they go black with distance.

Once the Dakota had us spotted, they came back and circled over us. They asked if we needed any supplies, but I said no, we just needed a ride. They couldn't land that size of aircraft, of course, but at least they knew we were where I had said we were.

The rest of our stay was tedious but at least uneventful. The weather turned foul again, and it was five days before Abe Dyke got in with the Beaver to pick us up. He flew us into Bathurst Inlet, where the first thing I did was to climb into a huge tub of hot water in the middle of the room at the Hudson's Bay headquarters and soak in the warmth.

The stricken Bellanca stayed there for weeks, until Associated Airways flew in a team of experts to fix her up and bring her back to Yellowknife.

For a year, I lived in the ex-CP Air building in Old Town, Yellowknife, along with several other pilots. Sheldon Luck, a long-time and outstanding early aviator, was also living in the building and flying out of Yellowknife. Luck had flown the bush for Grant McConachie, a super pilot whom I had always admired. In later years, I named one of Wardair's A-310s after him.

I ate in the restaurants around town, worked, saved, and wrote letters to Marjorie. She had remained in Lethbridge with the two girls, to sell the last two houses I had built. I also plotted my future. I was anxious to get out on my own again and build something. Having had a taste of running my own business, I could see the possibilities of creating a sound bush airline. I had my own ideas as to how an airline should be built and operated. I was ready to Go!

One day in mid-1952, I heard that Tommy Fox was on his way up from Edmonton specifically to make me manager of the operation in Yellowknife. I didn't want the job. More than that, I didn't want to have to tell Tommy why I didn't want it, so I simply made myself scarce, and was away on a flight all the time he was in Yellowknife. I later heard he was pretty ticked off at me for that. In fact, it turned out that he was so ticked off that, when I next turned up in Edmonton, he fired me.

I was sorry about that, but determined to strike out on my own. I decided to put in an application to start my own air service. I put together a very strong argument for the need for another airline in the area, citing the virtues of competition, the expansion of business, and the need for small and large operations all over the bush country. Then I went out to hire a lawyer. Naturally, my choice fell on Cy Becker, the man who had snookered me so successfully on behalf of Yellowknife Airways. He obviously knew something about air-transport law, and he was tough enough; let him go up against his former clients, who were bound to oppose the appearance of new competition, I thought.

While Cy got the wheels in motion, I went down to Toronto to see de Havilland about getting an aircraft for the airline I was so sure I was about to launch. I had heard about a new aircraft called the Otter, which was said to be something of a miracle, although it carried a price tag of $100,000, about two-and-a-half times the average cost of a bush plane at the time. It was bigger, faster, and could carry a much heavier payload than the Beaver. It had an effective range of six hundred miles, three times the range of my old Fox Moth. In Toronto, I went to call on C. H. "Punch" Dickins, Canada's most famous bush pilot and a long-time hero to me. He was Vice-President, Sales, for de Havilland, and he introduced me to George Neal, their senior test-and-development pilot, who tested all the aircraft types that de Havilland, Canada, built. George took me on my first Otter flight, and I'll never forget it.

We were lined up outside the de Havilland hangar at Malton, pointing directly at the hangar, which, to my eyes, seemed about ten feet away, when George hit the throttle. I thought to myself that we were probably going to have a short, nasty flight when that Otter just sort of leaped up in the air, jumped over the hangar, and soared. I lusted after that aircraft something terrible. It could carry fourteen passengers or two thousand pounds of freight, could go anywhere, had a fair turn of speed, handled well, and, I came to discover, would revolutionize not only flying in the North, but the way of life in the North itself.

I had lined up some financing, but it wouldn't be enough. I had done a lot of flying for Consolidated Discovery Gold Mines, and the president of that company, Jerry Byrne, was a good friend. He and his brother, Norm, a mining engineer who had a very effective mining-consulting business in Yellowknife, had agreed to help out with a company loan, although, of course, they couldn't provide more than a fraction of what I needed. So, I made the rounds of the commercial banks, and they wouldn't touch me with a barge-pole. They were sure that flying was just one of those fads that would quickly fade and, with characteristic bankers' vision, they stayed well away until others had taken the risks and proven the possibilities. Punch Dickins advised me to go to the Industrial Development Bank, which was established as a subsidiary of the Bank of Canada in 1944 – specifically to provide capital assistance for the development of new businesses such as mine.

In Toronto, I met an IDB loans officer, Ritchie Clark, who was to be my banker for years to come. I told him what I wanted to do: buy an Otter, start my own airline, pay off the Otter, buy another airplane, and keep on going.

"Fine," said Ritchie, "bring me in a financial pro forma that will show me how it's all going to work."

That was going to be a bit of a facer. I really didn't know, in detail, how it would be done. Still, I sat down with a pen and paper and began to work on it. From my own experience, I was able to put together a pro forma that looked very practical and promising. The main elements were not that hard to calculate: the charge for a mile of flying airfreight, the costs of fuel, capital, insurance, and administration, all things I had been dealing with for years. When I divided all the costs against the projected revenue, I came up with a net gain. Now, if I could only make it work out in practice.

I presented my handiwork to Ritchie, who looked it over for a long time, and then said, "All right, we'll put up the first seventy-five thousand dollars towards the Otter. Of course, we'll have security on the aircraft." With my twenty-five thousand dollars from Consolidated Discovery, I was able to put it all together.

Now I had the financing to make my dream go; all I needed was the licence. My application came before the Air Transport Board at a hearing in Edmonton. Cy and I produced a lot of evidence to show that another airline was required in Yellowknife, and Tommy Fox, on behalf of Associated Airways, opposed us on the grounds that a second airline would bring ruination, excessive costs, a shortness of breath, dizzy spells, and quite possibly an outbreak of wheat rust. John Hamilton was the lawyer on the other side, as he would be many times in the future. It was the usual sort of hearing, and I thought, as did the newspapermen who covered the hearing, that Cy Becker had done a great job, and we had made a convincing case. Foolish us. The Board turned us down flat. I suspected the problem was that we had no political connections. I had waited all through the winter of 1952–53 for the decision, a time made more anxious because we were also expecting our third child.

I learned something new about airplanes, something that I would have cause to observe many times in the future; you could get shot down without leaving the ground.

I decided to appeal the decision to the Minister of Transport, in Ottawa, and I followed the appeal down to the capital, where I went to see Lionel Chevrier, the minister. In those days, you didn't have to climb quite so high a thicket of assistants to get an appointment with a cabinet minister as you do today. I remember calling on him in his office on Parliament Hill, a silver-haired, well-groomed, handsome man, with impeccable manners and a pleasant smile.

I told him that I had been refused a licence and had put in an appeal, and now I wanted his help with it. He dispensed one of his smiles.

"Well, young man," he said. "I'm not sure, exactly, what I can do for you. The legislation to provide for appeals from the Air Transport Board is still being drafted."

He went on, "However, why don't you apply for your licence all over again, and see if you do better the second time around?"

It seemed worth a try. We had another hearing, in Yellowknife this time, in the spring of 1953, and the Air Transport Board announced that it would reserve its judgement, which would be released in due course in Ottawa. (During the course of this second hearing, when I was being cross-examined by John Hamilton, I remarked, prophetically, that "the fight has just begun," and on future occasions, he would repeat those words back to me. We became very good friends as years went by.) By this time, I was nearly frantic with worry; I had the financing lined up, but I still had bills to pay, and there was no guarantee I would come out of this hearing any better than I came out of the last one. As a matter of fact, I thought we had faced a lot tougher questioning during the second hearing, which seemed to suggest the board was going to turn us down again.

One day I was telling my troubles to Jerry Byrne, and we came to the conclusion, not surprisingly, that political pull might have more to do with these things than merit.

Jerry said, "Hey, my wife Mabel's father was Lionel Chevrier's campaign manager. Why not plug that fact into the equation?"

So, it was off to Ottawa again to a room at the Château Laurier again, a lot of nail-biting, again, and, finally, another interview with Chevrier. He received me with his usual affability, sat me down, and began to ask me a lot of detailed questions about the business, who would own it, how it would be financed, what connection his good friends the Byrnes were to have with it, and so on. I told him everything I could. It wasn't until much later that I realized he was only interested in learning one thing: Did the Byrnes family, whose connections had helped him, have anything to gain or lose in the deal? The answer to that was no. Consolidated Discovery Mines would put up twenty-five thousand dollars towards the Otter, covered by the value of the aircraft, but the family would have no further interest in the airline except in hiring the aircraft for their mining endeavours.

The next day, I was sitting in my hotel room when the phone rang. When I answered it, the caller identified himself as the Secretary of the Air Transport Board. "I've got good news for you," he said. "Your application has been approved, and a licence will be issued."

I shot back to Toronto, completed the financing arrangements for the Otter, and arranged to pick it up, on floats, at Toronto Island Airport. I accepted delivery of the fifth DHC-3 Otter off the line at de Havilland. It had the registration number CF-GBY, and it was painted to my specifications in blue with red and white trim. These were the colours I had picked out for my newly formed company, which I had decided to call Wardair – thus planting my own flag firmly where everyone could see it.

A friend of mine once told me that the colour scheme on my aircraft made them look like airborne Eaton's trucks.

"Fine," I said. I always thought the Eaton's colours had class. More importantly, the colour scheme I had chosen was also ideal to stand out against the snow, if, God forbid, a plane went down.

On June 1, 1953, I fired off a telegram to Marjorie – which she has kept, along with almost every other piece of paper connected to the business, to this day. It began, "Accepting delivery aircraft leaving Toronto Tuesday morning."

I still remember picking up the cheque for the money I used to put the down payment on the Otter. It was arranged that I would go to a little branch of the bank Jerry Byrne used at the corner of Bay and Temperance streets in downtown Toronto. I walked in and asked for the money, and the banker scowled and said in a loud voice, "Don't come back here for more after you've wasted this!" and shoved the cheque across his desk at me. He was really upset that Jerry would loan me that much money for such a crazy scheme. I just took the cheque, didn't say anything – except to myself – and went out to de Havilland to collect my aircraft.

The very first Wardair delivery flight was a real winner. My friend Toby Wood had flown to Toronto in order to be in on the big arrival, and he flew back with me. We didn't know what was waiting for us at Cooking Lake, outside Edmonton. A small, jubilant group, consisting of Marjorie, Gai and Blythe, Darrell and Janet Hayes, and a few other friends were there. They had brought along an old record player, and some fine Franz von Suppé marches, and we eased our beautiful new, blue, red, and white aircraft up to the dock to the sounds of music, cheers, and laughter. It was a grey, windy day, but there wasn't a cloud anywhere as far as we were concerned. We were to have many more inaugural flights over the years, but this was our finest.

From Cooking Lake, we headed north again and, to the shock and surprise of everyone in the North – including

Cy Becker – I landed on Back Bay with my shiny new aircraft, the first Otter to operate commercially in Western Canada.

The licence to operate my business was issued by the Air Transport Board on June 3, 1953, which thus became the official launch date of Wardair Limited, incorporated in Alberta. My competitors immediately announced that I would be broke by fall. There is no way, I was assured, time and again, that you can fly a $100,000 aircraft around the bush and make it pay.

I sure hoped they were wrong.

CHAPTER 9

▼

Takeoff!

I had learned a thing or two in my early years in the North, and I had formed a philosophy for my new company:

Take care of your customers. Their cargoes, those people in the seats, are paying your wages and the costs of your business.

Take care of your aircraft, and it will take care of you.

Buy the best equipment available to do the job.

Give the best service at the lowest possible price.

It was this philosophy I was determined to put into practice when, on June 6, 1953, a modest little ad appeared in the Yellowknife newspaper, *News of the North*, announcing that the Otter and I were in town, and ready for business, and inviting everyone to come down and have a look at the aircraft. Quite a few people did so, admired the machine, and told me, once again, that I was headed for financial ruin.

However, while the Otter cost more to fly, its productivity far exceeded that of any bush aircraft in Yellowknife. My necessarily higher charge per mile was more than offset by the fact that I could carry a larger load, and thus I could transport freight at far less per pound than my competitors.

The mining companies, at first, simply didn't believe this; they saw that the per-mile cost was higher, and stayed away in droves – with some exceptions. Frank Anderson, a mining engineer, very quickly caught on to the fact that he simply had to think in terms of putting together larger loads, and Norm Byrne used the aircraft to service all the mining camps he handled, but the first few weeks were a very scary time for me, as I had to build up the business. Indeed, the plane was never used at its top potential during that first summer.

I was doing the flying, naturally, but I had hired an engineer who was also a pilot: Johnny Dapp, who looked after the mechanical chores, took the bookings, and, occasionally, flew a run himself. As the bookings picked up, Johnny was run off his feet. He kept the aircraft in mint shape, and I couldn't have gotten along without him.

For back-up and overflow work, I leased a Fairchild Husky from Diversified Mining, a Toronto-based firm with interests in the North. The Husky wasn't nearly as useful an aircraft as the Otter, of course, but it didn't cost nearly as much, either, and was about all I could afford at the time. To fly her, I hired Jack "Rowdy" Rutherford, who was, like so many of us, ex-RCAF.

Now I had a business, employees, a large debt, and a growing number of contracts. It seemed time for me to have a building. I went out and bought an old bunkhouse from Jock McNiven, the manager of Negus Mines, and had it moved to the waterfront. It made quite a sight, hauled along by a truck. I had a frame of steel I-beams ready for the twenty-by-thirty-foot building, and this frame sat on large concrete spread-footings, because the waterfront was pretty well made of silt, and there was no way to build a cement foundation. I ordered a furnace, insulation, drywall, all to be installed as time permitted, cut new windows into the bunkhouse to let in light, installed fuel tanks, put up a sign, and said – to myself, of course – "CP Air, watch out!"

Marjorie and the kids were soon with me, in a house we rented from Norm Byrne. It was a two-bedroom place, not very well insulated, so that in the really cold weather frost formed on the inside walls, but it was home and we were glad to have it. By this time, the town had installed water and sewer lines and so, while we weren't living in the lap of luxury, we had at least graduated from the hovel stage.

Between my return in June with the Otter and September 15 of 1953, I flew 572 revenue hours; it is no longer legal for a pilot to do that much. I grossed $68,701.61, and made a net profit of $26,965.00 (you will understand the pleasure it gives me to go over these old accounts as I write). Pilots' wages, including my own, totalled $1,875.00 for three-and-a half-months' work. I was paying myself at the same rate as any other pilot: less than $300.00 a month. Included in my expenditures were modest sums for depreciation and replacement, as well as payments on the loans. When I toted it up, I said to myself, "By God, you did it."

I really had done it in other ways, too. On September 21 that year, Kim Maxwell Ward, our first son, put in an appearance, a week early. He arrived at full speed, and has never stopped. He walked at nine months, could open the fridge and help himself to ice cream at ten months, and had climbed and fallen off every piece of furniture we owned by the time he was a year old. He literally cut his teeth on airplanes, which he loved at first sight. He was an earth-shaker of a little boy, and to the everlasting credit of his two sisters, they adored him.

There were drawbacks, naturally. Once, I came back from a long series of flights, airlifting firefighters to battle the blazes that seemed to be a constant feature of the summer, and

I landed on Back Bay with a dozen bush men, on a break from their firefighting duties. I had radioed ahead for a truck to pick them up and take them over to the Consolidated bunkhouse, but it hadn't arrived when we touched down at 3:30 A.M. It was a cool morning, with the sun just starting up. The men straggled out of the Otter and went to stand by the road, watching out for their truck, while I set about the business of tying the plane safely to the dock. I looped one strand of rope around the front, and another around the back, then went to secure one of these lines to the main strut. I was so exhausted that I didn't watch what I was doing, and when I looked up, all I could see was a tangle of rope hanging down from the strut.

Irritated, I gave a mighty heave on the rope to clear this tangle, and discovered, too late, that it wasn't a knot, just a bunched rope, which came loose in my hand. Under the impetus of my mighty yank against empty air, I went lurching backwards, plomp, plomp, plomp across the dock, and into the water. When I came up spluttering, I saw the firefighters, all standing in a row with their backs to me – like sparrows on a telephone wire – and every head turned around to gaze solemnly at my damp disaster. They looked so startled and so funny that I began to laugh so hard I nearly drowned myself. That's what it takes to bring a guy around!

Don't think for a moment that Marjorie didn't see me arrive home in that condition. She's the lightest sleeper around and, due to the lateness of the hour, the door was locked. When I pounded on it, she looked through the small window at a cold, soggy sight on the entry-porch. I remember her reaction as sympathetic, although the temptation to laugh must have been overwhelming.

The Otter was a magnificent aircraft, not merely because it could carry passengers and a payload almost anywhere, but because it was, quite simply, fun to fly. With most bush planes, you spent a good deal of your time planning the takeoff run – could you avoid those rocks? Could you clear those trees? – that sort of thing. With a Bellanca or a Norseman, you might, quite often, have to make a sort of circular run to get up speed if there wasn't enough clear area straight ahead. But the Otter could lift off in a few times its own length. I often got a kick out of telling passengers, "See that hill straight ahead of us? We're going right over the top."

They wouldn't believe me, any more than I had believed George Neal when he told me we were going over the hangar at Malton, but I would give her the gun, and we'd hop the hill.

The Otter changed the way prospecting and mining were done. Before it came along, prospectors and miners out in the bush lived in very primitive conditions indeed. You would fly a couple of men in with a tent, an airtight stove, and a few boxes of supplies, and one of them would spend most of his time keeping the camp in order and the fire going, while the other worked. With the Otter, we could fly in complete frames for full-sized tents, with decent stoves to heat them.

One of the great revolutions in the North came about from the simple fact that the Otter could handle full sheets of four-by-eight-foot plywood and wallboard, and sixteen-foot lengths of framing material. For the prospectors, this meant that they could have a plywood floor to their tents. We had room enough in the plane to bring in cots, so they no longer had to sleep on spruce boughs; and they had a straight table, set on a flat floor, to work from, instead of some dinky rig that would fall over as soon as they leaned on it. For the mining men, it meant that the whole structure of mines changed, because they could be properly framed and surrounded by decent living quarters. Mining productivity was greatly increased.

I would be interested to see if some future archaeologist catches on to the fact that you can date almost any mining site in the North as pre- or post-Otter. A mining cabin built before the Otter was skimpily framed, and lined with two-by-eight-foot strips of a building material called "Donna-conna," not much better than pressed cardboard. Post-Otter places were properly framed, with full sheets of plywood on the outside and wallboard inside, almost like a city home. Once the mining fraternity recognized that they could move sixteen-foot lengths of lumber, they took to ordering it in at that length, just for the novelty of it, even if they were going to cut it afterwards.

Of course, you could move larger loads with the DC-3, another plane that helped to develop the North; but the DC-3 required a landing strip, and quite a long one at that. You could put it down in Yellowknife, but not in the dozens of tiny spots where I set the Otter down, and not on water.

That first winter of Wardair operation, 1953–54, was not as busy as the fall, and the down time gave me a chance to get the Yellowknife office in shape. I soon had a genuine airline building, thanks to my house-building experience, with a waiting room, a dispatcher's office, and two other offices. The executive suite was only about ten-by-ten, but it had a big window cut into it. In fact, the windows I cut around that building caused quite a stir in town. A number of the old-timers who came by gave me a blast because I would lose so much heat out the windows, and when I explained that I had double-glazed them, they looked at me as if I had taken leave of my senses. Small windows are what you have in the North, anybody knows that.

Not long after I finished the building, I had a visit from old Pete Baker, the only Arab then living in the Northwest Territories. Pete Baker, I hasten to add, was not his Arab name, but the one he had been given locally. I don't know how he landed in the Canadian bush, but he did, as a trader in Old Fort Rae. He did well for himself, and later became an elected member of the NWT Council. Pete had decided I needed his decorating advice, and he had already given me advance warning.

"Max," he said, "I hope you're not going to paint it some fancy colour."

What I had done, in fact, was to paint one wall a reddish brown pastel and the other a shade of blue. Pete came in, walked over to the wall, put his head about ten inches from the paint surface – he was quite short-sighted – shook his head sadly, and pronounced:

"Max," he said, "I don't like it."

I thanked him for his views, but left the paint-job as it was.

When we swung into high gear again in the summer of 1954, I still had the only Otter in commercial service in the western section of the territories, though there were others operating further east, and I was booked solid. The Fairchild Husky was not performing well; it was underpowered for its size, which made takeoffs somewhat chancy, and on one winter trip, Rowdy Rutherford knocked off the tail-ski, which wasn't hard to do. With this excuse, I had the Husky repaired and turned it back to Diversified Mining, with my thanks, then went out and bought a Beaver from de Havilland.

It was smaller than the Otter – with a payload of about 1,400 pounds – and much cheaper. I could use it on trips where I didn't need the Otter, because it was cheaper to fly. Once more, I got the financing from the Industrial Development Bank, but this time, I was much more confident of what I was doing. I was no longer quite such a beginner as I had been when I bought the Otter.

However, it was in the Otter, not the brand-new Beaver, that I took on what was to have been a trip full of drama and compassion in March of 1954. The headline that appeared in a subsequent issue of *News of the North* read,

"Starving Eskimos Getting Food" (nowadays the headline would read "Inuit," not Eskimos), but, as you will see, that is not precisely what happened.

One morning, I got a telephone call from L. A. C. O. "Laco" Hunt, the District Administrator at Fort Smith, who was terribly excited over word that there was a starving band of Eskimo at Flagstaff Island, a tiny, unmapped dot in the Arctic Ocean. He had come over to Yellowknife, located and purchased a large quantity of buffalo meat, and wanted me to fly it out to Flagstaff Island in my Otter.

Of course I said I would be delighted to take on this humanitarian and necessary chore. Think of Good King Wenceslas, aboard an Otter aircraft, and you get the idea. When we loaded up for takeoff early the next day, we had along, besides several hundred pounds of fairly odoriferous buffalo meat, Bert Boxer, a game warden, who wanted to know what had happened to the seals, the normal food for the Eskimos, to put them in such a fix, and Henry Busse, a local photographer, who had been commissioned by the government to record our heroism for posterity – to say nothing of the evening news.

I wished Henry the best of luck; he wouldn't see much out the aircraft window on a dull day in March. We flew first to Coppermine, at the mouth of the Coppermine River at the edge of Coronation Gulf, because Laco didn't like the idea of flying straight through to Cambridge Bay on Victoria Island, the closest settlement to the starving Eskimos. It was a cold and boring trip, and when we got to Cambridge Bay, Laco announced that he would wait for us there. A couple of the RCMP at Cambridge Bay had been to Flagstaff Island at one time or another by dog-team, and they would come along with us, to point the way; there were no readily visible landmarks. We waved goodbye and took off into the heavy haze that is so much a condition of flying over the Arctic Ocean in winter. The landscape below us was absolutely featureless, and within a few minutes, the RCMP fellows pronounced themselves baffled. Because they had always travelled on the surface, the view from the air didn't help them at all. They knew we were somewhere over the ocean, but other than that, they couldn't say. I had the map coordinates, however, so I flew by dead-reckoning, and when I figured we ought to be over Flagstaff Island, I descended in circles, telling everyone on board to keep watching for any signs of life.

Lower and lower we went, and suddenly, there was the Eskimo encampment, right below us. We had hit the nail on the head. The huts were all enclosed in blocks of snow, which is why they had been so hard to spot. We landed, and a flood of smiling Eskimos rushed up to greet us; it was so kind of us, they said, to come all this way to bring them food for their dogs.

"Dogs?" asked a bewildered Bert Boxer.

Oh, yes, their dogs. They weren't starving – what an idea! – but they were running out of meat for their dogs. They didn't want to waste their lovely seal meat on the animals, so they had sent out word, and here we were, with all this odoriferous buffalo meat, just the stuff for dogs.

"God help us," said one of the Mounties.

We hastily shoved several hundred pounds of buffalo meat out onto the ice and grinned ruefully at one another. Henry Busse, in pursuit of his story of humanitarian heroism for the government, took miles of tape of just about everything that moved, and quite a lot of things that didn't. Among the latter was a group of Eskimo women all sitting in a row on a long pole off to one side of the encampment. They all wore broad, toothless smiles, and Henry decided they provided the essential touch of colour he needed for the documentary, so he began rushing about, recording this pleasant scene of communal cordiality. I approached him quietly and asked, "Henry, have you any idea what those women are doing?"

Henry just shook his head and went on shooting. He didn't know much about Eskimos, but he knew a good shot when he saw one.

"They're sitting on the public latrine," I told Henry. "Their long parkas hide it from sight. You're photographing a public pee-in."

"Oh," said Henry. Still, it made a great photograph.

The subsequent news stories glossed over the fact that our rescue mission was in aid not of man but of man's best friend. Perhaps "Starving Eskimo Dogs Get Food" didn't make such a dramatic headline.

During that busy year, I was becoming more and more familiar with the terrain, not only around Yellowknife, but, thanks to the long range of the Otter, all over the North, a fact that came in handy in a dramatic fashion during one trip I flew in August 1954.

It started, as most of my adventures did, with a telephone call. Jean Lesage, then Minister of Northern Affairs, was going to make a tour of his empire, with Gordon Robertson, his deputy minister, the Commissioner of the Northwest Territories, and two other senior officials, one from Northern Affairs, the other from the Department of Finance.

Gordon Robertson was probably the most brilliant person I have ever met. He understood and had a firm grip on what was happening in the North in those days. He would go from Northern Affairs to become Secretary of the Privy Council, the Number One civil servant in Canada. Jean Lesage has gone into history as the Quebec premier who led the Quiet Revolution and coined the phrase "Maîtres chez nous," but he had a distinguished career in federal politics during the reign of Louis St. Laurent. He was Minister of Northern Affairs from 1953 until 1957, when he resigned to return to Quebec politics. This gaggle of officials was checking out potential townsites for a new town to take the place of Aklavik, then a government administration centre as well as a major transport and service centre in the area.

Aklavik was built on a silt river bank about a hundred miles north of the Arctic Circle, on the West Channel of the Mackenzie River. The warmth of settlement had begun to doom the place; as the permafrost began to melt from all the activity, the town was sinking. Whenever I went to Aklavik, I put my rubber boots in the back, because wherever you walked, unless on planks, you went into the ooze. The new town would be called Inuvik – the name means "place of man" – and the site eventually chosen was straight east of Aklavik, on the Mackenzie River's East Channel, but we were to look at a number of other sites, as well. The trip would take us from Yellowknife down the Mackenzie River, making stops en route. *Maclean's* magazine sent along a journalist with a particular interest in the North to cover the trip; his name was Pierre Berton.

It must be remembered that not many people flew as a matter of course in the 1950s, and, in general, most of them were very concerned about flying; some still are. Jean Lesage was a very nervous passenger, right from the start. He kept asking me whether I thought it was really safe to go swanning around such barren country with only one engine, and how certain was I that that one engine would keep on going? He worried about flying over the land with a float-equipped aircraft. I reassured him as best I could; the engine had never failed me yet, and if it did, I said, there was no problem in setting the plane down on any lake or river and sending out a radio call for help. He nodded, but didn't really believe me, and when we turned north after a quick look at Fort Simpson, and I cut straight across country to avoid having to follow the Big Bend in the Mackenzie, he was quickly up to visit me.

"I thought we were always going to be over water, so we could set down if we had to," he said anxiously.

I pointed out the window. "You are never far from water in this country," I told him.

He seemed to be glad to get onto *terra firma* when we arrived at Aklavik, although you have seldom seen *terra* less *firma* than the muddy muck at Aklavik when the frost is out of the ground. The officials all tromped around in their rubber boots, and then we flew off to visit a number of potential townsites, among which they favoured the present site of Inuvik. We circled back to Aklavik and then down to Norman Wells, on the Mackenzie not far north of Fort Norman. From here, our next stop was to be Coppermine, on Coronation Gulf, for refuelling. I had suggested going straight there from Aklavik, by following the coast of the Beaufort Sea, but that seemed too isolated for my passengers; so instead we stopped off at Norman Wells for the night, and, the next day, flew straight northeast across Great Bear Lake, and then up to Coppermine. This was a pleasant, easy flight, and the visit to Coppermine went very well, so that by the time we were on the last leg, heading south to return to Yellowknife, Jean Lesage was very much more relaxed about flying. He came up and sat in the co-pilot's seat and put on the radio earphones, and looked around and smiled at everything.

Suddenly, over his headset – and mine – came an urgent call from Coppermine radio. They were in contact with a twin-engine de Havilland Dove that was lost and hadn't the foggiest notion of where to go to land. What made the situation serious was that the Dove, while a dandy aircraft, was equipped only with wheels; they could not take the solution I had proposed to Jean Lesage, and set down on a lake somewhere. They needed a stretch of flat, level terrain. Unbeknownst to us, aboard the aircraft were the wives of three Eldorado and Atomic Energy of Canada executives, part of the official party to welcome His Royal Highness, the Duke of Edinburgh, on a ceremonial visit to Port Radium. They were Mrs. William Bennett, Mrs. Frank Broderick, and Mrs. Red Dutton. They had been headed from Yellowknife to the Eldorado landing strip at Sawmill Bay, near Eldorado and Port Radium at the southeast end of Great Bear Lake. They were already overdue at Sawmill Bay, and the people there were quite anxious – all the more so because they were grouped in the radio shack and could hear my conversation with Coppermine. Therefore, they knew the Dove was lost, although, like me, they couldn't talk to the distressed aircraft directly.

As soon as it was clear what was going on, Mr. Lesage whipped off the earphones and vacated the co-pilot's seat as if it had suddenly turned red-hot. He was well able to deal with pressure in the political arena, but he wanted no part of what looked like a looming tragedy. Pierre Berton took his place – fast.

I asked Coppermine radio to get the Dove's pilot to describe the terrain around him as best he could. He believed he was on the south shore of Great Bear Lake, having overshot Sawmill Bay, but when he described the terrain and the islands he could see to the north, I knew he had it wrong. I was sure he had drifted north and east and was cruising along the south shore of the Beaufort Sea. As he was now heading west, he was heading directly for Coppermine. He would never have enough gas to get to Sawmill Bay; his only chance was to land on a long sand-bar at Coppermine, dead ahead of him.

Coppermine passed this message on, the pilot continued west, and, sure enough, within a few minutes, he spotted Coppermine. However, he did not take my next piece of advice, which was to retract his landing gear and land on the sand on his belly; he kept the wheels down. The Dove landed, rolled a few feet, and came to an abrupt and undignified halt. Fortunately, no one was hurt, and a float aircraft came in to lift the officials out of there.

The Dove was the first aircraft I landed that I couldn't even see.

For every yin, of course, there is a yang, and some of the other ventures I undertook on behalf of the fledgling Wardair Limited didn't end so happily as the Jean Lesage tour. There were, for example, two incidents that I will deal with in the next chapter, which might be called "The Adventure of the Flying Muskoxen" and "The Gold Brick Affair."

CHAPTER 10

▼

The Flying Muskoxen

August of 1954 brought into my life, besides the episode with the forelorn Dove, a new face. It belonged to John Teal, a busy and energetic fellow from the state of Vermont, where he had a farm and a dream. The dream was to capture some muskoxen in northern Canada, fly them down to Vermont, and cross-breed them with Abderdeen Angus cows. I can't remember now what the new breed was to have been called – probably Musgus or Angox, or something equally revolting. The idea was sparked by the fact that the muskox produces enormously valuable wool, long and silky and incredibly warm; but if you want the wool off a muskox, you are quite likely to get the horns instead, which is why the material is usually gathered off the ground rather than off the animal. However, if you could cross-breed the beast with a domesticated creature such as the Aberdeen Angus, you would have a large, tranquil, walking wool factory of immense value. Even at this time, muskox wool sold for more than one hundred dollars a pound.

When John turned up with his, pardon me, "hair"-brained scheme, we talked about various ways you could capture a small sample of muskox on the hoof. Somebody suggested we could get a trained quarter horse, tie its legs, lay it in the Otter, fly it out to where we found some muskoxen, and use it to round them up. This did not appeal to me; I had visions of the horse getting loose and kicking the inside of my beautiful Otter to pieces.

We still hadn't solved this vexing problem when it more or less solved itself. John Teal was flying around the North on his quest with Harry Taylor, one of the pilots I had hired as the business expanded, and they found a small herd of the animals in the Barren Lands about three hundred miles north and east of Yellowknife. John had a permit from the federal government to export three muskoxen, so they decided then and there to go after them. On Harry's first pass, he buzzed the muskoxen, and of course they just went into their classic defensive circle, with the calves in the middle, and stood there. It was a bold soul who would go into that circle to try to pick out a few specimens. However, Harry noticed that when they became annoyed they would move out of the circle, so he would run the plane down almost on top of them, and a muskox would dash at his pontoons with its head down. Once the circle was broken, Harry could start the rest of the herd on the move.

With endless patience, he buzzed and harassed that herd until it started across a stretch of water; then he quickly landed on the water and he and John Teal grabbed a small male, hoisted it onto the floats, quickly lashed its legs, and hoisted it into the freight compartment. Although they could have been killed by even an immature animal, they did this three times, captured three of the beasts, and flew home to Yellowknife in triumph.

From Yellowknife, after suitable pictures and publicity, which didn't do Wardair any harm, the animals were put into crates for the long ride back to Vermont. Now we came to the tricky part. The muskoxen didn't look happy in their crates, and I didn't think they would last long unless we could get them out quickly – and that meant putting them on a scheduled airline. I approached Boris Onisko, then the manager for CP Air in Yellowknife, and asked him, as a personal favour, to allow them aboard the mainline DC-3 flight from Yellowknife to Edmonton. Boris explained to me that it was against company policy to put animals on the aircraft; especially, he added, on the aircraft with paying passengers.

However, after I pointed out the dilemma of these poor animals, the value of this experiment, and the need I had to get them out of here before they died on me, reluctantly he agreed, and the ox-boxes were duly loaded onto the DC-3, with the passengers, for the five-hour flight to Edmonton. They were not – did I mention this? – toilet-trained, and I gather that passengers on that memorable flight still talk about the aroma that wafted around the aircraft all the way to Edmonton. In due course, poor Boris got a rocket of the hottest and strongest variety from Grant McConachie, then President of CP Air, for doing me this favour.

But by that time, the muskoxen were in Vermont, and I went to visit them there. They looked strangely woebegone and out of place.

This should have been a great triumph, except that a couple of things went wrong. The first was that the experiment didn't work; the muskoxen and the Aberdeen Anguses were not interested in each other at all, much less romantically inclined, so there were no woolly Musguses to brighten the Vermont dawn. The second thing was that John Teal stuck me for the bill, which amounted to many thousands of dollars. It was my contribution to science, I guess.

Muskoxen and sled dogs were not the only animals I flew around the North. We flew cows from Hay River, on the south shore of Great Slave Lake, 110 miles across to Yellowknife, to start the first dairy farm there. We flew a number of flights delivering beavers from Prince Albert, Saskatchewan, to Fort Rae in the Northwest Territories, as part of the government's attempt to establish a beaver colony in the territory – an attempt that unfortunately failed. In short, we would fly anything anywhere, and frequently did. On one trip, I flew an upright piano, which I covered with canvas and tied to the float of the Otter, from Yellowknife to the Discovery Mines. One of the pilots, Hank Hicks, was playing the piano while we lashed it to the float. The landing, with about fifteen hundred pounds of piano on one side, had to be very slick indeed, or we would have struck a sour note.

By this time, there was a new hub of activity in northern Canada. In early 1955, the Americans began to build the first DEW (Distant Early Warning) line, a string of fifty tracking, warning, and control stations slung roughly along the 70th parallel from Alaska to Greenland, right across Canada's roof. There were a lot of flying and construction contracts being let in Edmonton and Yellowknife and, at first, I was anxious to get some of this work, which paid very well indeed. However, I didn't see how I could take on the kind of major commitment this work would entail and still continue to service the key customers I already had, like the Byrne brothers – and I sure as heck wasn't about to let them down. I made a few inquiries, but nothing came of them until the day I received a rather arrogant summons, demanding that I fly up to Cambridge Bay, ready to go to work for the Americans. I knew there was a handsome, quick profit to be made, but I was in this business now for the long haul, so I turned it down.

Later, I was glad I had; the work certainly paid, but it didn't last long, and in the meantime, I was building a steady business. By the time that frantic activity was over, I was well established in Yellowknife. There was also another factor in my decision that proved it to be the right one, I think. The arrogance of the summons I received was generally symptomatic of the way the Americans behaved on that project. For instance, Canadians were required to request permission from the United States government to land on our own territory at DEW-line sites. I frequently flew Mr. Justice Jack Sissons, the territorial Supreme Court Justice, into DEW-line stations, to look after judicial matters for the Inuit who worked on the line. He had four words for that piece of protocol – "To hell with them" – and we landed when and where we pleased.

Business was now going so well that I felt I could buy a second Otter. Or, to put it another way, I could mortgage a second Otter. The Industrial Development Bank continued to be my main backer, through the good offices of my friend Ritchie Clark, and when the IDB moved him, as they did from time to time, they insisted that he take my files with him to the next city on the list. Nobody else wanted to take a chance on us. However, Ritchie never flinched. Each time I came to him with another proposition, he would look up and say, "Well, how much this time?" and, after making sure my arguments were backed with paperwork, he would produce the money.

To fly this second Otter, registration number CF-IFP (these "call letters" may not mean much to the reader, I understand, but to me they are like the names of beloved children), I had enticed an outstanding pilot, Don Braun, to join me. An American, Don had flown on the staging route for the Alaska Highway during the war and stayed on to fly a Norseman for Northern Construction and Mannix, two

engineering and construction firms, during the building of
the hydro plant on Snare River. I naturally got to know
him very well during that project, when I was in and out
of Snare River all the time, and when he went back to the
United States at the end of the project, I phoned him, not
once, but many times, to ask him to come up and fly for
me.

To my intense delight, he finally agreed. He was expecting
to come up to Yellowknife and learn all about the aircraft
from me, but I had to fly out the very day he came in.
Our paths crossed at the airport, when he was getting off
the Edmonton mainliner and I was getting on. I told him
about the Otter.

"On takeoff, as soon as you get the aircraft off the water,
push the nose down, not up," I told him. This is the reverse
of normal practice on most aircraft – the Otter was the first
to which this applied – and Don looked at me as if I was
out of my tree. However, he did as I said, and by the time
I got back from my business trip to Edmonton a few days
later, he was handling the plane as if he'd been flying it
for years, and, like me, he had fallen in love with it.

Normally, I wouldn't let anyone else fly the Otter at this
time; the fact that I put Don into it sight unseen indicates
what I thought of him as a pilot – a confidence that proved
to be justified.

It might easily have been Don who got involved in the Gold
Brick affair, but it wasn't; it was me. One of my routine
jobs was to fly back and forth between Yellowknife and the
Byrne brothers' Consolidated Mine about fifty-five miles
straight north of the town. Discovery, you will recall, had
put up part of the money to finance the first Otter. I would
carry in needed supplies and passengers and bring out miners

going on leave, or leaving period, along with, once a week, two gold bricks – that week's output from the mine. They were always sewn into a canvas bag and placed in a mail sack. I just put them in the back with any other cargo, and paid no more attention to them than I would to any other freight.

On one fateful trip, on the way out after picking up the gold bricks and a few passengers, with their baggage, I was instructed to drop off supplies at Consolidated's wood-cutters' camp, a few miles south of the mine. Wood was the source of power for the gold mine; it was cut in the summer and fall and sleighed in during the winter, when travel was easier. On this trip, I was bringing in groceries to the camp, and picking up mail and a few other bits and pieces. During the stopover, I noticed there was some rearranging going on back in the aircraft, where the cargo sat just beyond the passengers, but I was out of the aircraft on the float, handing off the freight.

When we landed at Yellowknife, I taxied to the dock, tied up, and began heaving the cargo, including the passenger baggage, out onto the dock for pick-up. As I swung one passenger's bag off, it seemed so extraordinarily heavy that I said to its owner, "My God, what have you got in there, gold bricks?"

He laughed but made no comment.

The gold bricks were in their canvas bag, as usual, all wrapped up. I took them out and put them on the end of the dock, to be picked up by Frenchie's Transport, which was responsible for sending them on to Edmonton. Just as I was doing this, along came John H. Parker, then a mining engineer for Norm Byrne, later to become the Commissioner of the Northwest Territories, and always a good friend.

He'd never hefted a gold brick before, so he picked one up, and then turned to me and said, "Hey, what is this supposed to weigh?"

"Forty-eight pounds," I told him. "It's marked right on the outside of the bag."

"That doesn't weigh forty-eight pounds," said John.

"Don't be ridiculous," I replied.

That evening, a Friday night, a call came in to the office from one of our Discovery passengers, Tony Gregson. He insisted on chartering a Beaver to take him to Hay River, where the road from the south ended at that time. It seemed a little odd that he wouldn't wait for the much cheaper transport on the regular CP Air run, so I picked up the telephone to call the RCMP. I thought I would just check up on Gregson. We kept in touch with the RCMP on unusual movements. Just as I was beginning to dial, a cab pulled up in front of the office and out jumped a man who turned out to be Tony himself. I put the telephone down, in case he caught me making an embarrassing call, and a few minutes later, he flew off with Hank Hicks at the controls. They had a pleasant and uneventful trip.

On the following Monday morning, when I came in from a flight, Johnny Dapp was standing at the end of the dock, awaiting my arrival, grinning.

"Hey, guess what? Those gold bricks you brought in from Discovery on Friday weren't gold at all. The gold was swiped. They were lead!"

The clerk at Frenchie's Transport had taken the bricks out of the safe to check their weight and discovered that, as John Parker had tried to tell me, they didn't weigh enough. He then called Norm Byrne, who came rushing around. In his presence, the bags were opened. The men found themselves staring at two bars of the finest-quality lead.

Apparently Tony Gregson, who turned out to be a well-known criminal in his native Australia, had thought the scheme out long in advance, while working as a miner at Discovery. When he was set to leave for good, he made a quick trip down to Yellowknife, where he bought a quantity of lead – paid for it with a dud cheque, too – which he then melted and formed into bricks of exactly the right size. He bagged them so they looked and felt like the genuine article. Then, he simply switched the bags inside their canvas container at the wood-cutters' camp, in the dark of the aircraft, when no one was paying any attention.

He got off with two bricks worth about twenty-five thousand dollars each. (Gold at that time was sold at a set price of thirty-five dollars an ounce; today, it is worth more than ten times that.)

As soon as we had worked out what must have happened, the RCMP radioed Peace River, which is where the bus from Hay River goes, and the bus was stopped and searched. But Tony had gotten off somewhere along the way, and set out to spend his gold.

We later heard that he shaved small flakes off the bars for minor purchases, and cut off rather larger hunks to buy, among other things, a boat of his own in the Maritimes, which he sailed away to the Caribbean. Eventually, he wound up in Cuba, but the Cubans took his gold away from him, then kicked him out of the country, and where he is today, if he is still alive, I have no idea. If he ever turns up in Yellowknife, I will recognize him. He is not someone I am ever likely to forget, and, while the loss was covered by Discovery's insurance, the shock to my system when I found I had been duped was considerable.

Muskoxen and gold bricks aside, the business was doing progressively better as time went on. We were now employing seven people, making a steady and rising profit, and ploughing every cent back into Wardair. In 1955, among other things, we built a two-storey shop-building to service our growing fleet. It was set on trussed steel I-beams, and was the finest maintenance facility in Yellowknife by a country mile.

I was working, if anything, harder than ever. Sometimes, when I arrived back in the middle of the night after a long day's flying, I would sack out in exhaustion in a room upstairs in the maintenance shop for a few hours before my next flight. It wasn't worth while to go home, even though we lived only a few minutes' drive from the Wardair building.

Actually, I thrived on hard work, although I did not thrive on airplane crashes, one of which turned out to be the next big event in my life.

One evening in late November, I got a call from Northern Power Corporation, with a request that I be ready to fly first thing the next day. There was an intermittent break somewhere in the line between Yellowknife and the Snare River hydro plant, causing surges in the power in town. By this time, we were all utterly dependent on electricity, not only for light, but also to run our furnaces, so this was serious business indeed.

I decided the Beaver was the best aircraft for this kind of flight, and that night I fuelled her up, excluding the drop tank at the very bottom of the aircraft, a reserve tank that I filled only on long trips, and got everything ready to take off at first light.

The Power Corporation sent over a man to act as spotter. His name was Frank Thorpe, and he was very ill with inoperable cancer. There was a lot of hoar-frost on the aircraft when we started out the next morning, and, although I had put on wing covers and brushed off the body as best I could, some of it remained on the fuselage. It would cause a lot of skin friction and slow the aircraft down; on the other hand, the hoar-frost clinging to the power-line would make the break easier to spot.

We took off, I levelled off at a very low altitude, we picked up the line just south of town, and I flew within a few feet of the snaking black wire. We had barely settled to our work, about fifteen miles north of town, when the Beaver's engine suddenly quit dead. We had no height; I couldn't glide to safety, so the only thing I could do was to try to guide the plane to any flat area. I swung the aircraft quickly to the left, where I thought I spotted a lake. The airspeed was winding down. Suddenly the wing smashed into a pile of rocks, and as we began to slide down a slope, I braced myself as far away from the cabin door as I could get – my side of the aircraft was being shredded against the rocks. Then the grinding sound ceased, and we skidded out onto the frozen lake surface. We had been transformed, in seconds, from an operating aircraft into a wreck on the ice. Not just a wreck, but one that might, at any moment, turn into a funeral pyre, if all that fuel I had taken aboard caught fire. I still remember the silence of that cold, crisp morning, after the rumble and screech of our descent.

I was aware that I had taken a bit of a beating on the way down, but Frank obviously had a broken leg. The second the aircraft skidded to a halt, I grabbed him under the arms, and we both, somehow, got out of the plane and onto the ice, staggering away from the aircraft in case it decided to go up. But it didn't, and pretty soon it was clear that it wouldn't, so I set about trying to see what I could do about getting us rescued. The radio was smashed beyond hope, so that was out. I got Frank bedded down in a sleeping bag on the ice, and built as big a fire as I could with brush and fuel; it would serve both as a signal and as a way to keep us warm in temperatures that were now somewhere a long way below zero.

We hadn't been there more than a few minutes when I heard a distant, humming noise, which I was soon able to identify; we were still so close to Yellowknife that we could pick up the sounds of aircraft taking off and landing at the airport.

Nonetheless, it was many hours, in fact late afternoon, before the hydro people noticed that we hadn't turned up at Snare River and called the Wardair office to ask what had become of us. Within minutes, Don Braun was on his way in one of the Otters, and he soon spotted our fire. He later told me it was the biggest fire he had ever seen. By early evening, we were both comfortably ensconced in the hospital in Yellowknife. Frank had a lot of bruising along with his broken leg. I had several broken ribs and a couple of black eyes from bouncing off the rocks as we landed – something I was scarcely conscious of at the time.

That night, I was as thirsty as I have ever been in my life; I kept asking the nurses for fresh orange juice, and I probably set a new record for consumption of the stuff in the Arctic. I had obviously dehydrated out on the ice. It's interesting how the body tells you what it needs in circumstances like that.

The next day brought two new developments. The first was that an examination of my X-rays showed that I had, along with the smashed ribs, a crack in my skull. No one suspected this at first, because the usual sign of such a thing is a headache, and I had none. Every day for the week or so I was in the hospital, the doctor would come in and say, "Had a headache yet?"

I never did get one, which probably shows that I have a harder-than-ordinary head; it would come in handy in my business dealings later. I worked out of the hospital bed. In fact, a new secretary named Janet Lamb had just arrived from Edmonton. Janet still remembers taking her first dictation in my hospital room.

The second development of that second day was that, after being told that the Beaver was, as I suspected, a complete write-off, I sent a wire to de Havilland, and ordered another one, for delivery as soon as possible.

One of the fascinating jobs we had in 1963 was flying for the Geodetic survey with the Douglas DC-6B. We flew 3,000 miles round-trip per night starting at Thule, pivoting on the geographical North Pole, and ending in Alaska. We carried a magnetometer to plot lines of equal variation. Here we are going over our flight plan at Resolute. On the left is Al Graham; on the right, Phil Botley. (National Film Board)

"Take me, take my canoe," most of the prospectors said, so we did. Here is the Otter with a canoe strapped on the pontoon, warming up on Back Bay. (Photo courtesy Henry Busse/NWT Archives)

We could use our Boeing 707 as a passenger or freighter aircraft, and here you see it loaded down with nickel concentrate for an overseas flight, circa 1968. (Photo by George Hunter)

This is one of our early charter flights in the DC-6B, arriving in Copenhagen from Edmonton, June 1964. (Scandia Foto)

Now we were getting serious. I am hard at work in our office in the CN Tower at Edmonton. I love airplane models almost as much as airplanes, and the two shown are of our Boeing 727 (left) and the 707. (Jeen Pool Photo/*Edmonton Journal*)

Not all our engine changes were planned. Guenther Moellenbeck makes an unscheduled change on an Otter on a lake north of Yellowknife. The new engine sits on a tire at right. (Photo by Art Morrow)

While they were putting together our beautiful new 707 at the Boeing plant in Seattle, all our pilots were down for training and to look it over. From left are Dean Ostrander, Ab Freeman, Doug McKinlay, Phil Gaunt, Wilf Kyryluk, Doug Nicholson, Bob Gartshore. (Photo by Boeing)

Our engineers came down to check out the new aircraft, too, and gathered in the mid-section of the 707 under construction in Seattle. From left are Fred Woodhall, Ab Freeman, Peter Tollovsen, Wally McMillan, Doug Marfleet, George Bell, Art Lockwood. (Photo by Boeing)

The Wardair flight attendants were always first-class. A cheerful group is ready for a 727 flight from Edmonton. From bottom: Helen Watson, Pat Elkin, Susie Stern, Deanna McIntyre, Merri Valoe, Christine Petzold, Ragnild Lofgren, Elizabeth Chorney. (Photo by *Edmonton Journal*)

I thought you might like to see what the inside of an aircraft plant looks like. This is the de Havilland plant outside Toronto, where they're working on the first of six Twin Otters we purchased. (Photo by de Havilland)

Above: Sixteen miles from the geographic North Pole, Don Braun and two others landed the first wheeled aircraft, May 5, 1967. On May 9, another flight took fuel and supplies to the camp – plus the other three members of the team. Left to right: Wes Barron, co-pilot; Art Morrow, engineer; Del Hamilton, loader; Jeff Braithwaite, co-pilot; Don Braun, captain. Missing: Harry Kreider, engineer. (Photo by Art Morrow)

Opposite: The pineapples tell it all. Crew members hold them aloft on the arrival of our Boeing 707 at Gatwick Airport after an historic 7,776-statute-mile flight from Honolulu, the first non-stop flight on this route. (Photo by Pictures Honolulu)

Below: It was a cold but cheerful setup at the North Pole. You can see the Bristol 170 Freighter that established the record. (Photo by Art Morrow)

The smiles salute the delivery of our first Boeing 727, aptly registered CF-FUN, but called the *Cy Becker*, on April 28, 1966, in Seattle. From left are Marjorie, Pat Brault, our daughter Gai, Helen Maclagen, Hjordis Stevenson (my mother), and Pat Molyneux. (Photo by Boeing)

I hope I was cracking a joke; at least everybody seems to be smiling at the christening of the *C. H. "Punch" Dickins*, our 707-320C, in Seattle in May 1968. That's Punch and his wife, Connie, at right. We named all our aircraft for great names in aviation, and Punch was one of the top bush pilots of all time. (Photo by Michael Burns)

We found out later that a one-way flow valve between the main fuel tank and the drop tank had accumulated some ice, and overnight most of the fuel from the main tank had drained out into the drop tank, though the gauge was frozen at Full. We had piles of fuel in the aircraft, if only there had been time, after the engine cut out, to switch to the drop tank.

The following spring, Marjorie and I picked up a new Beaver on floats at Toronto Island Airport and flew off west with it. That first night, we got as far as Lac du Bonnet, Manitoba, north of Winnipeg. There, we decided to refuel and spend the night. I always liked to tie an aircraft to a dock, never to a buoy. However, there was no room for us at the dock, and the only space they could provide was out on a buoy in the lake. A line squall hit that evening, while we were at the movie theatre in town, and we were called out of the theatre in the midst of the show. We rushed down to the lakeside, to discover that in the high wind the aircraft had broken free from the buoy, drifted in to shore, and done considerable damage to the tailplane.

Marjorie and I ended up flying back to Yellowknife on the commercial line, leaving the aircraft for the McDonald brothers to repair.

Our second son and fourth child, Blake William Ward, arrived almost on schedule on June 3, 1956. Big brother Kim was a hard act to follow, so Blake did things in his own way, gently happy, quickly amused, big-eyed with wonder at all the antics going on around him.

Before he was tall enough to hoist himself up onto the sofa, I would lift him up beside me, at the end of the day, and he would settle in under my arm with a little book, while I read the paper. He always identified very strongly with me, and I often thought how, of the four children, he missed the most in my back-and-forth, in-and-out, career.

The next three years went very much as had 1954 and 1955. Marjorie and I and the four children lived in rented houses, because, though the firm was making money, it was gobbling it up just as fast in new equipment. We worked up a number of contracts, like the one with Consolidated, which brought in steady money to pay the rent and meet the increasing payroll, and we kept on with the special trips that are so much a part of the North. I am proud to say that Wardair was responsible for the transport that helped open mines at Hottah Lake, Taurcanis, and Rayrock.

Week faded into week and month into month. The children grew, and so did Wardair, in tandem.

As traffic was growing and demand was growing, I had decided that we needed a heavier aircraft to operate out of Yellowknife, and after consulting with my various customers as to the type of loads they had to transport, I settled on a Bristol Freighter. All the while I was very concerned with how I would ever get operating authority from the Air Transport Board to make this dream come true; already I had begun the process of asking the ATB for various operating permits, and had been turned down cold, usually with explanations that were either so vague as to be farcical, or simply made no sense. (The usual argument was that a new service was not necessary or that the area was well served.) This time, I was resolved to dot every "i" and cross every "t."

Thus, Cy Becker filed the necessary papers to obtain authorization for us to operate in the heavier class of aircraft. A long battle ensued, with the ATB holding a full-fledged hearing on the matter, and finally, after months, I was given permission to operate one – but no more than one – Bristol Freighter.

I already had the very aircraft in mind. It was not new, of course; they were no longer being manufactured, and anyway, I could never have afforded anything so ambitious as a new Bristol. The one I had my eye on belonged to Transair of Winnipeg, which had bought it, in turn, from Trans-Canada Airlines. I paid $300,000 for it, with most of the money, as usual, coming on loan from the Industrial Development Bank and the Byrne family. I later discovered that I got the necessary authority because the ATB were concerned about Transair's balance sheet, and we were the only ones who would buy the aircraft from them.

The Bristol Freighter is not a beautiful airplane – it has a bulgy nose – but it looked beautiful to me. It could carry six tons of freight, or forty-four passengers, or a combination of the two. I knew before I bought it that it had a difficult power-plant, a Hercules sleeve-valve engine that produced 1,980-brake horsepower. I note this for the record; it won't mean much to many readers, but what it amounted to was that the Bristol's very sophisticated sleeve-valve engine was problem-prone. Engines of the most advanced type were wonderful on scheduled airlines in the south, but you couldn't do much with them if they conked out on you on a frozen lake a couple of hundred miles away from the nearest telephone – let alone the nearest mechanic. The really strong point about the Bristol, however, was the fact that it had wide front-loading doors, which is what gave it that bulgy look. Thus you could run really impressive loads straight into her. It could handle D-4 tractors complete, as well as vehicles and awkward loads that were valuable to mining projects.

I knew I was taking a chance with the Bristol, but I had been taking chances steadily for years now, and, with the exception of the odd broken bone, I had come out all right. I also knew that the time was coming – had come – when the kind of payloads required in the North would be far beyond the capacity of the Otter, wonderful though that aircraft was. For example, Keith Deeble, a friend of mine who operated for Canadian Nickel Mines, said he could use the services of a plane large enough to haul small Caterpillar tractors, as well as heavy equipment and building materials, from site to site. A large diesel generator could weigh up to two tons, far too much for float planes but nothing for the Bristol Freighter, and diesel engines supply the electricity for drilling and mining projects all over the North. If I bought the plane, he had said, he would throw business my way – and he was as good as his word. Keith's requirements were very influential in my decision to buy the Bristol. There were also others in the mining business in the area who indicated that they would use my services, so I took the plunge.

The folks who had been sure the Otter would sink me were even more sure that the Bristol would be my undoing. You couldn't even put it on skis or floats; it was far too large for that. You could only use it on wheels. We got around that, at least for winter flying, by using the oversize tires then employed on C-130 Hercules aircraft, the transport giants favoured by the armed forces. The tires effectively doubled the "footprint" of the Bristol and simplified operating on ice, although we still had to have ice strips cleared for the aircraft.

When I went down to Winnipeg to pick up my beautiful new plane, I couldn't fly it, of course. (Come to think of it, once I got past the first Fox Moth, I seem to have made a habit of buying planes first and learning how to fly them later.) Transair's sales representative told me that they had a pilot they could let me have who was thoroughly familiar with the craft. So, it was in the right-hand seat that I took my first flight in the new aircraft.

When I first took the controls, I found the Bristol to be a tricky flyer. For one thing, it had air brakes, and I had been used to the much smoother hydraulics for years. With air brakes one had to "lead and lag," as the saying goes, when you were taxiing or stopping; that is, you had to anticipate that the brakes were not going to take immediate effect, so you put them on sooner than you would hydraulics, and they continued to bite after you let the pressure off. If you didn't account for this somewhat disconcerting performance, there was a pretty fair chance you would either wind up with the plane on its nose or trying to climb through a wall. Once I got used to the new aircraft's little habits, however, we became extremely good pals.

By the time the decade was drawing to a close, I had reason to think that I had done a wise thing in moving back to the North in 1951. From a job flying for Associated Airways, I had graduated to my own plane, my own air service, and even my own buildings. I had my name not only on the door but on the whole fleet. I had thirteen employees, more than half a million dollars in aircraft – much of which was paid for – and Marjorie and I were taking care of four healthy, beautiful kids. I had been through some dodgy experiences, had nearly lost my life twice, and I was still flirting with financial disaster if anything should go wrong, but by and large, I was doing very well indeed.

CHAPTER 11

▼

My Life as a Freighter Captain

The first job I had for my beautiful new Bristol Freighter, call letters CF-TFX, was to fly a D-4 Caterpillar tractor from Yellowknife to a lake in the September Mountains at the Big Bend of the Coppermine River for Canadian Nickel Mines. Ironically, the tractor was needed to prepare an airstrip for the mining company; there was no such thing as a proper landing spot when I descended out of a winter sky, just a crude area marked off with spruce boughs on the frozen sand flats beside the river. No aircraft smaller than the Bristol could have carried such a load as the tractor, and no aircraft less rugged than the Bristol could have survived the bouncing, heart-stopping arrival on that frozen sand and ice. We had entered a new era, one in which large equipment would be air-freighted all over the opening northland.

It was easy enough, later on, to see that the advent of the larger aircraft was inevitable, as was the role they would play in developing the mines that would become the lifeblood of the territory. However, at the time, most people – and all of my competitors – were sure I had made the blunder of a lifetime in sinking so much capital into the Bristol. If it didn't break me, they thought, it would probably kill me.

There were times when I agreed with them. The Byrne family, who had been so supportive of me, owned a gold-mining property about 170 miles northeast of Yellowknife, which could be fully developed only if they could get diesel power-plants and other heavy equipment to the site, so naturally I undertook to take the Bristol in. The property was formerly called "Bulldog" – later, they upgraded it to "Taurcanis," combining the Latin words for bull and dog – which was a fair way of indicating that it was somewhat rugged. They had scraped away a small strip on a sand esker, suitable for landing a standard bush plane, but rather tricky for my Bristol.

On the first trip, George Curley, who was working for the Byrnes in Yellowknife at the time, decided he would come along for the ride in the jump-seat behind the pilot, little knowing what he was letting himself in for. When we came in, fully loaded, there had been enough warming to soften the sand in spots, and as we bounced and rumbled across the ground, the heavy wheels would catch in the sand here and there, and the plane would give a mighty lurch, threatening to swing off the so-called runway. By the time we had staggered to a halt and unloaded the aircraft, and I was ready to head home, George had decided that he would wait, thank you very much, until a Beaver or some other smaller plane turned up. He was not anxious to find out if the takeoff was going to be as nerve-racking as the landing.

George had come to the North in the first place as a clerk for CP Air, and then went to work with the Byrne brothers, again in a clerical position. But he had ambition and brains and energy, and while working for the Byrnes he took a night-school course in accounting, which he passed with flying colours over three long, hard years of work. That allowed him to set up in business for himself as an accountant, just about the time I needed someone to manage the base for us in Yellowknife. I persuaded George to join Wardair as manager-cum-accountant-cum-everything-else and he became one of my staunchest allies through all the years of Wardair.

Even in routine flying onto the makeshift runways in the bush with which I was very familiar, it was necessary to position the aircraft perfectly every time. This point was illustrated by one incident at Consolidated Discovery Mines, fifty-three miles north of Yellowknife. Discovery had created quite a nice, but very short, little airstrip out of mine tailings, and I was making several flights a day to the site, hauling heavy equipment, oil, and other supplies to facilitate the mine's expansion. Several times a day, we would heave and haul six tons of freight into position in the belly of the aircraft, tie everything firmly down, and take off. It was only a twenty-minute flight to the mine, so there was no trick to getting there; the trick was to get down and stopped on the short runway.

The wind direction was usually such that I had to land towards the headframe of the mine, which was 130 feet high. That meant that if I made a mistake and couldn't get stopped in time it was going to be rather awkward. You couldn't easily pull up and hop over a 130-foot obstacle at the end of a short landing-run. I had asked Bob Kilgour, the mine manager, to provide markers for the beginning of the strip, so I could let down as quickly as possible and have the maximum possible stopping-room. Bob believed in doing things in a substantial way, so he had large triangular markers constructed out of three-quarter-inch plywood, and

I would drop down as close to these as I could. One day, I dropped down a little too close, caught my tailwheel on a marker and knocked the wheel off. The marker escaped unscathed, and so did I, but I had to replace the tailwheel right there on the airstrip before I could take off again.

Calamity was always hovering just off-stage when we flew in the Arctic; with primitive airstrips and communications, incidents were an almost routine part of the flying business – so much so that, after a while, all we pilots got relatively immune to disaster. When we had engine troubles, or when bad weather threatened, or when people were unable to perform as promised, the old adrenalin would rush into the system. Then, as we gained experience, it didn't rush quite as fast; while we never became cold-blooded or uncaring, we had seen so many upsets and heard so much bad news that we took it more or less in stride.

One day I had been up to Resolute Bay and to Isachsen on Ellef Ringnes Island in the High Arctic to pick up a Beaver that had been damaged. We took the wings and tailplane off the Beaver and stuffed the whole thing into the Bristol, and I flew it back down to Uranium City, on Lake Athabasca, in the northwest corner of Saskatchewan, for repairs. My flight path took me past Yellowknife, although well to the east, so I called our Yellowknife office on the company frequency, which was increasingly becoming our lifeline in the North, just to see how things were. I was told that one of our Otters had been destroyed in a fire up at Coral Harbour on Broughton Island.

"Boy," I said. "Is anybody hurt?" A few years and a few calamities earlier, my heart might have plummeted, but no one was hurt in the crash, I was no longer in the position where I could be wiped out by one destroyed aircraft, and my attitude was that human life was the main concern. While a property-damage accident might shake me up, I couldn't let it get me down.

As I became more and more used to the Bristol, I called on it to perform tasks that tested it to the extreme. On one occasion, we had a charter to move a tractor to a development site up on the Beaufort Sea, and I sent a pilot up in a smaller aircraft to check out the landing-strip, which was on a sloping stretch of glacier. He reported back that the strip was on the side of a hill, but okay. And so it was, when he reported. However, before we could get up there, three days later, a warm spell had softened the glacier. As I made my first pass over it, I could see water on the surface, always a bad sign. However, there was a strong wind blowing, and I calculated that by landing into the wind I could bring the aircraft to a stop before I got into really serious trouble.

It nearly worked. As I came bouncing and thrashing in across the rolls and grooves and slush of the glacier, I was just beginning to think everything was fine, when suddenly the plane came to a dead halt, severe enough to jolt me against the safety harness. The slush had grabbed the wheels.

"You've done it this time, Max," I told myself. "You're never going to get this aircraft out of here."

We unloaded the tractor and stripped everything that we could out of the Bristol – equipment, extra tools, anything that wasn't essential to the actual flying of the aircraft. Then I gulped several times, said a silent prayer to the gods of northern flying, warmed up the engines carefully, and opened the throttles to fifty-six inches. You don't normally use all the thrust available in an aircraft like the Bristol, so as to preserve engine life, but this time I did. The plane began to bounce slowly through the sherbet around her wheels, gradually gathering speed. She would run free for a few yards, then suddenly shudder as we hit a new patch of slush, then run free again. It would be interesting to see if we ran out of slush before we ran out of airstrip. I kept shifting my attention to my airspeed, then to the downhill slope, then back to the instruments again. Finally, I hit the split-flaps at less than single-engine takeoff speed, and we ballooned into the air. It was not a beautiful takeoff, but we were clear of the glacier.

However, I could not keep pushing the edges of fortune, even with a remarkable aircraft like the Bristol, without coming a cropper. I had a charter to fly from Yellowknife to Wrigley, on the Mackenzie River north and west of Yellowknife. When I was running up the engines prior to takeoff, one of them didn't sound quite right, but I thought it was just a matter of fouled spark-plugs, and that it would clear itself, which is often the case. I should never have left Yellowknife. The aircraft was fully loaded when we took off, and climbed, grudgingly, to five thousand feet. We flew just below a layer of cloud above the five-thousand-foot level. It was a bitterly cold mid-winter night, the kind of night on which airplane engines often perform surprisingly well – we used to talk about the propellors "biting the air off in chunks" when it got this cold – and everything went smoothly enough until I began the long climb to an altitude at which I could clear the McConnell Range, east of Wrigley. Just southwest of Great Bear Lake, the port engine started to act up again, and slowly died.

I was now about three-quarters of the way to Wrigley. There was nowhere else to set down an aircraft of this size, but, in order to get over the mountains to get to Wrigley, I needed to gain another twenty-five hundred feet. Feathering the wounded engine, I gradually increased power to the survivor, while easing the aircraft ever upwards. We dragged ourselves up, almost by our teeth. The old darling never faltered; I may have been skipping a few beats long before that climb was finished, but the steady Hercules power-plant hauled us clean over the mountains, and we sank gratefully down onto the airstrip at Wrigley.

The engine that had quit on me was shot. In fact, before I could fly the Bristol back out, we had to have the spare engine flown in from England, where it had been sent for overhaul. George Bell, my chief engineer, had the unenviable task of flying up from Yellowknife and swapping engines that weighed more than a ton each, under flapping canvas in a heavy wind in forty-below weather at Wrigley.

George not only knew the Bristol backwards and forwards, but he had a long history in aviation engineering and did a superb job in keeping our aircraft in first-class shape. When we moved into jet aircraft, George and the engineers who trained under him topped their training class at Boeing in jet-aircraft maintenance. George then ran our jet-maintenance operation for some years.

Pleased as I was with the Bristol, which was not only beginning to pay its way but to open up areas that had been scarcely touched before, I received a rude shock one morning in 1958 when the mail brought a notification that the spar-caps on the wing would have to be changed. The spar-caps are long steel strips, tapered from the wing-root to the wing-tip, and structurally vital for wing strength. If they had to be replaced, the task could only by accomplished in the United Kingdom, at the Bristol factory in a place called Weston-super-Mare on England's west coast. I had never been to England at this point, had never travelled overseas at all, in fact, so it was with a sense of adventure that I set off to pay my first visit by flying there in my own aircraft.

To help pay for the trip, I dug up a payload from de Havilland in Toronto. They had a Beaver on order for England, and since the Beaver couldn't make the trip itself,

I offered to carry it across, broken down as freight, in the belly of the Bristol. George Bell checked out the Freighter to within an inch of her life, and I flew from Yellowknife to Toronto to pick up both the Beaver and an experienced ferry pilot to help me on the overseas trip.

The pilot turned out to be an engaging character named Jack Ford, who had flown across the North Atlantic nearly a hundred times, and who proved to be a convivial companion. Our route would take us from Toronto to Goose Bay in Labrador, then across to Iceland, and down to England. I told Jack, when we talked on the phone, that I had a five-hundred gallon auxiliary tank installed to give us the necessary range for the leg from Goose Bay to Iceland; I also told him that since this was a ferry trip for the purposes of aircraft modification, there would only be the two of us on board. I don't recall what he said in reply to that, but he paid absolutely no attention, and when we met at de Havilland he had brought along a professional photographer friend of his and his girlfriend, a beautiful model. At that point, I could hardly say, "Well, the best of British luck to you," so they clambered on board, and away we went.

When we landed at Goose Bay, I discovered that in the air-force establishment there Jack knew everybody and everybody knew Jack, so we were given the royal treatment at the mess. Having a beautiful model along didn't hurt our reception, either. The next day we took off for Iceland, Jack whistling and humming to himself, and me worrying; worrying was not one of Jack's things. I knew we had enough fuel for the trip, but did we have enough oil? Each of the Bristol's power-plants burned oil quite heavily, especially when, as now, the plane was carrying a heavy load. I had calculated that I could increase the oil capacity by partially filling the expansion tank on the forty-five-gallon oil tank on each engine. The expansion tank holds a little more than ten gallons; I put an additional eight gallons of oil in each one, thus leaving little room for the expansion that would accompany greater heat. There was a cap at the top of each expansion tank, which I removed and left off, to allow room for the extra lubricant. However, leaving off the cap meant there was a danger that the tank would, at takeoff under heavy pressure, suddenly begin to pump oil overboard through the breather-pipe on the engine. The pipe could act as a siphon, and I could lose my entire oil supply while we were still lifting off.

Therefore, on takeoff, I had Jack peering out his window to keep an eye on the engine on his side, while I kept flashing a look at the one out of my side, and our two passengers, in the cabin down below, were instructed to scream if they spotted a tell-tale plume of black oil drifting down the side of the aircraft.

As it turned out, nothing happened; the aircraft performed flawlessly – Jack obviously wondered what all the fuss was about – and he talked to me cheerfully about all the people he knew in England and all the best places to stay and eat. The one thing Jack didn't know, though, was how to use an astro compass, which, to me, was absolutely essential for navigation over these wide expanses; we used it in the North all the time. His notion, apparently, was that you picked out a heading, pointed the aircraft in the direction of Iceland, and hoped for the best.

We were required to report our position to Air Traffic Control, which I did through the help of commercial carriers on the same routing. Once, I heard the pilot of a Canadian Pacific Britannia calling in, so I got him on the radio and asked him to relay our position to the air-traffic controllers. He was astonished to discover that just below him was an air-freighter out of Yellowknife, with a Beaver in its innards and a bush pilot at the controls, trying to find Iceland for the first time. We kept in touch for three or four hundred miles.

Soon we were crossing the southern tip of Greenland and the massive floes and icebergs of the Greenland current. I remember thinking, as I looked down on those gigantic lumps of ice and that almost vertical sea, that this would be an awkward time to have engine trouble. We landed at Keflevik in Iceland, where, once again, it turned out that everybody knew Jack and Jack knew everybody, and it was party-time again.

The next day we flew to Prestwick, in Scotland, and before I knew it, Jack and his pals were shaking hands and bidding me goodbye. They had an urgent appointment somewhere – probably another party – and I was abandoned for the trip down to Weston-super-Mare, which is on the Bristol Channel, just south and slightly west of the city of Bristol.

I checked with the transport people at Prestwick and was told that under British air regulations I could take the aircraft on without a co-pilot as long as I flew VFR – that is, by Visual Flight Rules, below the clouds and always in sight of land. I had a wonderful trip, flying at about two thousand feet down the length of England, gawking out the window at the countryside, getting a bird's-eye view of a couple of nuclear-power plants – I had never seen one before – and soaking up all the sights.

My first stop was to drop off the Beaver at de Havilland's headquarters at Hatfield, not far from London. I asked the crew, who gathered around when I landed, to bring over a forklift to unload the Beaver, and they just laughed. They didn't have such a thing as a forklift; however, we were able to jury-rig a lift and get the Beaver safely out and bolted back together again. Then I waved goodbye and headed once more for the Bristol Aircraft factory, where I landed on a beautifully manicured grass field at Weston-super-Mare. The aircraft workers who flocked out to greet me were absolutely astonished at the condition of my aircraft. Their records showed that they had never shipped any spare parts for this particular plane, so they were expecting to work on a bit of a wreck, and yet it looked as good as new. The answer to this was that Trans-Canada Airlines, in typical fashion, had bought enough spare parts when it took the original order to equip ten Bristol Freighters, and all these spares went from Trans-Canada to Transair and then to me, so there was never any need to send home for more.

I left the Freighter there, with orders not only to fix up the spar-caps but to give the plane a new paint job, and flew home commercial. I was back in England six weeks later, having arranged to meet Jack Ford at Weston-super-Mare for the trip home. Typically, he didn't show up on the appointed day, and I cooled my heels in a resort hotel for five days before he arrived.

We got back to Iceland and Goose Bay easily enough, with more parties for Jack, and then had a bit of a debate about how to proceed to Winnipeg straight across the Canadian Shield. Jack was petrified. He didn't mind flying over the open ocean, but the thought of coming down somewhere in the frozen North absolutely terrified him. It was a longer run from Goose Bay to Winnipeg than it was from Goose Bay to Iceland – a thought that first occurred to me on that trip, and gave me some notion of the immensity of my own country – and Jack thought we should go south, following the regular airways over the Great Lakes and southern Prairies, where there was at least somewhere reasonable to land.

"Heck, I cut my teeth flying this country," I told him. "Stop worrying."

He finally did stop worrying when a pleasant thought occurred to him as we were cutting across the top end of

James Bay. Jack was staring gloomily out the window at the bleak landscape below, when he suddenly brightened and said, "Hey, if we do get forced down, I've got a way to get us some help in a hurry."

"What is that?" I asked.

"I've got a bottle of gin and a bottle of vermouth in my suitcase," Jack explained. "If we have to land somewhere on the tundra, I'll get them out and start to mix a martini. Within five minutes, someone is bound to show up and tell me I've got the proportions wrong."

He clung to that thought all the way to Winnipeg, and when we got there, though he didn't exactly get out and kiss the ground, he did let me know how glad – and surprised – he was that we'd made it. We flew on to Edmonton, and Jack took a commercial flight back to the East. I never saw him again, and was sorry to learn later that he had died in a crash at sea, conducting one of his innumerable ferry operations out of Manila.

There is an air of romanticism about the flying feats of an earlier era in Canada, and, while I don't deny that there were great men and great deeds of derring-do, the truth is that much of what we did was hard, exacting work that required technical skill more than bravado.

Take the time in 1960 when we were asked by the Department of Northern Affairs (as it was then called) to haul sixty-five tons of materials from Dawson City to Old Crow in the Yukon, so they could build a new school. Old Crow is on the Porcupine River, almost up against the Alaskan border, and more than two hundred miles by air from Dawson. It was possible to move the material by water (at least, Erik Nielsen, in his memoirs, argued that it would be cheaper and better to do it that way, and he may well be right), but the decision had been made to air-freight it, several tons a trip, and I had no quarrel with that. I was glad to get the business.

There were other air-freighters around, of course, operating out of Yukon Territory, but they flew DC-3s; we could carry twice the payload and get the job done not only faster but cheaper. We flew from Yellowknife to Dawson, 750 miles, during which we saw only one settlement, Wrigley, climbed over a fourteen-thousand-foot mountain range, and ran into rough weather along the way. It was not exactly the same as calling up the local mover to come and haul your furniture away.

We worked out of Dawson, living in one of the original hotels built at the time of the gold rush. It was pretty decrepit; the foundation had sunk and cracked, leaving the floors so tilted that the room I shared with another pilot didn't have a door on it. You couldn't close a door, or even swing it across that tilting surface, so they had just slung a .curtain across the opening. But it was great.

We loaded the Bristol with five tons of materials – we were to haul desks, tables, blackboards, even the timber to build the school with and the wallboard to finish it with – and took off from Dawson. I had spoken to the officials of Northern Affairs, who assured me that there was an airstrip prepared at Old Crow, three thousand feet long and one hundred wide, perfectly adequate for my aircraft. I should have concluded that anything a bureaucrat said should be checked, but at the time I took their word for it, and it wasn't until I was circling the tiny hamlet, with the entire population out on the ice, running around and waving, that I discovered that my idea of what constitutes an airstrip and that of the department were somewhat at variance. It was true that an area had been marked off, but you couldn't call it an airstrip – just a stretch of frozen river slightly less bumpy than the surrounding land. Worse, as I circled lower,

I could see a shimmer of water on the surface, shining in the spring sun.

Perhaps this is the place to stop and explain a little about what the ice conditions mean to landing aircraft. When the weather is really cold, with temperatures well below zero, surface ice crystals act almost like tiny pieces of gravel and provide excellent braking action. Then you have no problem. When the ice starts to melt, however, you get two difficulties. The first is simply that the surface becomes so slippery that it is always a matter of conjecture whether you will get the aircraft stopped before pitching head first into a snowdrift at the end of the runway; the second is what is called "candling." In the spring, the meltwater drains through cracks, the sun reacts with these growing cracks, and the whole structure of the ice shifts vertically. You get shapes like an inverted candle flame throughout the ice, which consequently loses a good deal of its load-bearing strength.

I didn't really have much room to spare on that first landing at Old Crow, so the trick was to land short and stop before the aircraft skidded off the end of the runway. Of course, as I came in, the locals swarmed over the river banks and down to the edge of the strip, which made the landing all that much more interesting. There was a crosswind to contend with, too, which meant I had to apply heavy brakes on the right-hand wheel; within seconds, that wheel had locked to the surface, and the instant build-up of heat caused by the friction took the tread clean off a brand-new tire.

However, I got the plane stopped within a few yards of the end of the runway, and nobody but myself and my co-pilot, Joe McGilvray, realized how difficult it had been. Our takeoff, once we had unloaded, was a pretty rough one on that thumping wheel.

A cold snap settled in after that first trip, and our landings became rough but routine. We worked fourteen hours a day hauling materials, enjoying the hard work and the steady income. We were still being paid by the mile, including the mileage from Yellowknife, so, even if we were burning 125 gallons of gasoline an hour at a cruising speed of 170 mph, we did well out of that contract.

The Bristol was good for more than just hauling freight; she could hold up to forty-four passengers, although the seats were somewhat primitive. Once, when we had to move a group of schoolteachers from Yellowknife to Inuvik for a convention, we got the plane all loaded and discovered there were still a few teachers left over, with no place to sit. We tied a couple of kitchen chairs down in the aisle, and flew them that way. It was kind of illegal.

Another of our flights brought a bunch of football fans from Yellowknife to Edmonton, so they could watch the Grey Cup game on the TV set in the Château Lacombe bar, there being no TV in the North in those days.

Since the front door on the Bristol would swing wide enough that you could drive a truck right in, we developed a small business flying trucks and passenger cars from the end of the highway at Hay River across to Yellowknife during freeze-up and break-up. (When real winter sets in, you can drive across Great Slave Lake on the ice road, and in the summer, you can work your way around through Fort Providence and Fort Rae, but it was much faster to wheel your car into the Bristol and be whisked across the lake.)

Despite the fact that we did all the freighting between Hay River and Yellowknife for years, and despite the fact that no one else wanted to fly the route, our applications to run a scheduled service on this route were turned down, and that added to our problems. Without such a route, it was hard to generate enough traffic to pay down the heavy debt-load of the Bristol, so I went to call on my old friend at the Industrial Development Bank, Ritchie Clark, who was now working out of Calgary. I told him that I could still make my payments on the five-year loan, but it would leave me strapped for cash. Was there anything he could do? Ritchie restructured the loan so that, while the amortization period remained the same, I would pay more in the last two years, which reduced the current load. It was great doing business with someone like Ritchie, who had the imagination and the flexibility to make such a change. The new arrangement worked out splendidly, and I never missed a payment on that or on any other note I ever took out in over four decades of flying – and debt.

I have already mentioned that I didn't do much flying into the DEW-line sites during their construction, but I certainly wasn't going to turn down any work that came my way for the Bristol, and that led me into some controversy when I received a telex from an American company requesting me to take on the job of air-lifting parts of a damaged DC-3 out of DEW-line Site 26, on the Arctic Ocean. I replied that I would be happy to do so. Then I got another telex advising me that, before landing at any DEW-line site, I was to obtain permission from the U.S. company that had the contract to operate the site. I had already seen how Judge Sissons treated this kind of American arrogance – with contempt – so I quickly contacted Gordon Robertson, still Deputy Minister of Northern Affairs in Ottawa, and asked him to explain to me why a Canadian pilot would have to get American permission to land on Canadian soil. I got back a message through the Department of Transport that I was requested, when operating into a DEW-line station, to advise the Americans, "if convenient," as to my flight times.

Site 26, when I got there, proved to have a gravel airstrip three thousand feet long that started right at the edge of the sea and terminated in a great pile of boulders. It took a couple of days to get the fuselage of the damaged DC-3 and a great many parts loaded into the aircraft. The run-up before takeoff was perfectly normal, but when I got the aircraft pounding down the runway and headed for that pile of boulders at the end, the right engine suddenly slowed. The self-feathering feature took over and shut it down completely, so I was forced to haul myself into the air, with a full load and fuel topped up, on one engine. Again, the aircraft came through for me with flying colours; I was able to climb out, make a circuit, and land back on the strip safely. It was some time before we could get another engine in and the Bristol out again.

Maintaining an aircraft the size of the Freighter in the Arctic was no simple task, and it took dedicated, competent engineers, working often in snow storms, rain storms, wind storms, and temperatures of minus forty and plus ninety on the Farenheit scale, to do the job. This type of challenge draws a certain type of person, people like George Bell, Guenther Moellenbeck, George Bignell, Johnny Dapp, Ken Burgess, Art Lockwood – to name only a few of the northern adventurers who worked for Wardair. These were all men with the courage, resourcefulness, industry, and ingenuity that made an airline function.

We certainly couldn't afford to build a hangar at Yellow-knife, and I couldn't very well ask a mechanic to do an engine check, which takes many hours, in sixty-below weather. The solution was produced by a very bright engineer, Frank Rhumann, who designed a portable nose-hangar for me. It was about thirty feet high, sixteen feet wide, and twenty-five feet deep – large enough to cover one engine completely – and came on a set of truck wheels. You pushed it over one engine, lowered the top with a winch to fit tightly around the wing, and, with portable heaters, you could work in there for hours in your shirtsleeves. Then you backed it out and took it across to the other engine. It sounds simple and obvious now, but it was a surprising and incongruous sight when we first started to use it.

The result was that, with one trip a year down to Northwest Industries in Edmonton for a complete overhaul, we were able to operate with very little down time, and no accidents, from April 1957 into early 1969, with the Bristol. As the business in the North expanded, we bought more Bristols, until we had a fleet of five. It is the Beaver and the Otters that people in the south read about as the aircraft that opened the Arctic, but the Bristol played a key role, too, and it was with a combination of pride and regret that I would see our original Freighter retired from service in March 1969 and later hoisted to an honourable post atop a pedestal at Yellowknife, as a monument to her illustrious career.

Long before that took place, I was experiencing increasing frustration in my constant attempts to try to obtain a licence as a scheduled air carrier, and learning how tough flying could really be in this country – when you are trying to get over bureaucrats, instead of merely mountains.

CHAPTER 12

▼

The Move South

By 1961, we had gone as far as we could go in the North. The Air Transport Board's refusal to allow us a scheduled run to Hay River was only one of a score or more of the occasions, too tedious to enumerate, on which the Ottawa authorities who controlled our lives made it clear that we were simply not going to be allowed to expand beyond Yellowknife. My original licence had been for two aircraft only; every time we added a new aircraft to our fleet we faced another long, expensive fight with the ATB. Getting a licence for the Bristol Freighter had been like pulling teeth. The growth was good for the North, good for business, good for Canada, but if you were judging by the constant resistance you would have thought I was trying to do something shady, if not downright illegal. More and more of my time was spent, not building and running an increasingly important transportation service, but trying to figure out ways around the thickets of regulations that kept springing up before me. I would manage to find a way around one obstacle, only to discover that another and larger one had been put in its place. I was being frozen out of the North, if you'll pardon me, and it gradually dawned on me that I was going to have to find somewhere else to expand.

Despite the best efforts of the regulators, our operation was very successful, and we were building up a good surplus of money inside the business. By the end of the 1950s, we had four Otters and two Beavers operating throughout the territories (for about a year we had six single-engine Otters, until a crash wiped one of them out in May 1959), as well as the Bristol Freighter. The Yellowknife office was able to look after itself, under the capable guidance of the chief engineer, George Bell, the chief pilot, Don Braun, and an enthusiastic staff of fourteen, who all knew their stuff.

The base manager was Bob O'Hara. Through thirty years, Bob was to serve Wardair with enthusiasm and expertise, working in many capacities, moving from Yellowknife to Edmonton to Toronto to Edmonton and back to Toronto. When we were finally given the right to carry air cargo in our international operation years later, Bob became Vice-President, Cargo Sales, of this operation. Through his efforts and the efforts of his fine team, the cargo business became, in less than ten years, an important contributor to the airline's income. Bob became Wardair's longest-employed member, and he tackled retirement in the spring of 1989 with his usual enthusiasm. He now wears his thirty-year Wardair Wings of Excellence, the only set in existence, with well-deserved pride.

However, in 1961, it was time to move on and, although I had never said this aloud to anyone except Marjorie, it had always been my goal to run a full-fledged, scheduled airline. I decided that I would work my way towards realizing this ambition – which, in fact, I would not see for another twenty-five years – by starting with international charter operations, which were just then becoming popular in a number of countries. In fact, it was the sight of a KLM Constellation at the Edmonton airport on a charter flight that crystallized my rather vague thinking about this approach. Why should foreign carriers get all the Canadian business? (Not that there was much business, at this point; in the year before we went into international charters, there were only two overseas charter flights from the whole of Western Canada.)

As I contemplated a move to the South, I felt strongly that we must establish our image as we wanted it to be, right from the beginning. I chose the office space very carefully, and it was on the ground floor of the Macdonald Hotel. There was a drugstore operating out of the space, and I bought out its lease. The hotel manager was quite upset when he learned that a new tenant had moved in. I'm sure he thought this two-bit outfit from the northern bush would set up on a couple of apple boxes, with a collection of crates. However, I contacted a specialist on office interiors, Donn Larsen, and we built a small, but beautiful, wood-panelled sales office, containing the best of furniture. It was a little jewel. Donn Larsen later built and equipped many other offices for us in Edmonton as we expanded. He is a Dane, with impeccable taste and a flair for design. I always enjoyed working with him.

We soon acquired a fair-sized office upstairs in the Macdonald Hotel building, as well. It was not the showplace that the sales office was, but it was finished in good taste, with high-quality furniture and bright colours. Our sales offices in the New Town in Yellowknife were nice, but now we were launching a whole new service concept as we began to move into international operations, and we were determined to do it with style and grace. Our offices raised a fair amount of comment in Edmonton, which was good advertising for us.

I had formed a friendship with an extraordinary Canadian Pacific pilot, Jimmy Maguire, then flying the Amsterdam service in Britannia aircraft. Jimmy's experience flying overseas convinced him that holiday charters were going to be the coming thing, and of course he was dead right. We could combine these passenger charters with our air-freight business in the North, flying the customers to Europe in the summer and the fuel, machinery, and freight around the Arctic in the winter. Winter holiday charters still lay a long way in the future.

Jimmy suggested that to get a solid opinion on what was just a hunch on his part we should go to talk to a real expert on international aviation in Montreal, whose name he had been given. Thus, we both flew off to Montreal to talk to this aviation consultant, who told us, in rather less direct language, that we were out of our heads. The big airlines would always use their surplus capacity to run charters, he suggested, and no small start-up airline could ever compete with them.

We had a very glum flight back to Edmonton, and Jimmy went on to his home in Vancouver, convinced that the project was finished. However, the more I thought about the expert's advice, the less impressed I was. When was the last time, I asked myself, I had heard from an expert who turned out to be right? If I had taken all the best advice available, I would never have bought the first Beaver, the Otters, or the Bristol Freighter. If I was going to be guided by common sense, I would probably still be building houses in Lethbridge, Alberta. I phoned Jimmy and told him to forget about the experts, we were going to go ahead. Not long after this, Jimmy had a heart attack. When he had recovered, he came to work for me full time, and his opening assignment was to get a line on some aircraft.

Jimmy had heard that Trans-Canada was returning two Super G Constellation passenger aircraft to Lockheed Aircraft, under a buy-back arrangement they had with the manufacturer. This was because Trans-Canada was expecting delivery of Vanguard turbo-prop aircraft, which were faster, newer, and cheaper to fly than the Constellations.

It made perfect sense for us to step in and take up these aircraft for the charter operation, so I did two things at once. The first was to file an application with the Air Transport Board for a licence to operate out of Edmonton. The application was officially for a Class 4 charter service between Edmonton and other points in Canada and a Class 9–4 international non-scheduled charter service out of Edmonton. The second thing I did was to contact Kurt Yost, the head salesman at Lockheed, about buying Trans-Canada's returning planes.

Yost was something of a colourful character, who had a lot of dealings with Howard Hughes. He used to tell tales of trying to sell aircraft to Hughes, which usually involved waiting in a hotel room, night after night, until Hughes would suddenly summon him at about 3:00 A.M. and abruptly make an offer. Yost was clearly anxious to do business with us, and I had no reason to think the financing would be a problem, but the deal came unstuck for another reason.

Someone apparently tipped off Trans-Canada that we were interested in the aircraft (as I learned from other industry contacts), and a single phone call from an official high in the chain of command at Trans-Canada to an official high in the federal government was enough to finish our application for any licence out of Edmonton, right there. The official refusal didn't say anything of the sort, of course; it was wrapped in the usual bureaucratic language, but the meaning was plain enough: No.

You have to bear in mind that, in those days, it was received wisdom that we only really needed one air carrier in Canada, and that was the government airline. Canadian Pacific was reluctantly allowed to operate, too, because, well, it was CP, and CP had always had powerful friends in Ottawa. Pacific Western and other small-fry carriers were allowed to operate as regional airlines, as long as they didn't get too big for their britches. But no others need apply. The official reason given in the Air Transport Board decision handed down on February 15, 1961, was that, "The Board . . . is of the opinion that there are adequate charter commercial air services, both domestic and international, already operated out of the bases applied for." (Bunk.)

The Board was also of the opinion that the "diversion of traffic which would likely result from the licensing of an additional Group A Charter commercial air carrier from a base at Edmonton would prejudice the orderly and economic development of existing air services provided by air carriers serving the area and would not therefore be in the best interests of the public." (Also bunk.)

Translation: If we got a licence, competition was likely to rear its ugly head in the air-passenger industry, which would bring prices down and improve the service. We didn't want that, did we? Much better to leave everything in the hands of Trans-Canada Airlines. That would be "in the best interests of the public."

Bloody but unbowed, I fired off yet another application, with more data on future traffic possibilities, and settled down to see what happened to that. It was about this time that I learned that Trans-Canada had decided to hold on to the Constellations after all. This turned out to be a shrewd move, although whether it was aimed at anything other than keeping the planes out of our hands I never did learn. The Vanguards were not delivered on time, and if Trans-Canada had let the Constellations go, they would probably have had to lease them back from us to keep the airline on schedule. Wouldn't that have been fun!

My renewed application wandered around the corridors of Ottawa for about a year, until, surprise, surprise, the AirTransport Board looked upon it again, and found it good, and gave us at least part of what we wanted, namely a "Class 9–4 International Commercial Charter (non-scheduled) Licence." For quixotic reasons of its own, the Board gave us permission to operate out of Yellowknife, population four thousand, and a ridiculous place from which to operate an international charter service. However, a close reading of the licence indicated that, although the ATB issued the licence as from that city, we could, if we chose, operate from any point in Canada.

On June 22, 1961, we changed the name of the company officially to Wardair Canada Ltd., from a mere "Wardair," to indicate its new international ambitions. Now we had a licence, a new Edmonton head office (in the wrong place, according to the ATB, but we didn't mind about that), and a new name. What we didn't have was any aircraft capable of meeting the demand we hoped to find or create.

It was my old friend Cy Becker who led us to the solution of this latest problem. Cy, you will remember, had handled the early legal work for Wardair, and was still our lawyer. He had helped Grant McConachie, another of the old bush-pilot fraternity, to put together CP Air and to become president of the outfit, so they were very good friends. Cy set up an appointment for me to call on Grant in his Vancouver office, to try to buy from him one of the DC-6 aircraft, which Cy told me were then surplus to CP Air's requirements. (Like Trans-Canada, CP Air was busy acquiring turbo-props.)

The Douglas DC-6 was a four-engine aircraft, a passenger-freighter capable of carrying fourteen tons of freight or ninety-one passengers, or a combination of freight and passengers, at 300 mph. Grant McConachie agreed to let me have one of these, on a lease with an option to purchase. I can no longer remember how much we agreed to pay for it if we went through with the purchase (we didn't), except that, as usual, it was probably a lot more than our present traffic seemed likely to support.

As a matter of fact, at the time I accepted delivery of this aircraft (it had the euphonious registration CF-CZZ), the only firm contracts I had for it were to carry materials and equipment for Canadian Nickel and other mining companies, and to fly fuel and supplies from Resolute to Isachsen and Mould Bay in the high Arctic for the Polar Continental Shelf project. We started on that contract on March 16, 1962, and used Grant McConachie's own aircrews – which he always laid off in the winter – to get the work done.

Those early crews formed a nucleus for Wardair that was talented, dedicated, young, and enthusiastic: Don Saunders, Bob Gartshore, Doug McKinley, Phil Botley, Al Graham, Phil Gaunt, Harry March, Fred Woodhall, Ray Audette. By 1964, they were joined by Dean Ostrander, Wilf Kyryluk, and Doug Nicholson. They form a parade in my memory that I salute to this day. Most of them stayed with Wardair all through the years, writing our operations manuals, detailing the standards for aircrews. Their expertise was augmented as time passed by our northern bush-pilots: George Zlatnick, Jeff Braithwaite, Steve England, Steve Gillis, Ray Weaver, Rod Dyck, Darcy Fleming, and Murray Oakenfold, whose training and experience made me very confident of their ability.

We didn't fly a passenger charter until May 10, 1962, when we carried eighty-nine members of the Alberta School Patrol Band from Calgary to Ottawa and back – which was a seven-hour flight each way in those days. This was not an overseas charter, as described in our licence, but the ATB gave us special permission for this flight, and needless to say, the School Patrollers were elated and excited during that trip – almost as elated and excited as the Wardair people serving them.

Our first overseas charter came six weeks later, on June 22, 1962, when we took a group from Edmonton to Copenhagen, with stops at Frobisher Bay and Prestwick, Scotland, along the way. It took nearly seven and a half hours to reach Frobisher, and another eleven hours to get to Prestwick. In all, the flight took twenty hours and twenty-six minutes. Let the record show that the crew on that historic journey consisted of Captain Harry March, First Officer Bob Gartshore, Second Officer Ray Audette, Navigator Phil Botley, and Line Engineer Fred Woodhall. The cabin attendants were Pat Brault, Helen Maclagen, Patricia Molyneux, and Marianne McIndoe.

During that first summer, we completed eight overseas charters, and lost money on every one of them. We were pioneering, and pioneers have a tough time. The rules of the day provided that you could only fly "affinity" charters, that is, the entire aircraft would have to be filled with people who had all been members of the same club or association for at least six months. The government made it very clear that this rule had been established to prevent any serious competition with the only true, legitimate air carriers, the big boys who ran the scheduled services, and since they wouldn't allow us to fly any scheduled services, we were in a bit of a pickle. These rules led to some anomalous situations. We flew the Alberta Judo Club, whose members included little old ladies in wheelchairs; canoe clubs turned up with members who had never seen a paddle; and card-carrying mountaineers from the bald prairie put down their money and took their flight.

Since we had to charge rates below those of the scheduled carriers to attract customers, the DC-6 was not productive enough to operate at a profit, and to make matters worse, we had not yet developed the kind of market that would allow us to purchase a more productive plane.

It was a bitter pill to swallow when I had to return the DC-6 to Grant McConachie at the end of the first lease period, especially when I heard that he told Cy Becker he had made more money out of leasing the aircraft to me than he had ever made operating it. We lost $350,000 – all the money we had put down as part of the lease-purchase option. There was a particularly bitter side to this; we had made a larger down payment than required, so as to reduce our monthly costs, and now every cent of it was gone. So much for the learning curve. Moreover, in just one year's work, we had succeeded in wiping out most of the surplus built up so painstakingly over the previous fifteen years in the North.

That was another of the turning points in my life; I had to decide what to do next. One night, I stayed in our office on the first floor of the Macdonald Hotel in Edmonton after everyone else had gone home, pacing back and forth and trying to decide whether the time had come to cut my losses and give up.

On one side, the chartering business was only beginning. We had learned a lot from the flights we had done so far; we were in on the ground floor of what looked like a tremendous new business – we didn't have all the sophisticated surveys available now, but anyone of sense could see that, with the spread of jet aircraft, overseas travel was going to become commonplace within a few years – and, at the personal level, I wanted desperately to go on. More importantly, we knew what the costs were of operating an aircraft on the North Atlantic, and we knew what the problems were from our own experience – with accurate information we could count on.

The other side of the coin was the fact that, so far, we had failed; we had lost money and used up most of our reserves, and the only aircraft we could afford was never going to turn a profit in the charter business. That led to the logical conclusion that I had to buy a new and better aircraft – a jet. But there were two difficulties in the way.

In the first place, raising the money for a jet wasn't going to be easy for a man who, when he went through the front door of the bank, saw the bankers all piling out the back. I remember once during this period, an official with the Canadian Imperial Bank of Commerce told me he would never lend me any money because, "You don't care about money; you just use it." I was astounded. I thought that was what money was for, to use. Apparently, you were supposed to accumulate the stuff in ever-higher piles. Then, and only then, would the banks give you some more.

In the second place, I had now spent sixteen years in battles with the bureaucrats (I have mentioned only a few details of these skirmishes, because I have been trying to give the reader something of the flavour of life and work in the North at its most exciting time; the red-tape wars will move to the foreground as we proceed), and it was clear that if I could be blocked by either petty harassment or grand schemes, I would be.

Wouldn't it be simpler, I asked myself, just to forget about the whole crazy chartering business and go back North, where the bush operations were humming along smoothly?

Of course it would. I was glad I finally had all that straight in my mind. The sensible, prudent, responsible decision was to forget about charters and concentrate on the North. I cleaned up a few odds and ends on my desk, turned out the lights, and strode out into the gathering gloom. My mind was made up. I would somehow acquire another DC-6, and go into international charters in a really serious way. Someday, I would buy a jet aircraft. Arrogant thinking for a man who had just lost $350,000.

CHAPTER 13

▼

We Enter the Jet Stream

My thought processes weren't quite as perverse as they seemed. I reasoned that as long as I could keep the bills paid, by using the northern operations, in effect, to subsidize the charters, I could establish myself in the new business – provided I could get a reliable aircraft at the right price. I would have to roll with the punches, but this is what I would do, what I was used to doing. I knew that the Douglas DC-6 was reliable, so the trick was to find one at the right price. I wouldn't make money with the charters, but I would keep going and look for new opportunities to expand.

That resolved, I went to airplane brokers, first in New York and then all over the world. I flew to Helsinki, Brussels, London – each time on the trail of what looked like a deal, and each time in vain. Then I heard about a DC-6B that KLM had for sale; it was a straight passenger aircraft, not the mix of passenger and freight we had had before, and that was a drawback. On the other hand, the engines were what were called "low time" – they hadn't many hours on them – and the price was right – $300,000 U.S., a fraction of what a comparable aircraft would cost new.

Of course, Wardair Canada Ltd. didn't have that kind of money, not after the débâcle of the summer of 1962, so I soon had our sales staff of two – Rod Worrall and Art Gauthier – out selling charters to Europe for the next summer, to raise the money to buy the aircraft on which to fly! Our marketing people through the years performed remarkably, but none more so than Art and Rod, who, all that fall and winter, helped organize clubs and sold charters without an aircraft in sight. That takes real faith and real salesmanship. That was a time never to be forgotten. Everyone took a pay cut – engineers, flight attendants, pilots, president, secretaries, and on down the line. We had a "Hard Times Bean Bake" at our home in Edmonton. For the flights we did have going before the DC-6 lease ran out, Marjorie, my sister, Lillian, and most of the Wardair staff turned up at the hangar to clean, stuff pillows, replace chair covers and seats, and collaborate on the hundreds of jobs that helped to make it go. All of us were young, and the world was there to be challenged. In addition, I pulled some more cash through the northern operation and asked my ever-supportive father-in-law and sister to co-sign yet another bank loan for me. On the closing date for the purchase of the plane, I paid down $50,000 U.S., with the balance to be paid over three years, and flew over to Amsterdam to pick up the new aircraft.

I knew that if there was one thing we had to have in this business, it was reliability, so when we landed back in Edmonton in March 1963, I had the DC-6 – which wasn't in nearly as good shape as the one we had returned to CP Air – towed over to the Northwest Industries hangar and given a thorough overhaul. This cost another $100,000 and included everything from a check to make sure the aircraft was in tiptop mechanical shape to the replacement of upholstery and the elimination of anything shabby about the interior. In those days of the early charters, there were a number of fly-by-night operators in the United States whose antics were giving the business a very dodgy name. In addition, the customers would inevitably be comparing us to Trans-Canada Airlines and CP Air – we had to be better, and look better, to build up the credibility we required.

In 1963, flying was still something of a novelty. You would see pictures of people in the newspapers because they had made an overseas flight. It was a pretty expensive proposition, as well. The charters changed all that. As prices dropped, the aircraft got better and faster, and the excellent safety record of the charter carriers held up. We knew the time was right to develop a number of markets in Western Canada.

The first group to give us a lot of business, as it turned out, were the English war brides, who had come out to Canada in the period immediately after 1945 and had, in many cases, not been home since. They were now in their forties and anxious for – and able to afford – a trip back to England. Then there were all the European immigrants and their offspring, bursting to go home and show the old folks how prosperous they had become in Canada.

We opened offices in Vancouver and Calgary – eventually, we were even to open one in Toronto, to tap these markets. We flew charters from Calgary, Edmonton, Saskatoon, Vancouver, and Toronto to London, Manchester, Prestwick, Shannon, Belfast, Amsterdam, Oslo, Copenhagen, and Düsseldorf. From the first, we were determined that the service would be first-class and reliable and the crews cheerful – not just in the cracked-smile way you see in the ads, but cheerful because they were having a good time working hard. We couldn't afford to pay our crews what CP Air could pay, but we didn't dump them out on the street when winter or tough times came, and they responded.

We also provided really good food, in place of the drab and dismal plastic-encased fare that was often as much a part of the in-flight experience as the demonstration on how to use the life-vests. It didn't really cost that much more to serve good food rather than mediocre stuff, and my reasoning was that proper meals, well served, would give Wardair charters the stamp of excellence. It was a decision, and a policy, that I never varied. At first, when we were still operating in a small way, we got all our food from a superior Edmonton restaurant called The Steak Loft. (This restaurant was owned by Mitch Klimove and had a wonderful *maitre d'* named Corky, who liked to play the horses. He was the most improbable-looking *maitre d'* I ever ran into, but a real jewel.)

I believed that what the passenger wanted on every flight was a good steak – Mitch enthusiastically shared my opinion – and it seemed to me what was needed on these long trips was the stamina and comfort such a meal provided, so I provided it. The Steak Loft would prepare the meals, and we would truck them out to the aircraft and load them aboard at the last minute.

As the international operation began to build up, we inherited from CP Air not only the pilots and engineers that they laid off to save money during the winter season but also a number of its cabin attendants. It seems crazy now, when you think about it, but both Trans-Canada and CP Air had the rule that as soon as a female cabin attendant got married, she was fired. In any event, ridiculous as the rule was, it came to be of great benefit to us, because it meant there was a pool of talent out there, consisting of married ex-cabin attendants who were still eager to fly. Right at the beginning of the overseas charters, I was fortunate enough to meet one of these, Marianne McIndoe, who had worked for CP Air, and she was the one who recruited a number of her former colleagues and set up a training program for new recruits. A multi-talented woman, Marianne not only designed our first cabin-attendants' uniforms, she laid down the work ethic that eventually gave us, I am proud to say, a reputation as one of the best airlines in the world on which to fly.

In the summer, our peak season, we recruited university students as flight attendants and put them through a comprehensive training program. They responded wonderfully, never losing their cheerful calm on flights that could last as long as twenty-three hours, and the passengers in turn wrote us hundreds of letters to indicate how pleased they were with the standard of service. I always wondered how many mothers worried about their daughters flying with us in those early days.

Almost every business carries an item on its books called "goodwill," but sometimes it doesn't mean much; in the case of Wardair, it meant a lot, and the credit for that went in large measure to the staff. In those hectic days, despite all the pressures, irritations, and worries, we always seemed to be having a good time – at least while flying.

In the early years, most of Wardair was in my head, but as the company grew, I had to leave a great deal to my very competent staff of executives and their people. Wardair was always fortunate in being able to attract people who loved a challenge. I can't say enough in their praise. Many, many of us spent long hours of overtime endeavouring to build our company. I found staff in offices long after closing hours, or very early in the morning, when work could be done before the telephones began their interruptions and the offices hummed with busy crowds.

There was nothing of the ordinary about any aspect of the business I found myself in – including the attitude of some of our competitors towards us. I had a curious conversation one day with some of the sales clerks from Cunard Steamship Lines, who had a ticket office in a bank building across the street from the Macdonald Hotel. They told me that Wardair was one of the best things that had ever happened to them. I must say it startled me; I thought we were rivals.

"No," said one of these sales clerks. "You see, it's this way. A trip to Europe used to be only for the very rich, but you guys, with your charter flights, have sparked interest in overseas travel and put Europe within reach of almost everyone. People are going over, and coming back and talking about it, and we pick up some of the business, too, because, of course, some people are afraid to fly. In any event," he concluded, "we want to thank you for tripling our business."

"Any time," I replied.

We did a lot to make the trips cheerful. The conditions at the Edmonton airport at this time were pretty primitive, especially for us, the non-scheduled pariahs of the airline business. We had to load our passengers in a draughty, noisy hangar, with little in the way of seating space, telephones, or washrooms for the passengers while they waited. So, in defence, before flights we gathered the charter customers at the Macdonald Hotel and had a party – sandwiches and croissants and a beverage, nothing elaborate – before bussing them out to the aircraft. It started things with a swing, and the result was that the customers we took each trip became walking, talking advertisements for our service.

We gave the impression, I hope, of being a successful, smoothly honed, large, well-organized outfit, when the truth is, while we were well-organized – we had to be, to survive – we were rushed off our feet most of the time. The DC-6 would land in Edmonton after a trip to London, and we would descend on it en masse – crew, cleaners, Marjorie, myself, my sister, Lillian, and most of the Wardair office staff – to clear out the clutter and get it spotless for the next trip. Among his other chores, the company president – me – flew frequently as third officer on the DC-6, so I would understand the route and every part of the business of flying charters. The rest of the time, I worried about the finances, tried to drum up business, and helped to clean up the cabin. I wielded a pretty effective vacuum cleaner in those days, and fluffed a pretty pillow. The result was that we could get the aircraft back in the air in very short order and, always, neat and trim and stocked with fresh, good food. Because of the way we worked together, there was an air of camaraderie among the Wardair employees which was one of our most precious assets. And it was wonderful fun.

We had a crew that rushed from city to city by truck and van as occasion demanded, because we might have a charter going to London from Edmonton, then picking up passengers in Prestwick to bring them to Calgary, then taking off from Saskatoon for Manchester. Our flying squad of engineers and cleaners would swoop from city to city as required, because the whole point of the operation was to keep that aircraft in the air as much as possible. We had the major engine overhauls done by CP Air and paid very high prices for this. That was not so much because they were our competitors as because we insisted on a very high standard, and we were prepared to pay for it. If the work was not done exactly to specifications, we said, we would go elsewhere, and CP seemed to appreciate our determination.

On our long overseas flights we used to carry three pilots and four cabin attendants for eighty-eight passengers. One pilot and one cabin attendant had to be resting at any one time, because the flights took so long. When we were going from western Canada to Europe, we normally stopped in Sondre Stromfjord in Greenland for refuelling. It was right on the Great Circle Route to Europe; that way, our passengers could get out and stretch their legs and visit another country as a kind of added bonus. In the air, we played bingo, with a flight attendant calling out the numbers, or did calisthenics. Sometimes one of the passengers would entertain with a guitar or other music.

Gradually, we began to build up our business, and, while we weren't making money, we were able to keep up the payments to KLM for the aircraft right on schedule, at the same time as we were establishing a record for quality service and reliability among a growing clientele. And, the most important point of all, we were creating a market where none had existed. Trans-Canada didn't pay much attention to us, because we were flying out of Western Canada, and they couldn't see us from their headquarters in Montreal. I do recall one occasion, however, when we were loading passengers for an overseas charter in an Edmonton hangar, and there were a couple of Trans-Canada pilots standing around. One of them said, in a very loud voice, "Hey, what are you doing? Those are our passengers." As far as Trans-Canada was concerned, all passengers naturally belonged to them. CP Air was a little more aware of what we were doing, and, even as early as 1963, the obvious growth potential of the international charter business led to a sharp drop in their overseas airfares, which made the going that much rougher for us.

Bear in mind that the way these charters were operated and sold was crazy – no other word will do – and that the regulations were all laid down by one government body, the Air Transport Board, under clear direction from a federal government (then Liberal) that was determined to protect the interests of its own airline. Hence, the "affinity" charter rule mentioned earlier, which stipulated that only persons who had been linked together in a club for a period of at least six months before any given flight could apply for a charter. The club would charter the entire aircraft from us and divide up the cost among its members. This rule produced clubs for poetry reading, violin playing, real-estate brokering, and God knows what all. Then, after you paid your five dollars or whatever for the club membership, and waited six months, you could fly overseas for about half the regular price. The rules would not allow us to advertise charter flights at all to the general public, much less tell them what a bargain our flights were (it was about $275, Toronto – London return, at this time, about half the scheduled fare), for fear this would alert the public to the fact that this price and service were available.

We seemed to spend a lot of our time advising people on how to get up a club, sell memberships, hold meetings, and, incidentally, charter a plane for an overseas trip while they were about it. Inevitably, groups sprang up to operate as intermediaries, and often these groups made more money organizing clubs than we ever did flying them overseas. This is only to be expected when the government establishes artificial controls on the marketing of products.

Along with the legitimate operators, fast-buck artists soon got into the game, and one of these took us to the cleaners. This was an outfit called The Piccadilly Club, supposedly devoted to the glories of Old England, but actually formed to cash in on the charter business. The Club drummed up memberships from people, laid on a charter flight with us, and collected the return fare from each of the members in advance, along with a substantial fee for the Piccadilly Club for putting it all together. We were paid for the flight to London, as was the practice then, but when the time came for the return flight, three weeks later, there was nothing in the Piccadilly's till. What to do? Another charter airline, Caledonia, of England, had been caught in precisely this pickle, and they had backed away from the passengers, telling them, in effect, to pay again if they wanted to come home. There was no way we could do that; it was not only a crummy thing to do, it would underscore all the fears the scheduled airlines were circulating about the charter operators and their unreliability. We swallowed the costs and brought the club members home. One of the Piccadilly Club operators was charged with fraud – he was found not guilty, since there was no proof of an intent to commit fraud – and the club went bankrupt, but we never, ever saw another penny of the money owed to us. This happened to us once more in 1963, dooming any chance we might have had to turn a profit that year.

During the winter, we didn't have any overseas charters, and the aircraft wasn't suitable for carrying air-freight, so business was scarce indeed. However, we did dig up one charter that turned out to be quite interesting. This was to fly a magnetic survey some 40,000 miles for the Dominion Observatory, charting the 2.5 million square miles of the Arctic. We were charting what are called "isogonic lines" – magnetic lines of equal variation from the magnetic pole – to assist in the construction of maps that would make air and sea navigation safer. The task involved flying up and down, starting from a base in Thule, Greenland, with each pass a hundred miles from the last one, and pivoting on the geographic North Pole. The work was done entirely in the dark, with a fourteen-man team aboard the DC-6; each flight lasted about thirteen hours, and the whole operation took seventeen days. I was a crew member.

It was this winter, too, that we started to operate to Hawaii, although at first in a small way. Marjorie and I had visited Hawaii on a break from the bush one winter and we loved it. It was a world unto itself in those days and, lying on the beach and counting the flights heading into Honolulu, I couldn't help but reflect that, with new and faster aircraft, there would someday be a huge market for the operator who brought Canadians to Hawaii. We had come via CP Air on a DC-6, twenty-seven hundred miles from Vancouver, so it is not surprising that I decided to take our DC-6 on a charter the first chance I got.

As it happened, the first chance for such a charter turned out to be for a club formed in Saskatoon, so we took the plane from Edmonton to Saskatoon and loaded up one terrible winter's day, with the temperature registering something like sixty below zero Fahrenheit, counting in the wind-chill factor. The snow and ice caused one of the undercarriage doors to malfunction, and when the plane reached Los Angeles, well, that was as far as it went. We brought in the repairmen to work on our plane, while we bundled the Saskatoon crowd into seats on a jet that we booked in Los Angeles. It was not, to say the least, a money-making proposition. Just the same, I was convinced that the Hawaii connection had to be a major winter market for us.

That led, naturally enough, as 1964 developed to our satisfaction (despite such fiascos as the Piccadilly Club), to my exploring again the possibilities of buying a jet. These aircraft were clearly the coming thing, and, though they cost a lot more than either propellor-driven or turbo-prop types, they were also much more productive. That is, they were so much faster and more fuel-efficient that you could carry more people farther for less money, even if the initial investment was higher. In the airline industry, the best measure of success is the return per passenger-mile, and by this measure, the jets were bound to outmatch the earlier types. There was no way I could approach the bankers to explain that, once again, I wanted to buy a big new airplane with no money down, but I did contact the Boeing aircraft people in Seattle, who were instantly receptive, and even enthusiastic. They had been trying to sell jets to both Trans-Canada and CP Air, but without success.

One of the best prospects at that time, incidentally, was the stretched Douglas DC-8, but the McDonnell–Douglas people made it clear that they wouldn't even consider selling us one of those. McDonnell–Douglas told us that Trans-Canada was operating DC-8s, and they didn't want to anger the Crown airline by flirting with us. (Thirteen years later, Wardair would introduce the first Douglas DC-10 into Canada.) Boeing, however, had no such compunction, since they had never sold an airplane in Canada, and they suggested they would help us in any way they could to make the purchase work. There were two possible Boeing models that would meet our requirements, the 727 – a three-engine jet which was their newest model and could carry up to 120 passengers – and the much larger 707, which had four engines, could carry 186 passengers, and had a much longer range. In a 707, you could fly to Europe from anywhere in Canada non-stop, and you could fly from Toronto to Hawaii non-stop. The only trouble was that I didn't think the market was big enough yet to fill all those 186 seats continuously.

Even the 727, at five million dollars, excluding spare parts, was going to cost about fifteen times as much as we had ever laid out on an aircraft. Nevertheless, I decided we would go for the 727 – but not until 1966, when I hoped we would somehow find a way to swing the financing. Throughout 1965, we kept in contact with Boeing, without committing ourselves. There was another consideration in my mind when I put off the Boeing salesmen, and that was that the 727 had really just come onto the market; if it had any kinks, I wanted to be sure that they were worked out before we bought. In the end, I committed to buy a 727 in 1965, for delivery in April 1966.

In the meantime, Grant McConachie, over at CP Air, was beginning to get worried by the way we were not only creating an international charter market, but building up a reputation as a dependable airline with which to fly. He heard on the grapevine that we were about to purchase a 727; he didn't believe it, because he knew we didn't have the money, but he decided that he had better get into the chartering business in a big way. During the fall of 1965, he went to San Diego to buy short-range DC-6s from Western Airlines, so that he could release his long-range DC-6s to the charter market the next summer. It was while he was in the United States looking at aircraft that he had a sudden and fatal heart attack, and the aviation industry lost one of its most colourful and accomplished aviation pioneers. Grant was a competitor, but we got along very well indeed, and we shared the same views about the Ottawa bureaucracy, and about most other things. He was a competitor I admired and delighted in; we were both bush types and entrepreneurs. Under his leadership, CP Air had marvellous cabin services and a wonderful *esprit de corps*. We named one of our A-310s for Grant in 1988.

It was only after long and protracted negotiations that we were able to strike a deal through Noel Crawford of Greyhound Leasing to finance the 727. They would buy the aircraft from Boeing and lease it to us for ten years, giving us an option to purchase at the end of that time. We would get our aircraft without putting a penny down. Bay Street in Toronto was agog that a leasing company would buy a jet to lease to some unknown fly-by-night from Western Canada. It is certainly true that we paid through the nose; Greyhound was assuming a high risk, and were entitled to a commensurable return on their money. While we didn't put anything down, the lease cost us $61,419 a month in U.S. funds, a total of $7,370,280 over the ten-year period of the lease – and we had to buy the spares. If we missed

Beautiful, isn't it? This is a Twin Otter, loading at our float base at Yellowknife. (Photo by George Hunter)

Along the bank of the Mackenzie River, we took a brief pause during our search for a site for the new town of Inuvik in 1954. The man wiping his brow is Jean Lesage, then Minister of Northern Affairs; that's me, brushing mosquitoes off my cheek, standing on the pontoon of the Otter. The man to the right of Lesage is Frank Carmichael of the NWT Council, while seated next to him is Merv Hardie, the first MP for the Territory. Lee Post, the Area Administrator for Aklavik, stands at far right. This was the trip that involved the "Lonesome Dove" incident. (Photo by Michael J. Hewitt, Justice and Public Services, NWT)

The pictures on these two pages are a round-up of the uniforms of Wardair – my old high-school sweater doesn't count. This very handsome group in front of a very handsome plane comes from a publicity shoot. The snappy uniforms were featured in the late 1960s to the mid 1970s. (Photo by George Hunter)

Marianne McIndoe, our first cabin attendant, designed the uniform herself, and we used it throughout the 1960s. A great uniform on a great person.

From 1976 to 1988, our cabin personnel wore uniforms designed by Marilyn Brooks. The large bows at the neck were very chic for the time, as were the longer skirts.

These were the last Wardair uniforms. They were designed by Nina Ricci in time for the party – one of our best – at Toulouse, France, in 1987, when we accepted our new Airbus A-310s. These uniforms, alas, disappeared with the sale of Wardair.

One of our pleasant duties was to airlift members of the Royal Family around the North. This picture was taken during a tour of Northern Alberta by Her Majesty and the Duke of Edinburgh in 1978. We used the *Don Braun*, one of our Dash 7s.

I wanted to include this picture to give you some idea of the variety of aircraft we used, and the enormous difference in their sizes. The little chap is a replica of my original Fox Moth, and the giant Jumbo is a Boeing 747. This picture was taken when we got our first 747, the *Phil Garratt*, in 1973. The other planes, a Boeing 707 (right) and a Boeing 727, were used to ferry the guests to Seattle for the ceremony. (Photo by George Hunter)

My heart beats a little faster every time I look at this picture; a beautiful depiction of a wonderful aircraft. This is our first Dash 7, the *Don Braun,* going through her paces in 1978. (Photo by Terry Wildman, with permission of de Havilland Aircraft)

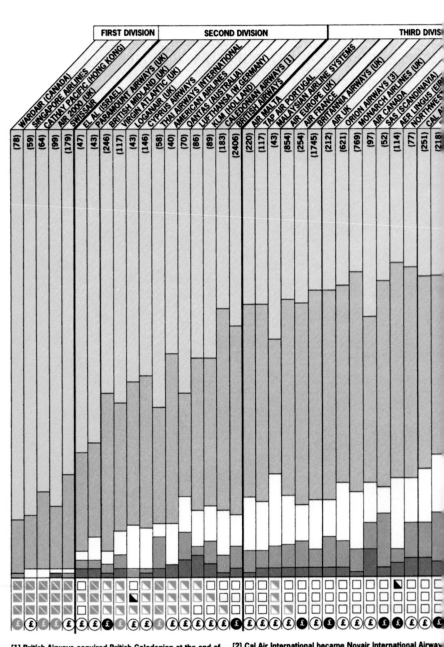

FIRST DIVISION   **SECOND DIVISION**   **THIRD DIVIS**

WARDAIR (CANADA) (78)
SINGAPORE AIRLINES (59)
CATHAY PACIFIC (HONG KONG) (64)
AIR 2000 (UK) (99)
SWISSAIR (179)
EL AL (ISRAEL) (47)
PARAMOUNT AIRWAYS (UK) (43)
BRITISH MIDLAND (UK) (246)
VIRGIN ATLANTIC (UK) (117)
LOGANAIR (UK) (43)
CYPRUS AIRWAYS (146)
THAI AIRWAYS INTERNATIONAL (58)
AMERICAN AIRLINES (40)
QANTAS (AUSTRALIA) (70)
LUFTHANSA (W.GERMANY) (86)
KLM (HOLLAND) (89)
CALEDONIAN AIRWAYS [1] (183)
BRITISH AIRWAYS (2406)
AIR MALTA (220)
TAP AIR PORTUGAL (117)
MALAYSIAN AIRLINE SYSTEMS (43)
AIR EUROPE (UK) (854)
AIR FRANCE (254)
BRITANNIA AIRWAYS (UK) (1745)
AIR UK (212)
ORION AIRWAYS (UK) (621)
MONARCH AIRLINES (UK) (769)
AIR CANADA (97)
SAS (SCANDINAVIA) (52)
AER LINGUS (EIRE) (114)
NORTHWEST (77)
CAL A (251)
(218)

[1] British Airways acquired British Caledonian at the end of 1987. In May 1988 Caledonian Airways replaced British Airtours as British Airways' new charter arm.

[2] Cal Air International became Novair International Airway December 1988 and is no longer owned by British Airways.

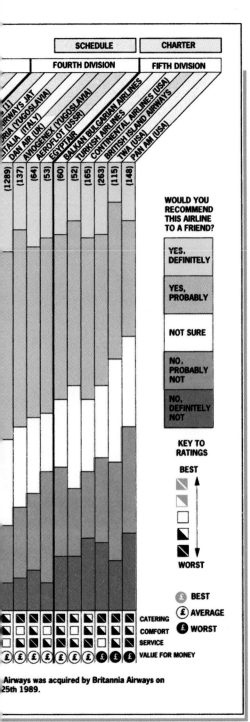

RWAYS JAT

RIA (YUGOSLAVIA)

TALIA (ITALY)

DAN AIR (UK)

AVIOGENEX (YUGOSLAVIA)

AEROFLOT (USSR)

EGYPTAIR

BALKAN BULGARIAN AIRLINES

TURKISH AIRLINES

CONTINENTAL AIRLINES (USA)

BRITISH ISLAND AIRWAYS

TWA (USA)

PAN AM (USA)

(1289) (137) (64) (53) (60) (52) (165) (263) (115) (148)

WOULD YOU
RECOMMEND
THIS AIRLINE
TO A FRIEND?

YES,
DEFINITELY

YES,
PROBABLY

NOT SURE

NO,
PROBABLY
NOT

NO,
DEFINITELY
NOT

KEY TO
RATINGS

BEST ↑

↓ WORST

🔵 BEST
£ AVERAGE
£ WORST

CATERING
COMFORT
SERVICE
VALUE FOR MONEY

Airways was acquired by Britannia Airways on
25th 1989.

This chart demonstrates the level to which we at Wardair brought our airline. No other Canadian airline ever achieved, or probably will achieve again, this kind of international recognition. The chart was assembled by the British consumer magazine *Holiday Which?* on the basis of a survey of 14,927 British travel agents, who completed questionnaires on everything from catering, service, and value for money to the key question: Would you recommend this airline to a friend? As you see, Wardair leads the list, and was declared "Best in 1988" and winner of the Golden Wings Award. This was our first, and only, full year of scheduled service. Please note which airline came in 28th (down in the Third Division, right behind Monarch Airlines). We won this same award in the two previous years, as a charter airline. (Both scheduled and charter lines are included; the yellow tone over the airline's name identifies a charter carrier.) In short, every time we were eligible, we walked off with top honours. (Reproduced with permission of *Holiday Which?*)

With his back to the camera is Bill Whitty, Manager of Maintenance, who is briefing me on a costly unscheduled engine change of a Pratt and Whitney JT D-7
engine, made necessary when we found metal particles on a magnetic sump plug.
Steve Moon is behind, holding the plug. Foreman Raoul Vicente is on Steve's
right, and foreman Bill Middleton on his left.

one payment, the whole scheme would come crashing down around our ears, but I don't recall being particularly nervous about that aspect. It seemed a reasonable risk, so I took it. Boeing were delighted; this was the first aircraft they had sold in Canada, and it would establish the quality of their aircraft – which was very high indeed – in the minds of Canadians.

Our worries weren't finished when we got the financing arranged. There was still the long and laborious and expensive process of obtaining the permission of the Canadian government to buy the aircraft, a process that neither of Canada's two larger airlines, Air Canada (as Trans-Canada had recently become) and CP Air, had to contend with. However, it was finally done, all the permissions granted, and all the papers signed.

It was during this period that I met Tom Spalding, the lawyer with responsibility for Boeing's contract administration, who had drawn up the legal arrangements for the 727 deal with Greyhound Leasing. Originally from Winnipeg, Tom had gone to Seattle for Boeing. Fortunately for Wardair, he was challenged by our small but ambitious airline, and in 1970, he decided to leave his very high-level position at Boeing and join us. Tom was a popular, multi-talented man, and he brought tremendous stability to Wardair management.

During the last six months of the adaptation of the line models of our 727 and the training of our crews at Boeing in Seattle, we put Ab Freeman, a captain recently acquired from Air Canada, in charge of training. A fine pilot himself, and a meticulous and fair manager of other pilots, Ab was for twenty years an anchor and strength for our crews and company.

On closing day, April 28, 1966, we flew the DC-6 down to Seattle, and had a wonderful party and a tour of the

Boeing plant. Then, with Captain Freeman in the left-hand seat, we flew back on a brand-new Boeing 727-11, with the official registration CF-FUN, and landed at the Edmonton Municipal Airport for an official inauguration ceremony. Cy Becker had died not long before, and we named the aircraft for him. It was an idea I extended later to all the new Wardair planes, which were named for great figures in Canadian aviation. His widow, Lucy Becker, had agreed to perform the ceremony by smashing a bottle of champagne against the nose of the new aircraft. In preparation, the engineering boys had cut through the neck of the bottle with glass-cutters, and it was so fragile we were afraid it would come apart in her hands. However, when she swung it against the fuselage, it wouldn't even come apart on the plane; all it did was thump home with a tremendous whack and leave a dent in my beautiful new five-million-dollar craft. Before Mrs. Becker could take another swing, we got a hammer; I held this up against the aircraft, and she hit the hammer with the bottle. We considered that the job had been officially done. After that, when we went to christen an aircraft, we emptied the champagne into a silver bowl. The christener sloshed this up against the aircraft and got to keep the bowl – a much more sensible system.

We had entered the jet age, and the fundamental difference, from the point of view of the operator of the aircraft, was Productivity, with a capital P. With the DC-6, we could make one trip to Europe in a day, and come back the next day. With the 727, we could make a round-trip in the same day, with hours to spare, and it cost us less to operate because of a lower fuel cost. From the passenger's point of view, the change was every bit as dramatic – flight times were cut by more than half (Edmonton to Prestwick took anywhere from eighteen to twenty-three hours in the DC-6, depending on winds, and seven to eight hours in the 727), with a stop in Sondre Stromfjord.

During that first summer, our aircraft had the highest utilization of any 727 in the world. The air-traffic controllers in Iceland thought we had a fleet of 727s, because every time they looked up, there was Wardair again.

Typically, we were told we had made a terrible mistake when we put the 727 on the North Atlantic route. No one had ever flown the 727, which was considered to be a medium-range aircraft, over this particular route. As usual, the experts were wrong; the aircraft performed flawlessly. About this same time, Pacific Western made a decision to get into the international charter business as well, and acquired a Douglas DC-7, a four-engine propellor-driven aircraft. It was not a patch on the 727, and one of our pilots told me a story that illustrated the difference between these two kinds of aircraft.

Our 727 was taking off from Calgary just behind the PWA DC-7, both of them headed for London with a charter group. Not long after the planes reached cruising height, the 727 passed the PWA plane and spoke to its pilot briefly. The Boeing flew over to England, unloaded its passengers, loaded up again, and headed back to Canada. Out over the Atlantic, it met the DC-7, still plodding gamely towards the U.K., and the PWA captain growled, "Pass me one more time and I'll ram you!"

One of the things that really bothered me all my career was the line I would hear from the Bay Street money-men in Toronto. "Ward runs a pretty good airline," the line went, "but he isn't really a businessman."

I guess it depends on what you mean by a businessman. It's true that I didn't have the talent, which seems so necessary these days, to hold out my hand for government grants and to fly my routes with the aid of somebody else's money (PWA would go that route in 1974, when it was taken over by the Alberta government). But I did have the foresight to understand the importance of obtaining the best equipment available, and I did have the guts to back my intuition with every dime I owned, and a lot I didn't. What would overwhelm my whole life's work, in the end, was not the competition of fellow businessmen, but the obstruction of governments.

In place of the eight charters we had flown in 1962, we flew 122 in 1966, of which 104 were with the 727 and 18 with the DC-6. In 1962, our passenger load had been 712; four years later, we carried 12,047 people. Wardair represented 2 per cent of the trans-Atlantic non-scheduled traffic in 1962, and 10 per cent in 1966.

The gamble had paid off, thanks in large part to the incredible efficiency of the jet power-plant and to the enthusiasm and hard work of our people. We were no longer hanging on by our thumbs; everything was going splendidly. What this meant, of course, was that we were headed for big trouble.

CHAPTER 14

Getting Mad and Going Public

As usual, I was working seven-day weeks, but on June 8, 1968, our elder daughter, Gai, was marrying a fine young man named Terry Bastin. It was a happy day, and I splurged and took the whole day off.

It turned out to be more dangerous than going to work, for that was the day I encountered my first, and last, hot-air balloon. An Edmonton friend of mine, Sandy MacTaggart, asked me in the morning of that great wedding day to go along in the chase car while he practised with his balloon. Apparently, he had to have a certain number of solo hours before he could take up any passengers, and the purpose of the day's exercise was to get in some of those solo hours. We drove out to a spot south of Edmonton, near the town of Wetaskawin, on a sunny, clear morning with very little wind, ideal weather for ballooning. Sandy did a couple of ups and downs, and by the time he hit the ground after the second trip, there was no way he was going to take off again without me on board. I piled into the basket uninvited, and away we went.

I loved it as we sailed aloft, with no sensation of movement at all: with the balloon, you are sailing with whatever wind there is, so you are never conscious of it, and can only tell that you are travelling by the shifting ground below. Sounds came up to us very clearly: people talking, dogs barking, a car backfiring down a country lane, and, in the background, the intermittent hiss of the propane-fired burner feeding hot air into the brilliantly bedecked expanse that swelled overhead.

Except that, suddenly, there wasn't any background hiss. We had run out of propane. The fire went out, and we started to descend majestically back to the bosom of Mother Earth – right smack-dab into a mess of high-tension wires on a major power line. Sandy said, "We're going to have to jump!" and, as the long metal wires that joined the basket to the balloon began to spit and crackle against the power-lines, I was instantly inclined to agree with him. It was jump, or fry.

I went over the edge of the basket and hooked my toes on the rim, so that I could lower myself as far as possible, with my head down, for the dive and roll that would, I hoped, get me to the ground in one piece. We were still moving slowly, bouncing along the wires about thirty feet above the ground – a good drop, but, I reckoned, not a fatal one – so I took a deep breath and let go. I saw Sandy, out of the corner of my eye, plunge to the ground, roll neatly, and come up standing, with no apparent harm done. My own landing was not so neat. I went into a roll, as he had done, but caught my left hand under me. "There goes something," I said, as I heard a sickening snap, and I sprawled in a tumbled heap on the ground.

I wound up with a broken wrist, two black eyes, and a lot of contusions, along with a few lumps on my dignity.

They gave me a powerful pain-killer during the ambulance ride back to town, and I remember that I babbled all the way there about the need to design a back-up system for balloons, with standby propane.

That evening, when Gai sailed serenely down the aisle, a vision of beauty, she travelled on the arm of what appeared to be a refugee from a bar-room brawl – black-eyed, bandaged, limping, and unlovely. As we heaved up in front of the minister, he looked from Gai to me, back to Gai, back to me, and broke into a totally unclerical cackle. The last time he had seen me, at the rehearsal the night before, I had looked somewhat different.

I have never been in a balloon since, but would like to be. I took no comfort whatever from the fact that Sandy MacTaggart's maniacal device was registered under the call-letters POP. I ought to have known it was a mistake to take a full day off the job; I seldom flirted with danger after that. Heaven knows, life on the ground was dangerous enough in the airline business.

With the addition of a pure jet aircraft, as I have already indicated, we really moved into a new age. It is my belief that when future historians come to look at our era, they will conclude that one of the keys to our advancement was the jet power-plant. The propellor engine is, in the end, a crude matter of metal banging on metal, and it cannot have either the productivity or the stamina of the jet engine, which operates through the propulsion of compressed air through rotors – much more efficient, and much less damaging. If there is anything in the past couple of decades that has been significant, it has been the development, improvement, and spread of this remarkable engine, which has not only cut distances but increased the size, comfort, and safety of aircraft beyond measure.

Let me put it this way: thanks to the development and improvement of the jet power-plant, we have gone through a revolution in transportation that has enabled us to fly faster, higher, longer, with larger loads, for less and less cost, and with the use of less and less fuel, burned more and more cleanly. Our entire way of life is now built on possibilities and geared to expectations that did not even exist in the human mind a few short years ago, and I cannot imagine why more has not been made of this phenomenon in the annals of our time.

Coming down to earth, the practical application of this advance was, quite simply, that we could put a jet engine on our Boeing 727, and, provided we kept it properly serviced, leave it there for four years, or for sixteen thousand hours of flying time, before it had to be removed for overhaul. Tiny Wardair, thanks to this marvellous efficiency, could compete with the giants – if we were allowed to do so, which we weren't.

During the winter of 1966–67, we really didn't have much business for the 727, so we leased it to National Airlines out of Miami, Florida. We did not yet have permission to fly to American destinations, so the best we could do was to put our aircraft out for lease, because we had to make the payments each month, though it didn't seem like a very creative use of the machine to me. We covered our costs, but that was about it. I resolved before long we would have something better to do. However, we were in for a fight.

Our growth and expansion caught the eye of the giants, and we were soon seeing what seemed to us to be planted stories in the press about the unreliability of the charter companies. We were a private company, and the word was passed around that if we went bankrupt, our passengers would be stranded far from home. I remember a particularly irritating piece by Allan Fotheringham, writing with his customary confidence, in which he assured his readers that the scheduled airlines would soon weary of the gnat-bites of the smaller operators and drop their overseas fares low enough and long enough to wipe us out. The message was clear: If you fly a charter, you risk getting stranded in some foreign clime.

Then there were the stories about the "unreliability" of the 727, our aircraft. There were four 727 crashes within a few months of its introduction to service in the United States; one, in Salt Lake City, which got a lot of publicity, resulted in forty-five deaths. These accidents all stemmed from fundamentally the same problem, which was not in the aircraft's design, but in pilot error. The 727 was the first commercial jet to work with a lift-drag wing rather than the conventional wing. The wing most pilots were used to was fundamentally a glider, fixed and unchanging. The 727 wing was designed with much more extensive flaps on the leading and trailing edges. You can see this out the window of almost any jet today, but it was new in the 1960s. Air-force pilots were used to this concept, but civilian aviators were not. What it meant was that the wing produced both lift and drag; you had to maintain much more engine thrust on landing than in the conventional aircraft, which just floats in and settles down.

The accidents were caused when too much power was taken off on approach and landing, and that could in turn be traced back to insufficient pilot training. The problem was discovered and sorted out, but at the time, besides the unnecessary tragedies, there was an uneasy feeling around that the aircraft simply wasn't safe. That feeling was yet another problem we had to overcome. The only poison-pen letter I ever received came to me at this time. It consisted of a message made up of words cut out of a newspaper, warning me that I would be punished for my action in bringing this new kind of aircraft into Canada.

*

To meet the concern that we might go belly-up some day and leave all the members of the Brotherhood for the Appreciation and Study of the Oboe, or whatever, stranded in Europe, we decided that we ought to publish our 1966 financial results in the newspapers. We thought it would reassure the public, and it did. It also infuriated Air Canada, which was losing money with a kind of steadfast doggedness, despite all the government help it was getting, and the end result was that, not only did the whisper campaign against us increase, but harassment from government agencies intensified.

We had to get permission from the government to buy the 727 aircraft in the first place, as we've seen. Then we had to apply for permission, months in advance, for each and every charter flight; very often, we would not get permission until the last minute. Sometimes, we were abruptly refused permission, which always produced a monumental scramble. Air Canada and CP Air did not have to get permission for their charters. If they wanted to fly one, they did.

During our early operation of the 727, CP Air had agents go to the air-traffic people in the control tower at Vancouver to secure copies of our flight plans. They were endeavouring to prove that we couldn't possibly have enough fuel on board to complete our overseas flights, although a full route analysis had been calculated and established by Boeing prior to our taking delivery of the aircraft. Then a rumour suddenly sprang up that on one flight we had had enough fuel to get to London, all right, but barely enough to taxi to the Arrivals area from the runway. It is hard to react to this sort of story, once it starts to circulate by word of mouth – and, believe me, it spread faster than gossip about a regal pregnancy. You don't want to issue a formal denial, because that will only give it greater publicity. We did the only thing we could do, which was to request the Ministry of Transport to conduct a thorough examination of our flying sheets and fuel logs and prove beyond any doubt that we could, indeed, make the flights we kept on making, in perfect safety. It took almost two years for that particular rumour to die down.

Then there was the insanity of the "affinity" charters rule. We couldn't fly passengers, only club members; we couldn't tell the public about our charters, we could only advertise to groups and organizations, and the regulations forbade us to tell these groups and organizations, or the public, how much it would cost per passenger for them to charter an overseas trip. The logic was perfectly remorseless. If the general public knew how cheaply they could fly overseas by going via Wardair instead of Air Canada, they would do so. Ergo, the Air Transport Board, a government body, set up the regulations in such a way as to protect the turf of Air Canada, a Crown corporation, and no politician could see what there was to get excited about in this conflict of interest.

I got around this restriction, briefly, with an idea dreamt up by an ad man in Calgary. We took out a series of ads in *Time* magazine and in a number of newspapers that read:

FLY TO EUROPE FOR $33,000
And Take Along 99 Friends.

You didn't have to be a mathematical genius to work out that the price per passenger in our 727, round-trip, was $330. This ad met the criteria of the regulations but, sure enough, the big airlines set up a howl, and we received a cease-and-desist order from the Air Transport Board. We had to remove this perfectly legal ad.

We helped to get a lot of the clubs and associations who were our only legitimate markets organized – the Shakespeare Club was one of ours, although we didn't say so at the time.

The Edmonton Symphony Society, on the other hand, was a genuine association, and it may even be that some of the investment clubs that sprang up in those days invested in something besides airplane tickets. We flew no less than fourteen different groups of Dutch Canadians back to Holland, and to keep from having to return to Canada empty on a number of flights, we arranged with the Danish and Norwegian governments to bring 220 agricultural students across the ocean to work for the summer on Alberta farms.

We were unpopular with our own government and unpopular with the International Air Transport Association (IATA), which was the international cartel for the major airlines, and the guardian of their regulated rates.

IATA is an international body made up of the world airlines, dominated by the major scheduled carriers, with headquarters in Montreal, and with its own sets of rules and regulations. It is not to be confused with ICAO, the International Civil Aviation Organization, a United Nations agency, also head-quartered in Montreal, which promotes international civil aviation regulations and standards, and to which 150 nations belong. IATA is strictly private, not governmental. The distinction between the two can be gathered from how they describe themselves: ICAO says it "promotes the safe and orderly growth of civil aviation," while IATA says it "fosters air commerce and studies the problems connected with it." IATA is the international airline lobby, and, to protect its members, it produces yet another layer of rules, most of them having to do with airfares, on top of all the others. The layers intermesh, in that IATA will set rules to cover rates and rules between countries, while individual governments control the prices within their own boundaries. Each refers to the other, and a great deal of horse-trading goes on behind the scenes, so that concessions won at IATA may be reflected in domestic arrangements. Again, the arrangements between nations are often negotiated bilaterally. Canada may give an American airline landing rights at Canadian airports in return for similar rights for one of our airlines at a U.S. airport. These deals can become incredibly complex, as bilateral negotiations, ICAO standards, and IATA rules are brought to bear on the already convoluted process of control by the national government regulators. The reader will be best served by thinking of IATA as a kind of OPEC with wings (although IATA won't like that comparison much). Its major but seldom-mentioned task is to keep ticket prices as high as possible.

We even managed to run afoul of other governments while we were at it. In 1965, we put in all the proper forms to fly a charter of Italian Canadians over to Rome, months ahead of the flight's schedule. The application worked its way through the murky channels of the ATB, crossed the ocean to Italy, returned, was duly approved, and everything was organized. Many of our passengers were going home for the first time in decades to tiny villages in the Italian countryside, and, for weeks ahead of the flight, they had been sending letters and wires and making arrangements for their friends and relatives to be on hand for the big landing.

The airplane was to take off from Toronto on a Monday. The Thursday before – that is, months after we thought all the paperwork had been cleared – I received a telegram from Felici Santini, Director-General of the Italian Civil Air Ministry, denying us permission to land anywhere in Italy. The Italian government owned a flagship airline, Alitalia, and, as far as Felici Santini was concerned, Alitalia didn't need any Canadian competition.

I was thunderstruck, to say the least. There was no way for us to get word to all our customers, who in some cases were travelling from well outside Toronto, and there was certainly no way for them to get word to their friends and relatives back in Italy to tell them that the flight was off and that the aircraft would merely be sitting on the ground throughout the period planned for the trip. Vacations had been planned, all kinds of arrangements had been made, on the basis of this flight going on time. If it didn't, I knew, word would soon be winging around the circuit that, once again, charter carriers were not to be trusted.

I telephoned the Canadian Embassy in Rome, and explained my predicament. No one actually said "So what?" but I got the distinct impression that my pleas were falling on deaf ears. They would get back to me if they had any good news to report, our gallant diplomats explained, but in the meantime, they thought it might be a good idea if we told our customers to start unpacking.

Frantic by this time, I put in a direct call to Paul Martin, then Secretary of State for External Affairs, and explained the situation to him. His reaction was much more humane, much more direct, and much more effective. I have no idea what brand of dynamite he stuck under the chairs in the Canadian Embassy, but, just twenty-two hours before the flight was due to take off, I received a call from Rome informing me that the whole thing had been one of those laughable misunderstandings, and we were cleared to land as scheduled.

I have had a high regard for Paul Martin ever since, but I must say that he is one of the few government figures, certainly on the Liberal side of the House of Commons, who ever showed the slightest sympathy or understanding of what I was trying to accomplish. I suppose what got me down, in the end, was not simply the mind-boggling stupidity of the regulations, but the persistence with which they were adapted to frustrate our attempts to comply. The pattern was always the same: a regulation would come out laying some new burden on us; we would change our operations to meet the regulation; a new regulation would promptly be drafted, and we would be back at square one again.

You think I'm making this up, don't you? Well, consider this.

We were required, under the "affinity" charter rules – I am now quoting from the gobbledegook that passes for English in these regulations – to

> obtain prior to embarkation a written declaration from every passenger on each of the group charter flights thereafter performed by Wardair under the provisions of Rule 26/66 amended by Rule 29/67, verifying that such passenger is qualified under the said Rules to participate in such flight.

Did you get that? It meant, in plain English, that we had to make each passenger on a given charter sign a declaration that he or she was, in fact, a dues-paying member of the Amalgamated Fellowship of Rose Sniffers and Blossom Blowers, or whatever the club might be, had been a member for six months, and was paid up.

Rose Sniffers and Blossom Blowers could storm aboard Air Canada, no questions asked, but, by golly, the government wasn't going to allow a Dandelion Puffer to slip past on a Wardair flight, and the expense and trouble of ensuring the purity of the process was entirely up to us. This was, to put it plainly, a monumental pain and cost, but the regulations were there, and, once we understood them, we complied. So, what did they do? They hit us with this one:

> That Wardair include with each application submitted to the Air Transport Committee for authority to operate a group charter flight pursuant to Rule 26/66 amended by Rule 27/67 an undertaking that the procedures outlined

in (d) above will be carried out and that Wardair Ltd. file with the Committee within fifteen days after the completion of each leg of a group charter flight an accurate list of the passengers transported, together with the declarations required under (d) above.

What that meant was that we had to keep track of a separate batch of paperwork, so anyone could go over our files and shout "Aha! Here's a Dandelion Sniffer!" I always had a mental image of teams of bureaucrats up in Ottawa poring over our files in a fever of excitement. On occasion, they sent their people to the check-in desk right at flight time, to go through the passenger list.

Then, just when we got used to that, they hit us with the crusher. We were required to produce, in addition to all the above:

The affidavit of a responsible officer of the chartering organization and its charter officer verifying that all of the said passengers were eligible for transportation on the flight as a member of a pro-rate charter group under the said rule.

Now we had to have two people swear, presumably under penalty of death, that the Rose Sniffers were indeed Rose Sniffers, and known to them to be so for the required period. The great temptation – and the government's clear intention – was that the chartering groups would decide it was simpler to fly Air Canada. As you will see, when we trifled with this asinine procedure, it very nearly destroyed the company.

There was, it seemed to me, a political vindictiveness behind some of the actions taken against us, based on the conviction of the Liberals in charge that Canada needed only one airline – their own. On the day it was announced in the Liberal caucus in Ottawa that Wardair had acquired a 727 jet aircraft, Prime Minister Lester Pearson told his colleagues in so many words that it was the last jet aircraft we would ever purchase, he would see to that. Within a few minutes of the break-up of that caucus, I received a telephone call reporting what had occurred from a western MP, Hu Harries, who was almost incoherent with rage.

I do not suggest for a moment that the Air Transport Board or its successor, the Canadian Transport Commission, undertook to carry out the implied threat in that prime-ministerial statement, but it is an undeniable fact, to anyone who cares to examine the record, that we were subjected to a constant program of harassment that very nearly pushed us into despair and bankruptcy and, not incidentally, turned my hair white by the age of forty-five.

The Canadian Transport Commission was established under the National Transportation Act a few months after we acquired our jet, replacing three boards: the Board of Transport Commissioners, the Air Transport Board, and the Canadian Maritime Commission. Jack Pickersgill, the Minister of Transport, a long-time friend and ally of prime ministers King and Pearson, recommended the establishment of the CTC, steered the legislation through the House of Commons, and then bobbed up as President of the CTC for its first five years. They were five very tough years for us. The arrogance of this man is hard for today's society to understand. He, in essence, dropped out of politics, but moved the Transport portfolio, or much of it, under his jurisdiction at the CTC. Even more interesting, I met a number of future ministers in the Transport portfolio who weren't even aware of how much of the portfolio had been shifted.

To meet the challenges we could see looming – buying new aircraft, marketing the charters through the regulations the government kept throwing up, and, not least, paying for the lawyers to deal with all this – we were going to need more money. I could get this by going back to the banks and trying again, which didn't seem a very profitable approach, by bleeding more and more out of the company, which didn't bode well for future purchases, or by going to the public.

There had already been a nibble at the company by no less a personage than Roy Thomson, the newspaper magnate, who had been, since 1964, "Lord Thomson of Fleet and of Northbridge in the City of Edinburgh." He summoned me, not to Edinburgh, but to Toronto, where he showed me his collection of Krieghoff paintings (later to be much expanded by his son, Ken) and told me he wanted to take my airline off my hands. He would buy it, and I would continue to be the president, but it would be run on Thomson lines, with Thomson money and Thomson methods. My way of running the airline was quite unsatisfactory, and he would handle Ottawa. In retrospect, he would have done a lot better in Ottawa than I could at that period, but I didn't believe that then.

I listened to him very politely, admired his paintings, and promised to consider his offer, but I never did. I had no interest whatever in having the Thomson accountants swarming over my airline and telling me that I didn't need to serve such good meals. I ran into Lord Thomson only once again, when I was invited to have dinner at the York Club, again in Toronto, by E. P. Taylor. He had a hotel in the Bahamas that he wanted to unload on me, but the land didn't go with the deal, so I was not interested. Lord Thomson came over to our table and had an amiable little chat with E.P. Taylor, but I got only a steely-eyed stare. Lord Thomson already owned a most successful U.K. airline, Britannia, and launched charters between Canada and the U.K., but he gave it up after a couple of years.

Even if I wouldn't surrender my airline, however, I did need an injection of cash, and if I didn't want it to come from one tycoon, it was better to raise it from the public in general. Accordingly, on September 18, 1967, Wardair Canada Limited became a public company. We raised $4,462,500 by issuing convertible debentures, which could be converted to 350,000 common shares in the company, at various rates between five and seven dollars, depending on when the holder decided to change his debenture from a loan to a share. We also issued 25,000 shares, to nine of our northern employees, who had been with us for so long – people like Don Braun, George Curley, my secretary, Doreen Rouse, and George Bell. We gave them an option to pick up shares in the company at twenty-five cents a share; if the public issue did well, they stood to gain by it, and if not, well, they lost nothing.

The response to our public issue was gratifying, and did bring in more operating capital; at the same time, I had not gone public in order to lose control of my own company. Of the five million authorized shares, I owned 2,391,588, and the Ward family holdings represented a clear majority. I notice from the information in our prospectus at that time that I was paid $55,000 in 1966, but took a pay cut to $50,000 in 1967. Neither I nor any other director was paid for serving on the board. In fact, most commercial pilots made more than I did, a pattern that continued for some time to come, and, whenever we did make any money, as Marjorie noted, patiently, it was ploughed back into the business for expansion.

As you will see in the chronology at the back of this book, we chose, by one of those wonderful ironies beloved by novelists, to go public on the very day that Jack Pickersgill took over the helm at the Canadian Transport Commission.

Shortly after we announced our public issue, we received some good news out of Ottawa for a change. The CTC, our transport master, approved the operation of "split charters." You no longer had to fill up your aircraft with members of the Ludwig van Beethoven Birthday Club; you could also bring along the Black Diamond Riders. You could not carry more than two groups, however, and all the rules about advertising and filing plans and requesting permission remained firmly in place. This change was of great benefit to the scheduled carriers, as they jumped after us into the charter business. This, of course, was the reason the amendment was put through, in my opinion, but it was bound to help us, too. The CTC also approved "Inclusive Tour Flights," through which we and our competitors could not only carry the bodies from place to place, but could offer packaged vacations of the kind now so common, which included hotels and some meals. That, too, was a boost for us.

Then, in December, we got a break from Washington, when the American Civil Aeronautics Board approved our request for a permit to operate inclusive tours to U.S. destinations. We could now put together a program in which we would fly charters in the summer to Europe and in the winter to Hawaii, Florida, and the Caribbean.

We thought we had the world by the tail – although it turned out that what we had was not the world, but a tiger. To get a clear picture of what was happening to us as a company, however, it is necessary to take another trip to the Arctic.

CHAPTER 15

▼

Meanwhile, Back in Yellowknife . . .

We now had two distinct operations under way. One was centred on the territories, hauling freight and passengers all over the Arctic. The other was operated out of Edmonton, and carried charters to Europe in the summer and to the sun in the winter. It was by far the bigger operation: in the first nine months of 1967, I can see from some old reports that we had a gross of $4,970,358 and made just over a million dollars in profit. The international business accounted for more than $4.3 million of the gross.

In this chapter, I will tell the story of the northern operations from the mid-sixties right through to 1979, when we finally had to close them down, before I return to pick up the thread of the other part of our operations, in the south.

The northern operation was still important to us, not merely for the cash flow it generated to help finance the charter business, but because it represented our start, our stability, our success. Over this period, we did everything we could to expand our operations north of the 60th parallel. However, we once more found the regulatory doors being slammed in our faces.

You will recall that we had asked for permission to run a scheduled service to Hay River from Yellowknife, using a Bristol Freighter. We had flown the route hundreds of times; we knew it, we had the right equipment, but we were denied the licence, which was held by Pacific Western, although they flew the route only very rarely and had little of the experience we did of freighting in the area. Nor did they have the right equipment for the route. However, we had come in third in the recommendations of the Air Transport Board for this route. We had also applied for a scheduled route between Pine Point and Yellowknife, and, again, we were turned down, although no one was as familiar with the route as we were. We had applied for a licence to serve Inuvik, Norman Wells, and Resolute Bay as a scheduled route, with bases we would construct at each spot. *After two years*, we were informed that "the Committee is not satisfied that the present and future public convenience and necessity require the granting of the application."

What did that mean? Presumably, if the present and future public convenience fell short on this route, we would lose our shirts, and/or we would have to curtail the service. But we would not be allowed to make that choice. The government would decide.

We had already courted disaster on one occasion, when a misunderstanding had resulted in the entire suspension of our operations in the North. We had carried some passengers from Yellowknife and Fort Smith to Inuvik, as part of a freight-hauling operation. We didn't charge for the people, but Pacific Western, which had the government monopoly to fly passengers on this route, found out about the trip, and laid a complaint before the ATB, accusing us of stealing their customers. Or potential customers. We didn't respond to the Board's telegram right away, for the very good reason that I was away when the crisis broke, so the Board simply lifted our entire licence. When I got back to Yellowknife and walked into the office one sunny morning, whistling and wishing a cheery good morning to the staff, I noticed there was kind of a stricken atmosphere around the place, but I didn't understand what it was all about until I went into my own office, sat down, and saw, right on top of all the stuff on my desk awaiting my attention, one of those telegrams from the Ottawa bureaucrats that seem to be written mostly in capital letters to set forth your sins in official prose: "WHEREAS IT HAS COME TO THE ATTENTION OF THE BOARD THAT . . ." They also always, in those days, seemed to end the same way, demanding my scalp on a plate. I tell you, it stopped my whistling in a hurry.

However, the complaint was so silly that I was able to frame a suitably soothing reply to explain that we hadn't done anything wrong, we hadn't stolen any Pacific Western passengers, and I did a complete crawl before the Board. Then, and only then, the licence was reinstated – after the loss of an entire week's work.

However, the northern business continued to survive in spite of the hurdles constantly in our path, and we had our share of triumphs along with the trials and tribulations provided by the weather and the regulations.

We added two more Twin Otters to the fleet in 1967, and later that same year, we managed to swing a deal to buy four Bristol Freighters at one swoop – and at a very good price – through Crown Assets in England, for delivery in 1968. The planes had belonged to the RCAF, and their addition to our growing fleet meant that we were ready to take on just about anything in the way of traffic the expanding northern economy could throw at us.

One of the most exciting tasks to come our way was something I had nothing whatever to do with, although it was one of the proudest moments of the Wardair saga and deserves a place in this story. In early 1967, the international Continental Polar Project mounted a joint Canadian–American expedition to the northern geographic Pole. This would require setting down a lot of equipment at the top of the world, and the obvious way to do this was to use a Bristol Freighter for the job, so we were contacted and asked to take it on.

Don Braun, our head pilot, was delighted at the opportunity to show what we could do, but, needless to say, he went about what could be a very dangerous task in a typically careful way. A single-engine Otter was chartered by the expedition through another company to fly from Resolute, on Cornwallis Island, to Alert, at the top of Ellesmere Island – our most northerly outpost – and, after a stop there, it would proceed, via a fuel cache laid down beforehand, to the geographical Pole, about five hundred miles away. The Otter would seek out a suitable landing place for the Bristol, and only when Don was satisfied that he could get the airplane in and out without trouble would he go ahead.

That was the theory.

In fact, for some reason, the Otter never arrived at Alert, and the expedition sat around and sat around and sat around, growing more and more frustrated as the limited time they had to set up their equipment and work at the pole seemed to be vanishing before their eyes. Finally, Dr. Fred Roots, the Canadian in charge of the expedition, begged Don at least to take them over the site, to see if they could find a landing spot. If they couldn't, Dr. Roots said, they would come back, and no hard feelings.

Okay, said Don, and on the morning of May 6, 1967, he and his crew, consisting of Jeff Braithwaite and Harry Kreider, took off from Alert. They carried five tons of scientific equipment and the seven-man international team, and pointed the Bristol's nose straight north. He carried an astro compass on his lap, because, obviously, a magnetic compass is of no use in that area. When they got close to the spot indicated by his instruments, Don spotted a lead in the ice that looked smooth enough to set down his twenty tons of aircraft. It was a split in the ice pack, which had been broken open by the action of the ice movement and then had frozen over again, quite recently, so it was still comparatively smooth. The problem, as always in these latitudes, was that the strip was covered with snow, and there was no way to tell how thick the ice was.

Don took his time about landing. In fact, he never did say he would land until he actually did. He was not using a ski-equipped aircraft; no wheeled aircraft had ever even attempted what he was about to do, and if anything went wrong in such a location, they were going to be in big trouble.

Don edged the Bristol down onto the ice, and, keeping a lot of power on the engines, ran the wheels along the ice for some distance before pulling up. Then he circled the spot to see if any water had been drawn to the surface by the pressure of the wheels. As far as he could tell, it looked clear. He went through the whole routine a second time, and this time, the prop wash had blown some of the surface clear of snow, to reveal a stretch of smooth blue ice that appeared sound. Finally, Don turned in for his final approach. However, first he gave orders that, as soon as he got the aircraft slowed down – but not stopped – before he turned the engines off, one of the scientists would jump out with an axe and take a few whacks at the ice to see how thick it was.

The landing went like clockwork, and a few heart-stopping moments later, they were all piling out onto the ice and setting up camp. They had landed within eighteen miles of the Pole itself. Don got on the radio to Alert, and via a computer base in Boston, Massachusetts, they were able to determine that the aircraft and its ice platform were moving at about five-and-a-half knots in the Arctic current.

The expedition was a great success, and we were given due credit for our role, but when Don first told me about it, my immediate reaction was, "My God, what if something had gone wrong? How would we have got you out of there?" The reply I got was, reasonably enough, that nothing did go wrong.

There was an interesting sidelight to this adventure. Don had asked the officials in Ottawa to contact the Soviet polar group, who had a scientific station not far away, on an ice island that had been floating around the Arctic Ocean for a number of years. Don wanted their permission, if something went wrong, to make an emergency landing at that station. The Russians wired back that they would be delighted to lend a hand, and made it clear that their offer of support included the offer of fuel, and – what was more impressive, or more sinister, depending on how you see these things – they knew what kind of plane Don was flying, and what kind of fuel he would need.

We had started replacing the Otters and Beavers of the early years with Twin Otters in 1963. These aircraft, of which we had six operating at one time, are turbo-props, larger, faster, and with a longer range than the single-engine version. They can carry fifteen passengers or thirty-five hundred pounds of freight, and proved ideal as the development prospects in the area turned from gold and uranium to copper, which was found spread all over the region. Later, we bought a Beechcraft 18 and a Mitsubishi MU-2, which was fast and sturdy, and able to operate out of relatively small strips. It was also pressurized, and we used it to transport executives and for medical evacuation work. We also bought a Grumman Gulfstream. The Grumman was used mainly for the government of the Northwest Territories. It was reliable, comfortable, and safe enough that it was considered a proper aircraft on which to transport members of the Royal Family on visits to the North. Every time the Royal Family were in northern Canada, they flew in our aircraft, and that included visits to small settlements, fishing trips, and all.

Once, when the Queen was visiting northern points with Stuart Hodgson, then the Commissioner of the NWT, we learned a little about protocol. Officially, Stu had to be at each point to receive Her Majesty when she disembarked. Since he was travelling on the same aircraft with her, this was a difficult feat. To do it, he had worked out a technique with the crew. After the airplane stopped on the tarmac, Stu would jump out the baggage door at the rear of the aircraft and run around to the front. When the stairs came down, he would present himself at the bottom to meet the Queen. This routine ran perfectly for the first two or three stops, but of course did not go unnoticed by Her Majesty. At the fourth stop, the Queen spoke to the crew and arranged to have her stairs go down the instant the aircraft had come to a stop. Then she popped down them, and, when Stu came rushing around to his designated position, she was already there.

"Beatcha!" she said.

We also used to take Prince Charles fishing after he was through with all the banquets and other formalities. Senior

RCMP officers would be in Yellowknife whenever Royals were on hand, and one evening when a couple of constables were going out with the Prince, I heard one of the senior men warn them, "If anything goes wrong out there, just don't bother coming back!"

We showed, I think, that we were dedicated to the region and to the business, that we were prepared to invest time, money, sweat, and reputation. Among other things, we showed how important we considered the North to be when we sent in our elder son, Kim, to fly and to help manage the Yellowknife operation. He was there for five years, and started right at the bottom. When he moved to the Toronto operation, he worked his way through many sectors of the company, so that he was extremely knowledgeable about many areas of the airline business before becoming Vice-President, Sales and Marketing, and a member of the Wardair board of directors. It was great having him alongside me. Later on, Gai and Blake also worked for Wardair. I had never urged any of our children to follow me into the company. I always felt that they would have to work twice as hard as anyone else to prove themselves. This they did, and I was proud to have them with us.

Blythe was content to leave the flying to the rest of us. She earned much of her university tuition as a professional model, became a teacher for children with special problems, and later ran a thriving modelling agency in partnership with a friend.

In the North, as in the charter business, we had a reputation for reliability and safety, although it was somewhat marred by two serious accidents to our Bristol Freighters. The first occurred at Snowdrift, a tiny settlement on Great Slave Lake, straight east of Yellowknife, on May 31, 1971, when a pilot negligently left the aircraft on the spring ice for a long period of time and it went through. It could not be recovered, but no one was hurt in this incident.

The second, and far more serious, accident took place at Hay River on November 20, 1977, when one of our crew, ignoring the standing orders we had laid down, failed to secure a load of sheet metal properly. The load shifted on takeoff and the plane crashed, killing the co-pilot, David Dalling, and injuring the pilot, Captain Robert Petkau.

Our firm commitment to the North was shown again in 1975, when we built a new hangar in Yellowknife, for about $1.5 million (this one had an official opening, on October 28), and when we ordered two Dash 7s from de Havilland, in the spring of 1978, specifically for northern service. De Havilland, a company I knew and respected as a first-class aircraft manufacturer, was taken over by the Canadian government in 1974, when the British parent firm, Hawker Siddeley, threatened to close down the Canadian operations, with a loss of hundreds of jobs. Once the government got hold of de Havilland, the company was headed for disaster. Within ten years, the Canadian taxpayer had poured $750 million into the company, with no sign that it would ever, as long as it was in government hands, turn a profit. The company was eventually to be sold back to the private sector, in 1985, when Boeing Corporation, the world's largest aircraft manufacturer, took it on. Boeing paid $155 million, and the major asset it got was the two aircraft – the Dash 7 and the smaller Dash 8. De Havilland's efforts to sell the Dash 7 in the early years had limited success, but it was and is an excellent machine. It is powered by four turbo-props and has splendid STOL (Short Take Off and Landing) capabilities. It is reliable, can carry fifty passengers or five tons of freight, and was intended primarily as a commuter aircraft, to be sold to airlines on feeder routes to their major lines. However, neither Air Canada nor CP Air found it suitable for their needs at the time.

De Havilland was almost tearful in its gratitude when we bought the first Dash 7s to be sold in this country, in May 1978. The then-Minister of Transport, Jean Chrétien, made an appearance with me at the Paris Air Show to announce our purchase and to show that the plane could be sold in Canada. Our plane was officially christened the *Don Braun* – the first of our northern fleet to carry a name – in a ceremony at Toronto. Don, who had just retired from Wardair (he now lives in St. Cloud, Minnesota), and his wife, Maria, were on hand for the occasion, which was a splendid, cheerful one, and it was Maria who christened the aircraft, which we stationed in Yellowknife.

In March of 1979, under the direction of Wardair's chief northern pilot, Dave Watson, we used the Dash 7 to help supply the Lorex Expedition at the North Pole. We made nineteen two-and-a-half-hour trips from Alert into the site, setting up the original base camp. This expedition was a fascinating, two-month mission under the direction of one of Canada's foremost Arctic experts, Dr. Hans Weber. Accompanied by geophysicists and oceanographers, he manned an ice station, gathering data on the Lomonosov Ridge, between Canada and the Soviet Union. This is a rock "partition," only twelve-and-a-half miles wide in places but 1,205 miles long and rising 10,000 feet from the floor of the Arctic Ocean. Our favourite photographer, George Hunter, who had recorded Wardair history almost since its beginning, accompanied one of our Dash 7 trips, supplying us afterwards with photographs of the operation.

On their last trip, before the strip became too softened by the increasing sunlight for landing, the Dash 7 crew took a position directly over the North Pole and, just for the fun of it, made the first round-the-world Dash 7 flight, before flying back to Yellowknife.

We had also hoped to use the Dash 7 for a series of charter flights that would have enabled southern Canadians to see and visit our beautiful northland. Kim and another Wardair executive, Brian Robertson, worked months on this project, but it had to be abandoned; the market was not yet ready. We were ten years ahead of the times with these tours, which, today, are flourishing in the North.

Despite the various ways we put the Dash 7 to work, this was one of the few times when buying the finest aircraft available for the purpose did not pay off for us. Our investment in these two aircraft, with spares and extras, came to just under four million dollars each. We had gone ahead with the Dash purchases on two assumptions. The first was that the federal government would, sooner or later, have to give way and allow us a scheduled route somewhere, sometime, somehow. We, along with a lot of other people, thought we detected a change in the political climate, signalled by the election of a Conservative minority government on May 22, 1979. Surely, we thought, this would mean an easing of some of the smothering web of regulation we struggled under.

We also assumed that the Mackenzie Valley Pipeline, which had been talked about, argued over, planned, and processed for years, would go ahead. We thought we were splendidly positioned in Yellowknife to take advantage of these two changes, and hoped that we would, at last, get a scheduled line to fly and, at the same time, make a steady income carrying supplies for the construction of the pipeline.

The pipeline project was hoisted when a Royal Commission headed by Mr. Justice Thomas Berger suggested a ten-year moratorium on the project; and the possibility of a scheduled route went glimmering when, at yet another in an endless series of hearings at Yellowknife, we were refused. We had applied to fly a regular service, with Dash 7 equipment, from Yellowknife to Rankin Inlet and on to Frobisher (now Iqaluit), the burgeoning capital of the eastern Arctic on Baffin Island. We had the aircraft, the experience, the record, the savvy –

but the CTC's Air Transport Committee gave the route to Northwest Territorial Airlines. We didn't even come second in the contest; once again, we came in last.

When I learned what had been done to us, something snapped. I knew that it didn't matter what we did, how hard we tried, how much of our own money we hazarded to try to make the northern enterprise grow, we would be stymied by the small minds and large bureaucracy of the CTC, which was still carrying out the old Liberal policy.

Had we been given a scheduled route, we could and would have stayed in the North, but as it was, I saw no other course but to close down the operations in Yellowknife. Overall, we were losing money; 1979 would leave Wardair with a net loss of $2,417,000, and this was not just my loss, any more; there were other shareholders to consider. The northern operation was marginally profitable but represented less than 2 per cent of our gross revenues. With the Dash 7s to pay for, it was likely to become a greater and greater drain of time, energy, and money. Mining exploration was on the increase, after a few years of moderate activity, but that gave us work only two or three months a year, and the oil-exploration work, which was far more extensive, was accomplished for the most part by giant companies that flew their own planes and had little need of us.

When I made the decision to close the Yellowknife office, we sent out a press release, which read: "Mr. Ward stated that his association with northern Canada started in Yellowknife in 1946 and he is sad indeed to see his close ties with the North end after all these years."

That was the understatement of the year. The closure of the base cost thirty-seven jobs, although some of these employees joined our international operations. The northern base had proved to be a good recruiting centre for management people. In 1968, George Curley, who was then the northern base manager, and who thoroughly enjoyed the North, reluctantly agreed to transfer from Yellowknife to our Edmonton operation, and thence to Sales and Marketing, finally becoming President of Wardair. His accounting background provided sound guidance to management decisions all through the years. When George left the North, Fred Dornan managed the base, contributing enormously to our growth there.

Ironically, when we started to sell the equipment, we discovered that a good deal of money could be made by selling aircraft. Unlike a car, a good airplane becomes more valuable with the passage of time, as long as it has been maintained in top condition, because it costs so much more to replace it.

In all, we gained $5,432,000 from selling off equipment and aircraft in Yellowknife, which was immediately gobbled up by the international operations. The piece of property on Back Bay, where we first started, was not of interest to anyone, so I held on to it. I still own it.

When we pulled out of Yellowknife in 1979, after so many years, it was as much a matter of exhaustion – physical, mental, and moral – as anything else. In the decade before that fateful decision was made, I spent so much time in fruitless battles with entrenched bureaucrats over the international charter operations, that I simply had nothing left for the North.

▼

CHAPTER 16

The Delusions of History

Throughout my battles with the various regulatory bodies, I constantly made the plea that I ought to be allowed to compete on level terms with the government-nurtured airline. Back would come the argument that Air Canada had to be protected as the nation's air carrier, bearing the burden of the scheduled routes, and that all Wardair wanted to do was skim off the cream.

"Then give me a scheduled route," I said. I never varied in my contention that I could run a better airline, leaner, more efficient, cheaper, and more pleasing to the consumer, than anyone else in the business. I was never given the chance; as you will see, by the time I did manage to get a scheduled licence, the industry had been overtaken by forces that meant I was doomed before I began.

The CTC was carrying out the policies of the government of Canada. Canadian aviation policy has been hampered over the past sixty years by a profound ignorance of how the business was actually developed in this country. It is part of the Canadian mythology that it was Trans-Canada Airlines, the government carrier, that set the pace, took the chances, opened the way. Like much of our mythology, that is simply untrue, and I do not believe we will ever arrive at a reasonable air-transport policy until we understand what really happened, rather than what we think happened, in the beginning.

In the 1920s and 1930s, it was the initiative and foresight of private individuals, never of the government, that inspired the development of the airline business. I am not merely speaking here of the development of the North and the exploits of the bush pilots. Shortly after the end of the First World War, two of its air heroes, Billy Bishop and W. G. Barker, started the Bishop–Barker Flying Company, to carry vacationers from Toronto to the resort country of Muskoka, a hundred miles north. It didn't work, because the time was not yet ripe, but they were in the air-passenger game, or trying to be, almost two decades ahead of the government.

There were dozens of other small, private air carriers, hauling freight and passengers and mail, long before any governments got into the act. In 1920, when robbers blew open the vault of a bank in Winkler, a Manitoba town southwest of Winnipeg, the city editor of the *Winnipeg Free Press* chartered an aircraft from the Canadian Air Company to fly a reporter down to cover the story. In its evening edition that day, the *Free Press* made much of the fact that this was the first time an aircraft had been used in news coverage in Canada.

Laurentide Air Services was formed in 1922 to patrol huge timber reserves in Quebec, and was later given a contract to map lakes and forests for the Ontario government. The task of spotting forest fires, and then of bringing in men and equipment to fight those fires, was soon added to the Laurentide workload.

It was Laurentide that established the first organized air-transport route in the nation, in 1924. This was in conjunction with a huge mining development at Rouyn, near the Ontario–Quebec border. Laurentide set up a regular service from the end of the rail at Haileybury, Ontario, to Rouyn, and brought in more than a thousand passengers, forty tons of freight, and thousands of letters and telegrams to the mining camp.

Private operators performed the crucial task of conducting Canada's first aerial mapping and surveys. In 1923, Fairchild Aerial Surveys of Canada was formed to provide photographs for national mapping surveys with the Fairchild aerial camera. Since the equipment needed protection, this led, in turn, to the development of the first cabin aircraft in Canada, called, not surprisingly, the Fairchild.

When government involvement did play a part, it was the provincial government of Ontario, not the federal bunch, who led the way. The success of the Laurentide contract led to the foundation, in 1924, of the Ontario Provincial Air Service, with fourteen aircraft flown almost entirely by former air-force pilots. The OPAS was originally set up for forestry protection, but it soon took on the tasks of transporting medical teams into remote areas and bringing patients out, conducting aerial mapping and surveys – especially in seeking out hydro sites – and aiding the Ontario Provincial Police in criminal investigations and in the location of missing people. It was also in the mandate of the OPAS to deliver government officials to reserves in various parts of the province, to fulfil the conditions of Indian treaties. This involved delivering money, mostly real, and promises, mostly fake, to the various tribes.

The first use of aircraft to aid prospectors occurred in the autumn of 1925, when gold was discovered at Red Lake, Ontario, about a hundred miles north of Lake of the Woods.

Rather than waiting until the lakes and rivers became frozen fast enough to allow for transportation over the ice, Jack Hammill, a prospector and company promoter, persuaded the OPAS to fly in ten tons of mining equipment and supplies to the site.

Bush-flying, as it came to be called, was essentially no more than commercial aviation on non-scheduled routes, and it was all of it performed by private individuals and companies. But it was not the romantic, slapdash, small-time operation it has become in the eyes of succeeding generations. I remember reading an article in an old *National Geographic* called "Gentlemen Adventurers of the Air" on the development of air transport in Canada, which pointed out that at that time – November 1929 – Canada moved more freight by air than any other nation in the world! None of it, although the article didn't say so, was shipped on a government airline, for there was none.

In the year 1928, Canadian Airways, owned by James Richardson of Winnipeg, carried 122,000 pounds of mail, 1.2 million pounds of freight, and about 10,000 passengers. And Richardson's outfit was only one of a number of successful bush airlines of the day.

By the time the government-run Trans-Canada Airlines was formed in 1937, later histories claimed, everything had come to a halt because of the Great Depression. This was nonsense. The Depression merely slowed down the development of a young air industry, which continued to grow right up to the beginning of the Second World War. The convenient side effect of this argument that independent air companies had closed down was that it justified the establishment of a national airline; there was never any need for it.

One historian, D. Corbett, in *Politics and the Airlines*, comments that "Canada seems to have established a publicly-owned monopoly of scheduled inter-urban air services in a fit of absence of mind, as Britain is said to have acquired her empire."

That explanation is more witty than rational; it was, in my view, not absence of mind but the *presence* of mind of a single individual that led to the formation of Trans-Canada Airlines in 1937, and that individual was C. D. Howe. He was an entrepreneur, and nothing was more exciting to him at that time than the thought of building an airline; he just couldn't resist.

Clarence Decatur Howe was born in Massachusetts and educated at the Massachusetts Institute of Technology. He came to Canada in 1907, when he was twenty-one, to study and teach at Dalhousie University in Halifax. He subsequently became a successful businessman, which led him into politics and to a post in Mackenzie King's cabinet. He was known as "the minister of everything," and in all he held eight cabinet portfolios, including the Department of Transport portfolio, which was formed in 1936.

I met him once and was struck by two things: the broad New England accent, which nothing in his years in Canada had ever softened, and his entrepreneurial approach. Howe was, and remained, a businessman *manqué*, and, deprived of a corporation of his own to play with, he created government corporations, which he treated exactly as if he were the president and owned all the shares. His fierce protectiveness towards Trans-Canada Airlines could not be explained, I believe, in any other way than that he regarded it as *his* airline and resented any attempts to compete with it as fiercely as would any private businessman.

I was later confirmed in this view by his biographers, Robert Bothwell and William Kilbourn, who wrote in

C. D. Howe: A Biography that Howe's vision of a Crown corporation was of a "publicly owned enterprise . . . to be managed as efficiently, absolutely, and aggressively as if he himself were the private entrepreneur at the head of it, and no nonsense about politicians meddling with the management."

But the most telling evidence came from the lips of Howe himself, when, during a House of Commons debate about the airline, an opposition MP reminded the minister that it was, after all, a public enterprise. Howe shot back, "That's not public enterprise; that's *my* enterprise." (Howe was, if nothing else, direct in his statements; when George Drew, the Conservative leader, noted that his party, too, had contributed to the development of TCA, Howe responded with one word: "Nuts.")

In point of fact, Howe appeared to have been turned away from private ownership of the airline by his personal antipathy to James Richardson, the president of Canadian Airways, the most likely contender to take on the job at that time. Howe insisted that no one firm, especially not Richardson's, could successfully fill the national need. Accordingly, the first proposal advanced by the federal Cabinet suggested a joint venture, involving Canadian National Railways, acting for the government, Canadian Pacific Railway, and Canadian Airways. Each of the member firms would be allowed to hold 10 per cent of the stock, with the rest held by a mix of government and private ownership. However, the proposal also contained a number of subsidies for the airline-to-be's operation, as well as a guarantee that the Post Office Department, as it then was, would use it as its sole mover of airmail. To offset that monopoly, the government insisted that the airline would have to have a control on its price structure, such that the return on invested capital could never exceed 5 per cent per annum. Neither Sir Edward Beatty of the CPR nor James Richardson of Canadian Airways was at all interested, and the joint venture notion faded from the scene.

The legislation introduced in March 1937 created fifty thousand shares, with a par value of five million dollars, or one hundred dollars a share, vested in the CNR. "Private interests . . . interested in aviation and approved by the minister," could buy up to 49.8 per cent of the outstanding shares. If any entrepreneurs wanted in, they were welcome to invest, but government would always retain control through the CNR. Under these conditions, there was no market for the shares, and, in fact, no shares were ever sold.

"However inadvertently," writes John L. Langford, in *Public Corporations and Public Policy in Canada*, "the Liberal government under Howe's strong influence created a thoroughly public airline."

The Trans-Canada Airlines Act created a monopoly on inter-city routes, all mail traffic, and all international air services, and gave that monopoly to the new airline. Only northern bush services and local feeder services were left for private enterprise, and much of the battle from that day to this has been to expand the private sector, which has always been more efficient and effective, into the areas carved out by the government for itself. This was always hard to do, given that the referee in this game also owned the home team and never seems to have had any hesitation in making the calls accordingly.

The rationale behind this monopolization was the argument that the government airline needed the profitable inter-city routes to pay for its services to the remote areas of Canada. "Cross-subsidization" is the term for this, and it represents a tenable economic argument. The flaw in this argument is that, in the case of Canadian air services, it is not true, and never has been. I saw this for myself. It wasn't TCA or Air Canada who opened the North, but private companies, including my own, every time. We were the ones who risked our lives, our equipment, our money, and our reputations, not the government. There were no TCA pilots beside me in the Fox Moth or the Bellanca as we began the task of servicing the development of the Arctic, and it took nearly three decades for an Air Canada aircraft to poke its nose into Yellowknife. That was after Air Canada bought into Northwest Territorial Airways in 1989, paying fourteen million dollars for a bunch of old aircraft.

I used to get a real kick out of hearing spokesmen from Air Canada point out at public hearings that the government had given them a mandate and the responsibility to create air transportation in Canada, when many of them had no idea of the history of aviation, or of the fabulous job done by private enterprise before C. D. Howe came down off the mountain with his collection of tablets in 1937. I often wonder how different the picture might be today had politics not inflicted itself on the airline industry with such a heavy hand. Canadian Pacific Air Lines would have been the nation's number-one carrier years ago, that is one certainty. Another certainty is that we would not have heard so much nonsense over the years about the need for Air Canada to have the world-wide routes to itself, to pay for the unprofitable lines into the hinterland of the country.

But don't take my word for it; I am, after all, a partisan in this debate. Read instead what Andrew J. Roman, a lawyer and student of history, says in his study, *Airline Deregulation in Canada: Why It Failed*:

In 1937, Trans-Canada Airlines, now called Air Canada, was created by the federal government. The official reasons were to provide air links with remote areas of Canada which might not be served economically by the private sector, to ensure that Canadians did not have to depend on existing American airlines to travel from coast to coast and, thus, to contribute to the national dream of uniting a geographically and sociologically diverse country. In fact, AC provided very little, if any, service to remote areas, which were actually served by the private sector, while AC was given the best routes as the national carrier, at the expense of private sector development.

When Canadian Pacific Air Lines was patched together in 1942 from twelve small bush lines, Lord Beaverbrook, a strong believer in free enterprise, and then chiefly responsible for organizing war supplies in Britain, proposed that CPA be given the task of running the Trans-Atlantic Ferry Service, which he had organized to airlift men and supplies over the Pole from Canada to the war theatres. It performed magnificently, and at the end of the war, under Grant McConachie's leadership, it began to knock the spots off the government-owned line. Howe responded not merely by refusing CPA's constantly reiterated requests for routes – it did not get permission to fly a transcontinental route until 1959 – but by making McConachie return new aircraft to the manufacturers when he had purchased planes that were bound to out-perform those owned by the government.

At a meeting of the CNR board of directors in 1937, before the TCA bill had even been passed, C. D. Howe had seen to it that six of his men from the CNR and the Department of Transport were placed on the TCA Board, had picked an American, Philip Johnson, to be Vice-President, Operations, of the airline-to-be (the president was to be S. J. Hungerford, who also just happened to be president of the CNR), and had even announced what aircraft the new airline would be allowed to buy. He had picked out, and ordered, seven planes from Lockheed aircraft, he said. The CNR would look after them until TCA was official and "could in turn be assigned the aircraft."

In effect, Howe picked his own aircraft, and those of anyone else who wanted to get into the business. Then he went on to set the rules. The enabling legislation allowed the Cabinet to amend the Trans-Canada Contract whenever it saw fit and to include whatever terms it chose. Routes, schedules, fares, mail contracts, aircraft choice – every aspect of running its own airline and that of any potential competitor was passed directly into the hands of the government. It was not until 1967 and the passage of the National Transportation Act that passenger fares, for example, were removed from the Trans-Canada Contract and made part of the responsibility of the Air Transport Committee of the Canadian Transport Commission. And this meant absolutely nothing.

There was still no real competition. As Andrew Roman remarks, "Air Canada continued to enjoy a favoured position as the result of financial assistance from the federal government, control of the major national reservation system, favoured treatment in access to airport terminals, and the operation of the government's central travel service." (The largest single pool of travel money in the country by far, this represents, in effect, all the travel of all the federal employees.)

And, he might have added, freedom from the kind of discrimination, bullying, and outright distortion that were heaped on the shoulders of anyone who tried to compete with Air Canada, as my own bitter experience attests. It is to that subject, with this brief history in mind, that I now return.

CHAPTER 17

▼

The Dance of Regulation

I come now to the part of my story that is hardest for me to tell, although it is also perhaps the most important part of the record. I cannot even bear to think, most times, about the endless years of battling bureaucracy, the countless trips to Ottawa to lay appeals before politicians and mandarins – all of them righteous, all of them sure, most of them just plodding along doing their jobs. At the beginning, I had the foolish and naive notion, since I was doing what every textbook and every political speech urged me to do – striking out on my own, exercising the muscles of free enterprise, creating employment through successful endeavour – that I would be, if not encouraged, at least not blocked by all of those who led me through the torturous dance of regulation.

Let me say at once that I understand the need for public bodies to impose certain standards of performance over any enterprise as complex, and, yes, dangerous, as commercial aviation. I was willing to abide by any rules, or any set of rules, and the interesting thing is that I never at any time had any trouble with the section of the Ministry of Transport responsible for the physical conduct of airline services, which embraced the entire industry. When we began to operate the 727, Walter McLeish, a senior official on the technical side, pointed out to me that we were the first operators of jet aircraft in the country, other than Air Canada and CP Air, who in fact ran their own maintenance. The MOT didn't even bother with them. He said to me, "We don't have the people with the knowledge of the aircraft and therefore the onus is upon you to operate and duly maintain it. And remember," he said, "that you will be setting the standards for other carriers to follow. We trust you not to let us down." Well, we didn't let him down, and in return, the technical people gave us support and encouragement.

But what I could never understand or accept was why Wardair should be singled out for what I was indiscreet enough in one speech to call "a program of constant harassment and discrimination" from the policy and political mandarins.

There are huge files in the office next to the one where I am writing this, devoted entirely to Canadian Transport Commission and Air Transport Committee dockets, a horrendous litany of the decisions that slowly strangled us, representing the private side of the Wardair story that has remained largely untold until now.

The twenty years from 1967 to 1987 were, on the surface, years of constant advancement, expansion, and achievement for Wardair, which grew, and multiplied, and begat subsidiary companies, and won awards for the excellence of its service and publicity for its deeds both of kindness and of derring-do. We went, in the public mind, from triumph to triumph. The chronology at the back of this book will give the interested reader some of the details of what appeared, in our publicity releases, to be the steady unrolling of successes – and we even made a little money along the way.

In 1971, I received the Billy Mitchell Award; in 1972, we set up International Vacations Limited (Intervac), to handle package tours, and Canada–U.K. Travel Centre Limited, to handle much of the business in England and Scotland. I was made a Companion of the Order of Icarus on March 31, 1973; on May 15, I was awarded the McKee Trophy at the Canadian Aeronautics and Space Institute meeting in Edmonton – the highest award you can receive in Canadian aviation – and, two weeks later, I was made Transportation Man of the Year for 1973 by the Northern Alberta Transportation Club. In 1974, I was inducted into the Aviation Hall of Fame, and a year later, I became an Officer of the Order of Canada. In 1978, I was given Honorary Life Membership in the Air Transport Association of Canada, and in 1979, I not only picked up an honorary doctorate from the University of Alberta, I was named Gordon R. McGregor Memorial Trophy winner by the Royal Canadian Air Force Association.

People who heard me speak during these years – and I was beginning to speak, with increasing bitterness, about the way the air-transport business was being run by the government in this country – must have wondered what I had to grouse about. The truth is that, behind the scenes, a very different kind of game was being played, and for each of these honours there was a contrary, and often ironical, counter-balance.

The Air Transport Association of Canada, for example, had thrown me and my company right out on our ears – in circumstances that will become clear – before they turned around and gave me a life membership. The 1979 awards (the McGregor Trophy, to give irony a bad name, was bestowed on behalf of the long-time president of Air Canada, my bitterest foe) came in the very year I had to close down our northern operations entirely.

Far from a triumphal march, those years represented a stagger from crisis to crisis. We were always in debt, often in a rage, forever wondering if we were about to be put out of business by the whim of a bureaucrat or the decree of a politician, at the very moment we were leading the industry in both the methods of our marketing and the choice of our aircraft. By one of those twists that novelists enjoy, we were both rewarded and punished for our audacity in challenging the established kings of the air-transport business, and some of the trophies seemed to be handed over with smiles that came through gritted teeth. Let me again say frankly here what I thought a thousand times during those years: if we had been allowed to operate our business without the constant Chinese water-torture of interference, restriction, and regulation, I believe Wardair could have emerged as one of the premier airlines of the world.

As it was, although I was too stubborn to acknowledge this for decades, we never stood a chance in the long run. Our competitors could well afford to see us named "Airline of the Year" by industry magazines and travel agencies, praised in the press, fêted at award dinners, because in the end, they knew, we weren't going anywhere serious.

Let me lay before you, now, as instances of my thesis, two cases from my files that created some fuss at the time, but which have never, to this day, been properly explained to the public. We can call them, for convenience, "The Air Canada Sting" and "The Affair of the Broken Trust."

In 1967, you may recall, the only way we could fly the charters that were becoming our lifeblood was to round up members of the Amalgamated Brotherhood of Clock-Watchers or the Rooftree Society and sell them a charter flight to wherever they chose to go to watch clocks or check out roofs. We could not advertise the flights, nor let the club members know the price, lest the moon turn to blood, and civilization perish. Air Canada and CP Air, which were both edging into the business, were under the same restrictions, with some notable exceptions. They did not have to apply for approval for each and every charter, nor did they have to prove, and prove and prove again, that only bona fide members, with at least six months' standing in the relevant club, were aboard the aircraft.

On March 4, 1968, when our summer season was shaping up to be the best we had ever had, I received a registered letter from the Air Transport Committee of the Canadian Transport Commission, which, in effect, threatened to put us out of business forthwith. It ordered that Wardair Canada Ltd. appear before the Committee in Ottawa on March 19, to "show cause why its Licence . . . should not be suspended or cancelled."

The document laid out our sins for all the world to see. There were five pages of them, and I will quote a tiny portion of the indictment to show you, not merely the horrible nature of our offences, but the wonderful language in which they were cloaked:

> (1) AND WHEREAS it has come to the attention of the Committee;
> (a) That an officer or servant of Wardair Canada Ltd. did on November 20th, 1967, at the Vancouver office of Wardair Canada Ltd. hold out to a member of the public on behalf of Wardair Canada Ltd. an offer of charter transportation by air from Vancouver to London on April 14, 1968, as a member of the North-

West Section, American Vacuum Society, when the said member of the public was to the knowledge of the said officer of Wardair Canada Ltd. not a member of the said Society. . . .

This was, of course, the sin of sins. One of our sales people, who may have been overwhelmed by the mere existence of a society as wonderful as the North-West Section, American Vacuum Society, had offered to sell a society member a charter flight, when he ought to have known that he wasn't entitled to go on the flight.

However, our transgression did not end there:

(b) THAT the said member of the public pursuant to the suggestion of an officer or servant of Wardair Canada Ltd. wrote to a Mr. M. Wareham, addressed 3023 Fremont Avenue, N., Seattle, Washington, a letter dated 20th November 1967 requesting particulars of the said flight; that the said letter was returned marked "no such number" and that the said member of the public then wrote Wardair's Vancouver Office a letter dated 2nd December 1967 requesting Mr. Wareham's correct address; that in an envelope postmarked "Vancouver 6 December '67" addressed to the said member of the public, the said member received a brochure giving particulars of the flight and an Application Form for membership in the Pacific North-West Section of the American Vacuum Society.

If you can follow this – it took me three readings, in my distressed and shocked state – you will see that our salesperson tried to put the "member of the public" in touch with the vacuum gang, screwed up the address (actually, just reversed two numbers), and then got it straight. The persistent "member of the public" kept after us until we did, indeed, put him in touch with the society, and he got a membership form.

This ought to have been enough to condemn us in the eyes of any right-thinking person, but there was worse to come:

> (c) THAT on December 12, 1967, the said member of the public completed the said Application and mailed it together with the requested annual dues of $2.00 by letter dated 14 December 1967, addressed to Mr. B. M. Wareham, 3203 Fremont Ave. N., Seattle, Wash., 98103, being the address on the Application Form; that the said member of the public in an envelope addressed to him and post-marked "Seattle, Wash., Dec. 28, 1967" received inter alia, a membership card in the said Society dated Oct. 14, 1967, and an application for the said Charter flight, and . . .

To cut a long story short, the "said member of the public" was signed up for a flight in April, when our servant, in Vancouver, knew full well the said member of the public had not been a member of the vacuum searchers, or sellers, or whatever they were, for six months, because he, our servant, had only sent the said member of the public the address, for purposes of joining, on December 2.

We were accused, charged, and convicted of making a mockery of a regulation that was itself a mockery, and we would pay heavily for it.

This is the point where you are entitled to know that the "said member of the public" who played such a stellar role in all this was, in fact, an Air Canada employee who didn't even, I would hazard a guess, care much about vacuums.

We had been stung. As the pages of the indictment rolled on, it became clear that an employee, in our Edmonton office, had signed up another said member of the public for a trip to Amsterdam as a member of the Canadian Amateur Ski Association, and had passed along his application to join the club (it cost three dollars), with which he became eligible for a skiing trip to the mountains of Holland, without even checking out the man's skis. In Calgary, the Alberta Mutual Benefit Association sold one of its memberships through us – for five dollars – to put another said member of the public onto a charter flight of persons seeking Mutual Benefits under similarly suspicious circumstances.

The Foreign Fashion and Culture Exchange organization had its ranks swollen by one new member, through the efforts of another of our salespersons in Vancouver (it normally cost twenty dollars for this membership, but we were able to arrange an associate membership for five dollars), and we performed the same office for the English-Speaking Union (ten dollars), when we had good reason to know that the said members of the public were interested in cheap charters, not culture and language.

In all, the busy group of Air Canada employees were able to document six occasions between November 1967 and February 8, 1968, when we had tried to skate around the asinine rules governing "affinity" charters.

I never dreamed Air Canada would be sending a swarm of spies out to do us in, because their charter groups had no more integrity than ours. Shows how naive I was, I guess. I was later asked by a journalist why I didn't send some Wardair employees out to sting Air Canada back by trying to find out if their sales staff were bending any rules, too. I replied rather shortly that it had never occurred to me, and that, if it had occurred to me, I would have rejected it as an inappropriate and silly way to conduct a serious business. If I had thought Air Canada or anyone else was acting in a way likely to cause hardship, anxiety, or danger to the public, I would have taken any action required to set the matter right, but I was too busy trying to run an airline to play these sorts of games.

In the end, there was a hearing in Ottawa, which was much like so many hearings I attended over the years. It was held in a courtroom, and the ATC Board members sat on a podium in courtroom style, with court reporters. There were two long tables below for the victims – pardon me, the respondents – and the complainants, in this case the security people from Air Canada who had gathered the incriminating evidence. There was really not much we could say at this hearing, once the case against us had been read into the record. We did not contest the facts. I received advice from our lawyer, Jake Howard, to the effect that I ought to fight the regulations, on the basis of their innate stupidity, and because they were clearly not drawn up to protect the consumer, but rather to harm the consumer by protecting the Air Canada position. However, we were soon to take delivery of our first 707 aircraft, and we couldn't afford either the time or the money to enter a battle I thought we were probably doomed to lose anyway. When you have a nine-million-dollar hot potato on your hands, you get pretty frightened that you are actually going to be closed down entirely. I was also conscious of the fact that we had just become a public company, in September 1967, and the longer this matter was allowed to drag on, the more it would hurt our shareholders.

We said we were very sorry and promised never to do it again. The suspension of our licence while this was sorted out cost us nineteen days out of the best part of our season, and nearly destroyed us. Copies of the "show cause" documents and the details of our sins were in the hands of both Air Canada and CP Air as quickly as we got them – it was one of my standing concerns over the years that almost every confidential document we received from Ottawa was somehow transmitted to the offices of our rivals – and the newspapers blossomed with headlines that read "ATC Slaps Wardair."

How could we sell charters in those circumstances?

There was more, and worse, to come. We had a flight organized by the Alberta Petroleum Recreation Society – which actually was a genuine club – scheduled for May 15, but the CTC demanded that we produce documentation to prove that every club membership had been signed by an executive of the club, and we were required to have the club's officers swear that they knew every person on the charter had been a member for six months. When the club's officers refused to be bothered with such nonsense, the trip was abruptly cancelled by the CTC, four days before takeoff. All the arrangements people had made (it was too late even for those who could afford it to switch to Air Canada) were just thrown into the dustbin.

Once again, we were given a public black eye. We survived that season for one reason alone: we were providing the public with a service they wanted at a price they could afford to pay, so they came back to us. I wrote a few letters and gave some interviews, one of which resulted in a headline in the *Calgary Herald* that read "Wardair Asks for New Deal for Charters" – with which, plus twenty-five cents, you could then have bought a cup of coffee.

The *Herald* went out and interviewed a number of the people whose vacation plans had just gone up in smoke, and uncovered a good deal of heartache. Mrs. John Hogeslag of Calgary, who had been saving for her trip for five years, told the newspaper, "We have a daughter in Holland who has built an extra room for us. My mother is waiting; she is eighty." Tough.

Other disappointed passengers included an elderly farm couple who were going to visit their birthplace in Denmark after an absence of thirty years, and a young Dutch widow, whose husband had just been killed in an accident and who wanted to go home to see her parents. Too bad.

There were a number of travellers who had pre-paid for trips within Europe and were unable to get any of the money from this part of the trip back. (Everyone got his or her money back from us, but not from European operators who had taken non-refundable advances.) So what? Jack Pickersgill, who at this point had recently taken over as President of the CTC, put the Commission's point of view tersely when he told a journalist, "it is not a governmental responsibility to protect the flying public against financial losses."

The Alberta Mutual Benefit Association sent one telegram to the CTC and another to Paul Hellyer, the new Minister of Transport, asking for a reversal of the cancellation. The minister never even bothered to respond; the CTC sent back a telegram that said: "The answer is No, repeat, No."

Thousands of people wrote to me, to the airlines, to the politicians, complaining about the crazy affinity rules, and Jack Pickersgill came in for his share of knocks. Robert L. Perry, in the *Financial Post*, wrote, "In aviation, Jack Pickersgill is Mr. Big. His Canadian Transport Commission is prosecutor, judge, jury – and executioner."

The CTC's actions cost us millions of dollars in the loss of already-contracted revenue. To this day, I am convinced that the intent was to close Wardair down permanently. Fortunately for us, Western Canadian politicians received so much heat from their constituents over the grounding of Wardair that the government found it politically expedient to limit its duration to nineteen days.

In the middle of the fuss, the Air Transport Association of Canada, a grouping of the Canadian air carriers that is run, in effect, by Air Canada, expelled Wardair for our transgressions. I said, when asked about this, that I couldn't have cared less. Later, I was asked to rejoin and refused for many years, although finally I did rejoin. There must have been some members who regretted our original expulsion. Tom Spalding, Wardair's Executive Vice-President, was made a director of ATAC, and was ultimately made Chairman of the Board – the first charter airline chairman!

Eventually, the affinity charters would be abandoned, first, for Air Canada, in October 1969, and finally, for everyone, on January 1, 1973 – that is, four months after Jack Pickersgill stepped down as President of the CTC. The entire exercise had been a waste.

The charter business was booming in the middle and late 1960s. The first response of Canada's two giants was to concentrate on getting the charter passenger onto their scheduled flights instead; but to sop up the kind of demand that was now becoming apparent, they would have had to lower their prices substantially to try to match us. Between mid-May and October of 1968, we flew 16,000 people to and from Europe, which was only a patch on what we knew we could do.

As I noted earlier, with the changes made in 1969, we were now allowed to sell "Inclusive Tours," which helped us greatly in developing the business to Hawaii, and we did not have to sign up members of the same club – or, as we had under the "split charters" rule, two clubs – to fill an airplane, but we were still subjected to a great many rules that did not apply to our competitors. We couldn't run our own package holidays; we could only arrange them through a third party. Again, under Pickersgill's new rules, we could fly Advanced Booking Charters (they were almost always referred to as "ABCs"), and we could not pick up other than ABC passengers anywhere we flew. The crucial qualification for an ABC was that the flight arrangements had to be made at least thirty days in advance of the flight, and had to be fully paid for seven days before takeoff. This meant that, as often as not, we would be obliged to come back from Europe with an empty plane in the middle of summer, while Air Canada was operating under an entirely different set of rules.

In January 1969, we bought another Boeing 707, which was convertible and could carry either passengers or freight, but the CTC met that attempt to inject efficiency into the business by passing regulations under which we could not mix passengers and freight on the same aircraft. Fine, we said, we'll schedule the planes so that a charter can unload its passengers, then go on to pick up freight and return. So, of course, they passed a rule saying that we could not stop to pick up freight on any flight that began as a passenger flight. We had to come home empty instead.

All this time, Air Canada was saying that it had to keep its prices up on the overseas run or lose money. However, it was having an increasingly difficult time making the argument stick, and, sure enough, in 1969, overseas fares were dropped abruptly, to meet our fares. A first-class ticket from Toronto to London and return was going for $803, but now Air Canada was allowed to create twenty-one-day group inclusive tours in economy (with a minimum of twenty-five members in a group) for which they sold tickets as low as $345. We dropped our charges to $215, with off-season rates as low as $177.44. Air Canada then cut their fares to $181, with a summer rate of $219.

Newspapers began to wonder why, if Air Canada hadn't been able to lower fares before, they suddenly could fly to London so cheaply once Wardair was up and running. Don Hunt, in the Toronto *Telegram*, wrote, "Until Max Ward and others forced their hand, the airlines are now admitting, their charges were exorbitant. It would be a tragedy if Wardair is forced out of business because of its lead in this fight."

Tragedy or not, that is exactly what was promised by the next abrupt action of the CTC.

As more companies got into the charter business, inevitably fly-by-night operators appeared, and, inevitably, some Canadians who took charter flights to Europe found, when the time came to leave for home, that the chartering company had disappeared and they were stranded. To meet this problem, a regulation was established that required the charter operator to open a trust account covering each flight and to deposit money in the trust account to cover the cost of the return trip. We had no objection to this sensible precaution – indeed, we applauded it – but we did object to the way in which the CTC began to apply it. They wanted us to put the entire cost of a flight in trust and leave it there until the return trip had been accomplished, which I said was just silly. There was no point in holding funds on hand to cover the cost of a flight to, say, Europe, that had already been made; what you were guarding against was an operator skipping out with the funds for the return trip – that was all the money you needed to keep in a trust fund. By the way, neither Air Canada nor CP Air, nor any other scheduled carrier, was required to keep funds in trust for charters, or to go through the paperwork to satisfy the CTC.

We were unhappy with the CTC, and they, as usual, were unhappy with us, and we exchanged a number of letters on the subject, but I was in no way prepared for the blow that fell on January 5, 1971, by Order No. 1971-A-1 (the first business of the year). The Air Transport Committee of the CTC suddenly announced that it was not satisfied that Wardair was keeping enough money in its trust funds. Wardair was therefore ordered to cease all international charter flights to anywhere except the continental United States, as of February 15, 1971, "unless it has filed and maintains in good standing an Agreement of Guarantee or a Performance Bond acceptable to the Committee."

We were out of business; we were out of business on the grounds that we were a bunch of crooks, although the CTC were too careful to put the matter in a way that would have allowed us some recourse to the libel laws. We were not accused, we were convicted; we were not being tested, we had already been failed. The newspapers rang with the stuff: "Wardair Must Stop Its Foreign Flights," "Wardair Ordered to Stop Overseas Charter Flights," and the killer, "Wardair Head Denies Trust Fund Violation."

The careful wording of the Committee Order contained two deadly paragraphs:

> WHEREAS the Committee has noted past failures of Wardair Canada Limited to maintain required amounts IN TRUST until completion of charter contracts; and
>
> WHEREAS the Committee has examined the submissions made by Wardair Canada Limited and from the information contained therein is not satisfied that Wardair Canada Limited will be in a position in the future to maintain IN TRUST the prepayments received on charter flight contracts to the full amount required by its undertakings in the applications to the Committee for approval of charter flight contracts. . . .

There was only one way for the ordinary reader – and potential charter customer – to read those two paragraphs, and that was to assume that we had somehow rifled the trust accounts and had been caught at it. In wonderful, ironical fact, the trust accounts at the moment that the order was issued were not merely in balance, they contained excess funds. The quarrel we had with the CTC was over the crazy contention that the money be kept in for both legs of the flight after one leg had been completed. We told the CTC we would take out the money for the first leg of the flight when it was completed, and they accepted this. Then, and for reasons that were never made clear, they suddenly decided *all* the money had to be kept in until the return flight had been completed, and we were still quarrelling about this interpretation when they suspended us.

The damage to us was increased when the CTC began to leak stories that made it look much worse. Southam News Services ran an article quoting an unnamed – naturally – official from the CTC as reporting that "its inspectors had discovered Wardair was violating trust fund regulations for charter flights," which was simply untrue. The story read in part: "The CTC official said Wardair had been withdrawing passengers' fares out of the trust funds before the permitted time." Untrue again. "All we are trying to do is protect the people flying on these planes. We are worried about the public interest."

Two months earlier, Jack Pickersgill had been saying that it was not up to government to protect the passenger; now it was apparently central to the CTC's role, and the fact that we had never abandoned a passenger, and never would, and that we had flown home, free, passengers abandoned by other charter operators, was nowhere mentioned.

I reacted angrily, telling the Southam reporter that "every damn penny has been left in."

A little more calmly, Tom Spalding, our Executive Vice-President, and I released to the press a statement that said:

> All prepayments for Wardair charter flights are currently in trust and all such funds will remain in trust in keeping with our obligations to the public.

The [Canadian] Transport Commission has seen fit, in its bureaucratic wisdom, to guess that Wardair will not be able to maintain these funds in trust.

This order blithely ignores a record of excellent performance in the past and assumes a fact in the future which simply does not exist.

I might as well have saved my breath to cool my porridge. The CTC's version of events became the version of record. Worse was to follow. Another leaked story out of Ottawa, a few days later, appeared under the intriguing head "Wardair Faced Suspension 6 Months Ago."

This story said that "Wardair's licence to operate charter flights could have been suspended more than six months ago because of an alleged shortfall in the airline's trust accounts, Southam News Services learned Tuesday."

Two CTC inspectors had visited Edmonton the previous June, the story said, and found the money in the trust accounts was "short by several hundreds of thousands of dollars."

If you read this carefully, you could see that it all had to do with the same incident, the same inspection, and the same argument about how much money we had to maintain in the trust accounts. But who read it carefully? We looked, again, like a bunch of crooks who had been given a chance to reform by the generous CTC six months before, but who had continued in our dangerous ways.

The CTC inspection was absolutely routine; they had done it before, they would do it again. We never heard of Air Canada or CP Air being inspected this way, but never mind; we knew we would be inspected, and we were fully up to date. We told the inspectors, as we told the CTC, that we didn't agree with the policy of having to hold the entire amount of the flight money in trust when one half of it had been earned, no matter what happened to the airline –

and they had agreed, at least at the time. The money was important to us, because taking so much out of our earned cash flow hurt. The amount in the trust account on January 6, 1971, was $1,033,255.55; whatever we could get back from that to put back to work was obviously going to help.

To ease the concerns of the Committee, if they were real concerns, we had got a new line of credit, rearranged our financing, and ensured that every dollar we received as prepayments on transportation went into the account and stayed there, just as the CTC wanted. For this, we were made to look like deadbeats and con artists, and I resented it with a bitterness I carry to this day.

On the instructions of our legal counsel, I had prepared and sent to the CTC a long document setting forth our objection to the way they wanted us to keep our books. It said, in part:

> The Committee has indicated that Wardair did not present a forecast position of the trust account from October 19 to December 31, 1970. Such a forecast at best would be hypothetical. We contend that as we cannot accurately forecast the timing of prepayments, the only representative forecast would be the value of the charter contract for groups awaiting return to point of origin. It was precisely these points that Wardair's President tried to convey to the Committee on October 8, 1970.

In that same document, I included copies of our financial statements, projections of cash flow, and copies of debentures issued on our behalf with the Royal Bank of Canada, Imperial Oil Limited, and the Industrial Development Bank, showing the availability of over seven million dollars to us to prove, as I said in the document, "that Wardair is and will continue to be a viable operation."

There was never a danger that any passenger would ever be stranded, and the Committee knew it at the very time they slammed the gavel down on us "to protect the public."

This was simply one more demonstrated attempt on the part of the Liberal government of the day to destroy our company. They had been receiving complaint after complaint from the scheduled airlines as to the damage we were doing to them in the marketplace. The absolutely false and damning stories made us look like thugs and bankrupts, and the innuendoes were always released behind the squid-ink of "unnamed CTC sources."

We tried to appeal the ruling to the courts, on the grounds that the CTC had far exceeded its legal role, but we were denied even the right to appeal, and no reasons for the denial were ever given. We appealed to the new Minister of Transport, Don Jamieson, and he made polite and sympathetic noises, and did very little, although the CTC subsequently gave us until March 1, rather than February 15, to satisfy them that we were not about to go bankrupt.

I went before the CTC's Air Transport Committee, and they told me, flatly, that I was to do what I was told, or they would close me down. And then, suddenly, they announced that they weren't concerned about the trust accounts at all; all they really wanted was proof that we wouldn't strand our customers.

I believe this change in position came, again, because of an incredible outpouring of sympathy and outrage that accompanied the publication of the ruling, particularly from the West. We had built up a solid core of customers who liked us and who were prepared to raise hell on our behalf. Without them, the CTC's predictions would have taken on the weight of self-fulfilling prophecy, and we would indeed have gone bankrupt (although, even then, our customers would still have been covered). I have boxes and boxes of letters in my office, in which ordinary people poured out their support for us and their disdain for the CTC and the Liberal government behind it. The newspapers' Letters to the Editor columns, especially in Western Canada, were awash with comments such as:

I know that once Wardair is forced out of business the People's Airline will make sure that no other airline such as Wardair will be allowed to start up again and private passengers such as myself will be left to the tender mercy of Air Canada. Monopoly corrupts and absolute monopoly corrupts absolutely!

To this day, I've heard Trust Account ruling referred to in the airline business as "the ruling that was designed to put Wardair out of business."

During this stressful period, I received a number of very touching letters, including one from an elderly lady who wrote that she and her husband managed to take a trip to England only because of the lower charter fares. She said that though they were retired and didn't have too much money, they had managed to save two thousand dollars, and would it be any use to us in the present situation?

There was not much we could do but swallow our pride and hasten to meet the unreasonable demands laid on us. Accordingly, we arranged for our insurance underwriters to go before the Air Transport Committee to explain, yet again, the arrangements that had been put in place to ensure our continued existence, and we arranged for an expensive blanket insurance policy that would cover anyone who flew with us, to an amount of fifteen thousand dollars, to ensure that he or she would be able to get home again. Imagine our astonishment when we received a message from one of the CTC commissioners, to whom the ATC reported, informing us that he was "too busy" to meet with us, and that an oral presentation by our underwriters was refused.

Tom Spalding fired off a blistering telex to J. R. Belcher, the Committee Chairman, in which he said, among other things, "we can come to no other conclusion except to believe it is the intention of the committee to delay this matter beyond a point of no return."

We finally got our meeting, on January 29, two weeks before the original deadline, and the CTC accepted that the insurance satisfied their demands for a guarantee that we would be able to meet our obligations. The President of the CTC always referred to that as a financial guarantee against Wardair's bankruptcy, and was floored that we could get such a coverage. There was no more talk whatever about the trust fund.

The end result of the whole episode was simply to increase our costs of doing business without having the slightest effect on the financial security or otherwise of the consumer.

We had been brought to heel.

CHAPTER 18

▼

Flying High While Dragging Our Feet

By the early 1970s, I was spending more than half of my time running from pillar to post to try to keep up with the various regulatory rulings the CTC kept showering upon us. I finally lost track of the number of times they threatened us with suspension. We were buying new aircraft, trying new marketing approaches, and doing our best to keep up a standard of service far above other carriers; we certainly didn't need the hassles that were constantly our lot in life. I therefore concluded, after the trust account incident, that I was never going to be able to operate on my own. I had already set the wheels in motion to purchase a Boeing 747 Jumbo Jet, with a price tag of twenty-five million dollars U.S.; if we got hit with another crisis in the midst of that purchase, we would go under.

I contacted Claude Taylor, then President (and later Chairman) at Air Canada, and he set up a meeting with Ralph Vaughan, who was both a senior official with Air Canada and a director of the CNR. We met in the Place

Ville Marie in Montreal, and I proposed to them that Air Canada might be interested in buying into Wardair, and we would become, in effect, the charter arm of the national airline. They were very much interested. Air Canada had a number of advantages over us in the handling of charters, the most obvious one being that it could shuffle various aircraft back and forth between its scheduled routes and the charters to make the best possible use of them, but it was an undeniable fact that customers preferred to fly with Wardair, and Air Canada knew it.

The talks went on – and on and on – until we seemed to be ready to strike a deal. During one of my visits to Montreal, I ran into one of the top men from the CTC, who let me know that such a merger would have approval from the government, and from the Air Transport Committee, but of course there would have to be a public hearing before anything was concluded.

Complications set in, as is usually the case in anything that involves a government body. Word got out that Air Canada was planning to transfer the 747s it already had on order to the Wardair charter operation. A spokesperson for the Canadian Airline Pilots' Association announced that, if they did that, there would be a picket line around the Air Canada headquarters the very next morning. To be captain of a 747 in those days was to be a god; there was no way they were going to let this two-bit charter operation get control of the most prestigious jobs in the business.

A public hearing was finally held, and the Consumers' Association of Canada filed an objection to the merger, on the grounds that it would lessen competition (of course it would; that was why it would have been approved by the CTC). The other airlines objected, and politicians on all sides got into the act – 1972 was an election year. So the CTC did what it has always done best, and sat on its hands, without making any decision whatever, while 1972 turned into 1973. We received the 747 we had purchased, and we were no further ahead with our talks than we had ever been.

I began to wonder if a merger would work, anyway. The Air Canada people were very nice to me, and pleasant to deal with, but every now and then something would happen that would drive it home to me that we came from the other side of the tracks. After one of our meetings in Place Ville Marie, I strolled over to the railway station in the basement of the Queen Elizabeth Hotel with Ralph Vaughan, who was taking the train back to his home on the East Coast. Waiting for him in the railway station was his own sumptuously appointed private railway car.

The deal that was eventually structured had been much improved along the way, for both sides, by Yves Pratt, who was a shrewd and knowledgeable lawyer and, at that time, Air Canada's Chairman. It would have given Air Canada one third of the shares in Wardair, with an option to purchase another third. The price offered, by the way, for effective control of Wardair, was $2.7 million, or about 10 per cent of the cost of one 747.

I have no idea how this joint-ownership arrangement would have worked had it gone through. Perhaps at this time my offer to sell out was more a signal of frustration than a serious attempt to get out of the business. I had made one earlier attempt to sell Wardair – to CP Air, when Jack Gilmour was running the airline, after Grant McConachie's death. Gilmour was very enthusiastic, and took the deal to Ian Sinclair, then the Chairman and Chief Operating Officer of Canadian Pacific. Sinclair was not sympathetic to the idea.

John Hamilton, representing CP Air at many of the hearings I was forced to attend, once claimed that "every time Max Ward gets into trouble, there is a deal cooking off-stage with CP, and as soon as he gets out of trouble, the stove gets turned off." There was a certain amount of truth to the statement.

What turned the stove off on the Air Canada deal, besides the constant delays, was the impact of the new changes in regulations that Jack Pickersgill had agreed to. With the passing of the affinity charters and their replacement with Advanced Booking Charters (ABCs), followed by the introduction of new, better, faster (and more expensive) jets, I became convinced, once more, that I could make it on my own, and I wrote a letter to Air Canada, withdrawing from all future negotiations.

My motto went from "If you can't lick 'em, join 'em," to "If you can't join 'em, lick 'em," and we proceeded to do just that.

Nothing gave me more pleasure, during all this hectic time, than to get away from the hearings and the regulations and the controversies, and go out and buy a new airplane. I have always loved machinery, and to me the airplane is the epitome of what can be accomplished by the human mind and hand. Every time we added to our fleet, I used to say, "They're so nice, it's too bad we have to use them," but when I got the bill, I soon changed my mind.

We had been the first in Canada to put a Boeing jetliner into service – the 727. Then we had moved upscale to the 707, in 1968. I had had our first 707 christened the C. H. "Punch" Dickins, for the most famous of our early bush pilots, and the second christened the W. R. "Wop" May, for another famous bush pilot, a year later. There was a reception at the Boeing plant when we took over the 707, and a plant tour. The highlight of this tour was a mock-up of the 747 Jumbo Jet, which was just then coming on line. The side of the mock-up was emblazoned with the names of all the airlines that had signed up to buy this machine, starting with Pan Am. Then there was a tiny sticker with the word "Wardair" hopefully displayed. We hoped so, too.

The 707 took us to the forefront of charter operations. Powered by four Pratt and Whitney engines, it could hold 183 passengers, could cruise at 560 mph, and had a range of 6,000 miles. It was the *"Punch" Dickins* that set a range record on October 7, 1972, making the first non-stop flight between Honolulu, Hawaii, and London's Gatwick airport, a distance of 7,746 statute miles, in an air time of 13 hours and 49 minutes. The crew was made up of Captain Dean Ostrander, First Officer Wim Wolfe, Flight Engineer Art Lockwood, and Navigator Lloyd Pinder.

We took delivery of our first 747, the *Phil Garratt*, on April 23, 1973, at Seattle, in a blaze of glory and with another great party. At that party, I announced, proudly, that this was, so far as I knew, the first major aircraft purchase funded entirely in Canada. We had also found a little Fox Moth, just like my original, and Guenther Moellenbeck and his great crew had rebuilt it so that it flew again, and we trucked it down for the ceremony. Its call letters were CF-DJB; the 747 had the call letters CF-DJC, which were the call letters of my original Fox Moth in 1946. After the ceremony, the little Moth went back to Edmonton, and one of our pilots, Garth Martin, flew it on to Toronto. Later, during Aviation Week at the Canadian National Exhibition, it crashed into Lake Ontario. We were very lucky that the pilot and his passenger were only injured, not killed. But with whatever pieces we could salvage or make, and with parts of Fox Moths from all over the country, our engineers in Toronto put together another one for us. Paramount in that effort were Kenny Allen, George Benedik, and Dan McNiven. Hans Peuker built the complicated wooden fuselage. After Wardair was sold, I donated it to the National Aviation Museum in Ottawa. On May 10, 1989, at the former Wardair hangar in Toronto, George Neal climbed into the pilot's seat, accompanied by Doug Weaver as passenger. I swung the prop, and the little Moth climbed easily into the blue just as one of our Boeing 747s rose majestically into the sky from another part of the field. As Marjorie and I watched the two aircraft, we knew at last that Wardair was really gone. It took us a long time to say goodbye – if, in fact, we ever have.

The 747 was an aircraft that was worth a good deal more, at $25 million U.S., than the entire Wardair company. The largest airplane ever designed for commercial service, it could carry 455 passengers, cruise at 41,000 feet, fly 6,000 miles non-stop, and, if you could keep it full, make a great deal of money. It was also a beautiful machine, and I loved it.

Heretofore we had filled our jets with brightly coloured seats. Now we extended the colours to the wall panels as well, starting with the 747. Gone were grey or beige or neutral shades. In their places were sections in orange, yellow, blue, turquoise, and hot pink. The colours gave the aircraft a holiday air that was recognized by our passengers the minute they stepped aboard. We discovered an interesting phenomenon with the redecorated plane – the orange section always had the best and noisiest "party" going on in it!

A year and a half later, on December 12, 1974, we took delivery of our second 747, which we named for a French-Canadian bush pilot, the *Romeo Vachon*. Now we had been twelve years in the marketplace with low-cost charter fares.

Two crucial things had been happening during those years from 1962 to 1974. First, the charter market was expanding by leaps and bounds. A huge market that had not, hitherto, been able to consider air travel discovered the low-cost charter carrier. Second, the scheduled carriers became aware of this new wave and were moving more and more into the charter carriers' market, while government regulations completely protected their own scheduled market from the charter carriers. The scheduled carriers were able to cross-subsidize their low charter airfares with high-yield business airfares on the same flight. To the scheduled carriers, it didn't matter that the charter fares provided only an incremental revenue, as long as they covered their direct operating costs, and thus contributed to overhead. And, because they could subsidize the low fare, the scheduled carriers could control and depress the charter fare in an attempt to prevent the charter carriers from operating profitably. This they did.

But, as time went on, I thought I could foresee something positive glimmering on the horizon. The price spread between scheduled and charter fares grew larger and larger as our competitors continued to increase their scheduled fares while depressing their charter fares. I felt strongly that, as the percentage of charter passengers flying on scheduled airlines increased, these airlines would be forced to increase their charter airfares somewhat, as they became an increasingly significant part of their traffic.

I decided to thrust ahead with a fleet expansion, predicated on this philosophy, and ordered two Boeing 747s and two McDonnell–Douglas DC-10s. This would expand our fleet to four 747s to service the larger markets, while the DC-10s would serve the smaller markets that could not support a 455-seat aircraft.

Freddy Laker had just begun to operate on the North Atlantic route to Canada with Laker Airways, at the same time as other operators were springing up with "no frills," cheap charter flights. (Freddy received a knighthood before he went bankrupt, and I acknowledged this with a telegram in which I asked him, "Good God, does this mean I have to call you Sir?" Freddy replied, "Not even God would ask you to call me Sir.")

With all of this charter capacity on the North Atlantic, I felt we could eventually establish the market price for charter airfares at a remunerative level, that we would be able to move the prices up to a point where we were actually making money. This technique worked only to a degree. Unfortunately, the fares did not move up enough for us to create the financial resources we needed to enable us to continue operating the latest-model airliners.

With our four new aircraft, delivered between 1975 and the end of 1978, we had become a dominant force in the international charter market, but the scheduled airlines continued to increase economy and first-class airfares, leaving the fares that competed with charter carriers low. They had no intention of living with charter airlines, and the Canadian government continued to condone this position. The scheduled carriers had access to our markets, but government regulations prohibited us from operating in theirs.

We were now carrying more than a million passengers annually, flying nearly four billion passenger-miles, employing more than 2,000 people, and bringing in revenues of more than $250 million. That was the good news; the bad news was that we had operating losses of over $6 million in 1978 and nearly $11 million in 1979; we only balanced the books by buying and selling aircraft wisely. It must be pointed out that, unlike our competitors, we had no government-guaranteed loans with low interest rates. Our interest expenses were very high, as we could get only short-term loans. We had to purchase our aircraft – not lease them – in order to realize the appreciation on our equipment to remain in business. In other words, we had to squeeze profit from every available source to compete at the extremely low per-passenger-seat-mile yields in the single market to which we were restricted. We weren't horse-traders, we were plane-traders, and we had to be good at it to stay in business.

Still, we were making progress; certainly our market share had improved, and if we could hold on long enough to get into the scheduled-airline business, the $250-million gamble might just pay off. Just about the time I was starting to congratulate myself on my shrewdness, a DC-10 owned by American Airlines shed an engine at Chicago, on May 29, 1979, and 273 people died in the crash. We were shocked and upset, as anyone is by such a tragedy, but we did not expect any immediate repercussions on our operation, because we were flying brand-new aircraft with a later-model power-plant. We were instructed to conduct inspections on our machines, we did so, and they passed with flying colours. Then the Civil Aeronautics Board issued a directive from Washington, grounding all DC-10s until further notice.

Once again, it was panic time. We were right into the summer North Atlantic season. All our aircraft were booked on tight schedules, and we had to scramble to move everyone on the 747s. The juggling involved setting up a shuttle service between airports in Europe and Canada. A 747 would land in London and have to be turned around and headed back to Canada within an hour. It was sheer chaos for the ground personnel, but they worked magnificently, and we met every one of our obligations to our passengers. Our London station manager, Derrick Galpin, told me that he saw our 747s head out for Canada when he started his shift, and then come back, reload, and be off again before he ended it.

The grounding order was in force for twenty-five days, from June 5 to June 30, 1979, and, on the first flight after it was lifted, I thought I had better go along to quiet any fears among the passengers that might arise. It was a flight from Toronto to London, and when I got to the check-in desk at Toronto, there were the TV cameras and the interviewers, trying to scare the daylights out of our passengers. One man, bless him, said that he didn't know about the technical aspects of the DC-10, but "if Wardair is flying them again, that's good enough for me."

I noticed one elderly woman who seemed to be very reluctant to board the aircraft, although she wasn't saying anything much, so I went over and told her all about the aircraft, and what a safe plane it was. She looked at me and said, "Oh, is this a DC-10? I don't care about that, I'm just afraid of flying, period."

I persuaded her to come along, and I hope she had a good time.

It turned out after an investigation that the problem with the DC-10 was not in the design of the aircraft at all. The bolts attaching the engine to the pylon had been incorrectly installed on the Chicago jet, and after a certain amount of use, they gave way and the engine fell off. The solution was a replacement bolt that could not possibly be put in wrong.

The DC-10 gained an undeserved reputation as an unsafe aircraft, because of a number of incidents, but the only fatal accident attributable to the design of the airplane itself occurred very early on, on a Turkish airline, when a door flew off one of the first models. In our own experience, the DC-10 was about the most reliable aircraft we had.

Incidentally, the popular engine on the DC-10 was the General Electric CF6-50, and the popular power-plant on the Boeing 747 at that time was the Pratt and Whitney. We decided to standardize both types of aircraft with the GE CF6-50. By doing so, we introduced the General Electric power-plant to Canada, and it turned out to be an excellent decision, as its reliability even exceeded our expectations. Negotiating for the engine type was certainly an interesting exercise and there was, of course, much disappointment at Pratt and Whitney to see the GE engine entering the Canadian marketplace for the first time. Pratt and Whitney power-plants are excellent, and gave us good service on our first two 747s, but at the time we purchased the four additional aircraft, we felt the General Electric was a little ahead in the state of the art. And a wonderful art it is.

*

Now that we were, during these years of the late 1970s, at last assembling the aircraft we needed, I realized that the next step was to get better control of the package holidays that were a large part of what attracted many of our customers.

Hawaii was a favourite destination for Canadians, especially Westerners. We had a superb staff at the Honolulu airport, headed by Cheryl Lavoie, an engaging, practical, but compassionate woman who served Wardair's passengers for twenty-five years. Two of her unforgettable ground hostesses were Mercedes "Mercy" Hinokawa and Yvonne Boissoneau. I hope they are still greeting passengers. For kindness and caring, these three smiling women were top of the line, and literally hundreds of passengers benefited, in times of perplexity or genuine trouble, from their care. When I think of Hawaii, I cannot help but remember all the wonderful workers there – Gary Aoki, Phil Gard, Julie, Peli, Clarence, and many, many others.

We were soon flying sixteen Boeing 747 trips a week to Hawaii, but we often heard that our customers, once they got to their hotels in Hawaii, were not happy with the accommodation; the prices were too high, or the rooms were dirty, or the food was inedible. We couldn't control this, because we were not allowed to market these packages ourselves – we had to work through tour companies – and yet these details often ruined the trip for the customer. The "Inclusive Tour" charters we offered after the slight easing of the rules by Jack Pickersgill meant that we chartered the aircraft to a tour operator or package-holiday company. We would provide first-class air transportation, but some of these operators scraped a living by carving something off the airline ticket and something out of the hotel package, with the result that the accommodations were, on many occasions, not up to the standard of the flight. To put it bluntly, sometimes the customer would be wafted to a place in the sun in surroundings of pleasurable comfort, only to wind up in a flea-bag hotel with lousy food. Not surprisingly, we came in for criticism for something we couldn't, by CTC decree, control.

For years, I tried to persuade the Air Transport Board, and then the Air Transport Committee of the CTC, that the world would not come to an end if we sold and ran our own package tours, but my arguments were always in vain. We therefore bankrolled a company called Fun Seekers, to operate as a tour company on our behalf, and to ensure, we thought, that the customer would get a good deal. We put up the money, but did not control it. Fun Seekers was run by two individuals who quickly worked out that, since we were picking up all the bills, there was no need for them to stint themselves on expenses. I remember, sometimes, signing their tabs and wishing I could afford to live the way they did, at my expense. In the end, we had to bring Fun Seekers to a halt before it did the same to us. I decided to go ahead and incorporate International Vacations Limited – Intervac – as a direct subsidiary of Wardair and have it take over the role of the outside tour operator, but under our control.

The ATC soon put a stop to that: "Certainly it was never contemplated that a carrier be involved in any way in the sale of its own ABC tickets," the Committee huffed, so we were back to square one again, booking inclusive tours through outside operators. One of the other restrictions on the inclusive tour was that the tour price could not be lower than 115 per cent of the lowest scheduled airline fare to the destination. Once again, the regulations were not to benefit the consumer, but to protect the scheduled carriers.

We tried to give the customer an incentive by offering a credit of forty-eight dollars to people who took one of our packages to Barbados, the forty-eight dollars to be applied not to the hotel accommodation but to add-on services only, such as a meal or drinks or the rental of a bike. To protect ourselves further, we made it a rule that the customer could not get the money back; he had to use the credit right there in the hotel, or lose it.

The ATC immediately glommed on to the important fact that the customer was likely, if we persisted in this course of action, to get a break:

> WHEREAS the Committee is of the opinion that notwithstanding the fact that the bonus cannot be refunded, that the Licensee is in effect offering Inclusive Tour transportation at an Inclusive Tour price below 115% of the lowest scheduled unit toll return fare available contrary to Sections 41(b) and 41(e) of the Air Carrier Regulations. . . . IT IS ORDERED THAT:
> Wardair Canada Ltd. is hereby directed to cease and desist from offering a hotel bonus.

The complaint that launched this was filed by Air Canada, the scheduled carrier to Barbados.

So that was that. The Committee was vigilantly on guard against any attempt to aid the consumer, whether the dirty deed was done by us or by one of the outside operators.

An inclusive-tour firm called Elkin Tours, which operated out of Detroit, chartered a great many of our aircraft from time to time. We didn't own Elkin, or any part of it, and it was not subject to the directions of the ATC, but we were threatened with closure because Elkin had done something wrong. Elkin, the ATC had discovered, was running ads in the Detroit newspapers that offered tours at less than 115 per cent of the return scheduled airfare from Windsor, Ontario, to Acapulco. We had nothing to do with these ads; we didn't even know about them, in fact, until one of the other airlines spotted them and laid a complaint before the ATC. We were forthwith directed "to show cause why approvals for flights . . . issued to Wardair in conjunction with Elkin Tours Limited . . . should not be cancelled."

We, of course, went to Elkin and told them to stop being so nice to the customer; Elkin jacked up its prices, pocketed the money, and the ATC lifted the ban. Thus Canada's aviation regulators struck another blow for the air industry. We resolved to be even more careful in the future, but it didn't do us any good.

Skylark Holidays, like Elkin one of the tour operators, produced a brochure, a copy of which was sent to us, that offered a free ticket to any "group leader" who would organize a charter trip. The ABC regulations at that time allowed you to give a free ride to a "tour conductor." Skylark took the position that a "group leader" and a "tour conductor" were basically the same thing, although there was the crucial difference that a tour conductor was not charged with filling up the aircraft and a group leader apparently was. This made us nervous, given the past conduct of the ATC, so we wrote to Skylark and got from them a written assurance that henceforth "No person described as a 'group leader' will be carried free of charge."

We thought the matter was closed, but Skylark then went ahead and gave free flights to group leaders, by renaming them tour conductors; the other airlines spotted the ads and went running to the ATC, which came down on us like a ton of bricks. I very quickly got one of those famous "do-it-or-we'll-put-you-out-of-business" directives that read: "Wardair Canada Ltd. is hereby directed to ensure that Skylark Holidays Ltd. cease and desist from such advertisements."

It was no use pointing out that we didn't own or control Skylark, or that the whole thing could have been avoided by letting us run the tours ourselves. Nor did it do any good to ask, "What the hell has this got to do with air transport?" which is what the ATC was supposed to be about.

An editorial in the *Globe and Mail* on May 10, 1973, put the point nicely:

> Passenger convenience is of no moment to Ottawa. Neither is the passenger's purse. The national airlines and the Government of Canada, with the assistance of their international conspirators, maintain costs of travel for Canadians that make no sense at all, unless it is sense to pour the money of individuals into Air Canada coffers.
>
> Incredibly, it is possible for a Canadian to buy a round-trip charter ticket to London from Toronto, and a round-trip charter ticket to Toronto from London, throw the return portion of each away, and still pay less than the single economy return.

The move from "affinity" charters (the six-month club regulation) to Advance Booking Charters (ABCs) relieved charter carriers of a senseless, unworkable burden, but there were still many regulations the charter carriers faced that did not apply to the scheduled carriers who, as mentioned, were rapidly getting into the charter market:

We could not carry passengers with Inclusive Fare Tickets (ITCs) and those with ABCs on the same flight. Why not? Fear of contamination, I guess. The scheduled airline could.

We couldn't even carry British passengers and Canadian passengers on the same flight, because all passengers had to have the same point of origin. This was not a problem for the scheduled airlines.

We couldn't sell a one-week charter to Hawaii, although our scheduled competitors could. (Fortunately, most of our passengers loved Hawaii and found it no great hardship to stay longer than one week.)

We had to use a tour operator such as Elkin to charter our aircraft; then they sold the seats. Scheduled carriers could book in any way they wished.

We could not carry cargo, although we had all the capacity, desire, and ability to do so. Our competitors, of course, could.

In addition, there were harassments that we never could understand. We took a charter flight from Vancouver to London, England, and, so far as we know, everything went splendidly. Then, after our return to Canada, I came in to work one day to find one of those heart-stopping notices from the CTC. There had been, the bureaucrats noted, an "infraction" during this flight. We had, somehow, it seemed, run afoul of one or another regulation in the skein that now surrounded us. We would therefore have to write to each and every person on the charter and inform him or her that, because of this infraction, they were entitled to receive back from us the money spent on the return portion of the flight. Or, to put it another way, they were to get half their fares back, courtesy of the CTC but paid by Wardair. We sent out the letters, and received back exactly one demand for a refund. I telephoned the man who wrote us and asked him if he was happy with the flight.

"It was great," he said, "really great."

Then why did he think he should get half his money back?

"Those are the breaks," he said. We sent him back the money. I always regarded it as a testament to the airline that so many other passengers simply ignored this opportunity to collect from us.

Governments, not only in Canada, but elsewhere in the world, had funded and given their airlines a mandate to provide a network of scheduled flight services that had not anticipated, and could not handle, the demand for low-cost charter seats. They had no real understanding of the transportation market.

For years, Canadians were told that it was the leadership of Air Canada, and Air Canada's willingness to serve the hinterland, that had built up air transport in this country. Open Air Canada to competition, the argument ran, and all will be lost. Untrue.

However, the public sorted the matter down to the basics – low airfares. They knew only that it cost less to fly to Europe and back than it cost to fly from Western Canada to Eastern Canada. The public wanted and needed two types of services – scheduled services *and* charter services, because this worked for *them*. But the government placed its vested interest in a national airline ahead of the public need, and continually blocked the possibility of charter carriers surviving.

The success of the government policy was, of course, predicated upon refusing charter carriers access to the scheduled-airfare-paying passenger. Had we been allowed to compete head-to-head during the formative years of the aviation industry, certainly the private sector's necessity to operate efficiently would have put them in control of the industry. But the net result of discriminatory government regulations was that in one year alone, 1978, we flew nearly 44,000 empty round-trip seats between Canada and the United Kingdom, while, at the airports, passengers waited for charter seats on scheduled carriers.

We could no longer go on like this; we knew Wardair must either be allowed to change its mode of operation to that of a scheduled carrier to compete, or go out of business.

How ironic it is that today, in the spring of 1991, as I read newspapers and articles discussing open skies between U.S. and Canadian carriers, the term "level playing field" appears again and again. And I think how different this story would be if the federal government had permitted Wardair to compete on a fair and "level playing field."

CHAPTER 19

▼

Amazing Maz

The scheme to eliminate charter airlines was obvious back in 1977, but Transport Canada (as the MOT now calls itself) persisted in pretending there was no change in the competitive status between scheduled and charter carriers. In the United States, matters went quite differently. There, the government recognized that what was happening posed a threat to the very operators who had, by building up the charter business, brought down airfares. Let the competition be carried out on an equal basis, the Americans said, and the result was the Airline Deregulation Act of 1977. It was introduced with a statement that said the government "was not going to sit back and allow those airlines that provided low cost air transportation to the American public to be destroyed."

In Britain, too, the charter airlines operating on the North Atlantic route were authorized to conduct scheduled airline services – except to Canada, of course.

But there was no relief for the Canadian charter carrier.

In August 1978, I wrote, rather desperately, to Prime Minister Pierre Trudeau, to point out that deregulation had arrived in the United States and was bound to have an impact on our competitiveness in the international sphere. In Canada, we had grown to be the nation's third largest air carrier, and we had served the consumer by bringing travel to Europe, the Caribbean, Mexico, Hawaii, and other U.S. points within reach of ordinary Canadians, not merely the rich.

In response, I pointed out, we were treated as a threat to the national carriers, a blot on the national escutcheon, a danger to the public weal. We had put $250 million into expanding our fleet, had introduced a computer passenger-reservations system, and had expanded, upgraded, and staffed airport handling facilities all along our routes to meet intense scheduled-airline competition for the charter passenger – without one cent of government money.

While Air Canada and CP Air could charge the customer twice as much per passenger-mile on domestic routes as on routes where they faced competition, and could use the money gained thereby to subsidize fares on the North Atlantic that were far below their cost of providing the service, we had no such government-furnished cushion to fall back on. In a transportation world that was changing with bewildering speed, we could not continue without the flexibility that had been accorded to charter carriers in other countries, I told the Prime Minister. I begged him to direct the CTC to loosen the rules that were binding us, and I asked, not for the first time, that Wardair be designated Canada's third international scheduled carrier. I knew the charter business would not sustain, over the long run, the kinds of investments in aircraft that we were going to have to make; we needed the steady income of scheduled services to compete with British Airways, KLM, Swissair, and the other international carriers who were moving ever more successfully into the

North Atlantic charter traffic. If we could not have any scheduled routes within our own country – and the Air Transport Committee seemed to have made it clear that we could not – we ought at least to be able to compete on the international scene.

On September 5, the Minister of Transport, Otto Lang (one of the many problems of dealing with transport policy matters in this country is that we seem to change ministers as often as some people change socks), as if in answer to my prayer, announced that the department was implementing a new series of regulations aimed at increasing competition and opening up the air industry to global changes, which included increasing deregulation. They were not the changes I wanted, needed, and had asked for, but at least they would be something, a start.

And absolutely nothing happened. The Air Transport Committee of the Canadian Transport Commission declined to take any action whatever on the new policy. In fact, it was not until May 16, 1979, that the CTC even moved to consider implementation of some of the changes in Lang's policy paper, and very little came of that.

I couldn't believe it. Didn't politicians make the rules and bureaucrats follow them? Didn't responsible ministers lay down the fundamental policy for implementation by the hired professionals? Were we entirely at the mercy of the bureaucrats? The answers to these questions are No, No, and Yes.

The Chairman of the ATC had the answer to our problems; he said that if we were finding the going rough, we ought to sell off some of our aircraft. At the time, we were projecting a load factor of 80 per cent, which was a lot better than Air Canada was doing, and we had not, like the national airline, had to have the government swallow our debt.

The Chairman's comments so incensed me that I made a speech in Toronto in which I said, "Power and authority do weird things to some people." I was not gaining a reputation for diplomacy, but I figured I had nothing to lose by being frank.

I was willing to admit, I said in that same speech, that there was no longer a role for a charter airline of Wardair's size and with late-model aircraft in the modern aviation scene – that was precisely why I had been pressing for years for a scheduled service. We were already, I noted, scheduling our aircraft a year in advance, but we couldn't advertise our charters because the ATC was constantly finding "phoney methods to delay our programs," so we never knew if a given flight would ever take off.

The problems we were running into had nothing to do with our capacity to operate an airline; rather, they arose from the fact that the same body that was responsible for governing the air regulations had a conflicting interest, which was to look after the well-being of the state airline. No wonder the rules were slanted against us. I went on: "The roots of Canadian government air transport policy are so deeply entrenched in government bureaucracy that I question if there will be a politician strong enough to uproot that bureaucracy."

I didn't know it at the time, but there was a politician strong enough, if not to uproot the bureaucracy, at least to stir them up with the end of his stick – Donald Frank Mazankowski, a dark-haired, good-looking man with a friendly smile, a firm handshake, and, it would develop, an iron will. He showed me how a single individual can prevail and carry out his convictions, and what that can mean to a nation's industry.

It was not my letter to the Prime Minister that had unleashed the feeble and doomed policy paper that Otto Lang laid on the mat in September 1978, as I realized when I finally – four and a half months later – got a letter from him, in response to my August missive. Lang rejected out of hand the notion that Wardair might become an international scheduled carrier. If he were to allow that, the effect would be "to replace Air Canada and CP Air" in these markets – a tacit acknowledgement that, in any straight competition, we would win out. He told us to tend to our knitting: "Look to the charter market (with prospects of a somewhat looser regulatory regime) for the increased traffic you desire."

I wrote back, citing the harassment that was hindering the development of our summer marketing plan for 1979 – the ATC continued to shower us with "show cause" orders in a way that, I told Otto Lang, "saps all our managerial strengths and is unbelievably costly to this company."

I also noted that British Airways was pushing to establish a scheduled airline service between the United Kingdom and Western Canada, a market we had spent fifteen years developing, and I suggested that, if the government were going to give in to this request, they ought to demand, in return, a similar entrée for Wardair into Britain – a suggestion I had made before, and which had gone over like a lead balloon.

I didn't hear back from the minister this time. The May 22, 1979, election intervened a mere four months later, before he had had a chance to gather his thoughts. That election produced a minority Progressive Conservative government, a new Prime Minister, Joe Clark, and a new Minister of Transport, Don Mazankowski, of Vegreville, Alberta. My heart leapt up; Mazankowski is a businessman (very few Ministers of Transport have had any working knowledge of business), and a confessed proponent of deregulation. I would get a sympathetic hearing, at last.

I went to see Don Mazankowski in September, explained my philosophy, and said I needed freedom to operate and sell my services to the Canadian public. His simple response was: "I have no trouble with that."

When I dragged myself up from the floor, because I had never heard anything like that in an office in Ottawa in all my career, I raised with him the complaint that I had been making, with drum-beat regularity, before the Air Transport Committee. Air Canada and CP Air were both allowed to mix charter and scheduled passengers on the same aircraft for the same flight (a process which has given us "Charter Class Fares"), while every one of our passengers had to go through the thirty-day waiting period laid down by the Advanced Booking Charter rules. They had simply invaded the charter territory, skated around the rules, and got away with it.

In fact, British Airways were doing the same thing, filling up their scheduled flights to North America with charter passengers, a process that allowed them to offer charter-class fares to top up their revenues on any given flight. This was not the open competition I had been calling for, it was a rigging of the rules, once more, for the benefit of the scheduled carriers, whether Canadian or foreign.

I did not ask the minister for any special favours, but I did ask him to put us on the same footing as our rivals, at least to a degree. Let us sell up to one third of our seats on a first-come-first-served basis, without the waiting period, I asked. We would "top up" our charter flights the same way our competitors could top up their scheduled flights, and we would charge the latecomers a higher rate, to accomplish the same end (higher per-flight revenue).

There was a great deal of concern about energy conservation at this time – the second of the world's two oil-crunch crises occurred in 1979 – and it made little sense for us to be flying with aircraft half empty because of the bizarre rules laid down in a pre-crisis world.

The minister was clearly sympathetic, but the officials in the Canadian Transport Commission were not. The CTC was going through the process of rewriting the Air Carrier

Regulations, in order to try to catch up to the rapidly changing world of air transport. When their proposals were released, in early November, they made no mention whatever of the topping-up proposal, and Mazankowski, in a press conference at the time, made a direct reference to the omission, when he said:

> We have a situation where scheduled carriers probably invaded the fertile ground of the charter carriers, both international and domestic. So you have scheduled carriers providing both types of services. What is unfair is that the charter operator does not receive a similar *quid pro quo*. I am not sure that the new policy of the CTC will address that.

That hint ought to have been enough, in a parliamentary system where the politicians, supposedly, direct, and the bureaucrats respond, to cause some redrafting of the proposals, but the CTC paid not the slightest heed, either to this, or to another issue I had raised with Don Mazankowski.

I had asked to be allowed to carry freight, to make the best use of our aircraft, and I had been blocked by the regulations that said we couldn't carry freight in the same aircraft – let alone on the same flight – as passengers. Even an empty passenger plane could not be used for freight. If the world was running short of oil, as the newspaper headlines kept shrieking, what was the sense of such rules? We often had excess capacity in our cargo holds, and we knew the shipping companies were complaining that they couldn't move air-freight when they wanted to, but all of us were bound by the same outmoded rules. The rationale was perfectly straightforward. If we were allowed to carry cargo, it would undermine the cargo market for Air Canada and CP Air. In a sane world, that was no rationale whatever, but even in our bureaucratic madhouse it made no sense, as I demonstrated. Pan Am had started an air-truck service from Montreal and Toronto to Kennedy Airport in New York, precisely because air-freight customers couldn't get their goods moved out of the Canadian cities by the Canadian carriers. There was no threat to the scheduled carriers. They couldn't even handle the business they had. The policy was a waste of energy, of money, and of carrying capacity, and I said so as forcefully as I could to the minister.

The minister directed the bureaucrats to address this issue "without undue delay" on November 5, 1979.

When the new air regulations devised by the CTC were promulgated on December 5, 1979, the air-freight issue was completely ignored, and the topping-off question was met with a solution that betrayed either profound ignorance or a lack of good faith on the part of the Committee. One solution offered was to eliminate the requirement for advance booking on flights taking off between 10:00 P.M. and 5:00 A.M. At this time, as the Committee should have known, there was an unofficial curfew on late-night flights and landings at Vancouver airport and an official ban on such flights between 11:00 P.M. and 7:00 A.M. in Toronto. We were being given one hour per day in which to operate competitively – if we could get our flights in and out within that hour.

I became truly alarmed when I saw the new regulations. We had shown a loss on operations for seven years in a row, keeping afloat by our shrewd trading in aircraft; there was no way of knowing how much longer we could survive if we didn't begin to see some change in the regulatory environment. I had been banking heavily on the fact that we had a new government with a different approach to regulation and a new minister whose heart was obviously in the right place. If he couldn't change anything, because of the entrenched views of the established bureaucracy, Wardair was headed for bankruptcy. I wrote to the minister early in 1980 to tell him that, unless something was done quickly, we would be in desperate trouble. I did not need to spell out, to a Western politician, that our demise would not be well received in Western Canada.

I laid two proposals before him. I had learned at least enough about politics to know that you must present the relevant authority with options.

The first was a suggestion that Wardair be allowed to operate a scheduled carrier service from Western Canada to the United Kingdom. I was not enthusiastic about this one.

The second suggestion was that charter carriers like us should be allowed to top-off up to one third of our loads with scheduled passengers on flights that either originated or terminated in Canada. I spelled this out in more detail than at other times, but it was essentially the same idea, with one addition. As part of what I called a "new charter concept," I proposed that charter carriers be allowed to sell empty seats at the last minute to stand-by passengers. They could go one way at less than the charter fare, but on the return, they would pay the same rate as the "top-off" passengers.

These suggestions were passed along by Don Mazankowski to the Ministry of Transport, where, predictably, they ran into stiff opposition. If either of these proposals was accepted, the bureaucrats wailed, it would "probably lead to strong demands for changes on the domestic side." (That was undoubtedly true, although it had nothing whatever to do with the merits or otherwise of my argument.) Moreover, the change would lead to a decrease in regular airfares (always to be avoided in the philosophy of the department), while allowing "discount airfares to go up." (Ditto.) The ministry's response did note that the Consumers' Association of

Canada, among others, was pushing for a relaxation of the rules as a way to bring down fares and stimulate domestic Canadian tourism, but its overall reaction was one of distaste.

What happened next was a lesson, I think, in what a determined politician can do if he refuses to be bulldozed by his own experts. The Conservatives, you will recall, lost a vote of confidence in the House of Commons on December 13, 1979, and an election was called for February 18. Now the Minister of Transport, who was heavily involved in the election campaign, would have to take time off to force through the Cabinet rule changes that were opposed by his own bureaucrats – bureaucrats who had won every battle on the regulatory front since the department was formed in 1936.

And he did it.

Two members of his personal staff, Jamie Burns and Fred Von Veh, had researched the issue and were strongly in favour of the changes I talked about. So, despite the continuing resistance of Ministry of Transport officials, the department was instructed to, and did, prepare a document for the Cabinet that would implement a new and more open regulatory regime. Four senior staffers at the department, in fact, worked long hours to prepare a detailed order-in-council to implement these changes, which was to be presented to Cabinet on February 1, 1980. Unfortunately, the minister could not attend that meeting, but he gave written instructions to a colleague to shepherd the order-in-council through the Cabinet.

They very nearly didn't make it. David Kilgour, the outspoken Conservative MP from Edmonton, has written in his book, *Uneasy Patriots: Western Canadians in Confederation*, that just before Cabinet met, Alain Desfosses, a career civil-servant who had worked for the Canadian Transport

Commission and was then seconded to the Privy Council Office, raised a number of technical objections to the working of the order-in-council. With Don Mazankowski away, the Cabinet was persuaded to remove the matter from consideration until a week later.

Within a couple of hours of the Cabinet meeting's adjournment, Kilgour notes, Alain Desfosses, the PCO official who had thrown up the roadblock, phoned the minister's office to ask that someone on his personal staff attend a meeting to propose an alternative solution to the difficulties besetting Wardair. This request was refused; the minister had made his views clear, and he wanted them dealt with by Cabinet, not by a collection of bureaucrats.

Don Mazankowski, out on the campaign trail, was furious when he found out that Prime Minister Clark had agreed to put off the passage of the order-in-council, although no one around the Cabinet table except a PCO official had had a word to say against it. According to Kilgour, the minister "expressed his vexation to the Prime Minister that night in a long distance call from Vancouver."

Then, again according to Kilgour (I knew nothing of these matters at the time), Alain Desfosses assembled a six-member interdepartmental group to draw up a new document for the Prime Minister. It purported to be a summation of the positions taken by ministers at the February 1 meeting, although it is hard to find any evidence that any positions were taken, or expressed, there. This new memo proposed to hoist the whole subject until after the election:

Ministers' preference was to reconsider the proposal at some later time on the basis of a thorough assessment of all its implications including its impact on the structure of the Canadian Air Transportation industry and on Canada's negotiating stand on bilateral air agreements.

This made it sound as if the Cabinet members had decided that the best thing to do was to cool it, but the key minister, Don Mazankowski, had never been consulted and didn't even know this memorandum existed until one of his staff turned up a copy by accident. Peter Thomson, a Mazankowski aide, had asked for copies of anything that had been received in writing from the department. He was handed a copy of Desfosses's group's memo, together with a note from Hans Lovink, Director of Domestic Policy/Air in the Ministry of Transport, in which Lovink said that he objected to a good deal of what Desfosses had to say but gave the memo his okay because he had not had any "negative response . . . from the Minister." Nor had he. The minister didn't even know the document existed. That was rectified about five minutes after Thomson got a look at his find, and Mazan-kowski, thoroughly roused, put his foot down.

A request to the MOT's legal writers to draw up a new order-in-council based on the Desfosses paper was quashed. In its place, the minister insisted that his original submission and order-in-council go before Cabinet on February 8, and that was done. The new rules were passed with no significant changes and were announced on February 13, five days before the federal election.

The charter rules were relaxed generally but, far more to my delight and astonishment, the order-in-council regulations allowed Wardair to enter the domestic market for the first time. We were allowed to fly charters between Canadian cities, subject to fourteen days' advance booking and a proviso that the traveller must stay over at least one Saturday night. There was also a rule that the charters could only operate between two of the three main regions of Canada (East, Central, and West), the effect of which was to freeze us out of the Toronto–Ottawa–Montreal triangle, Canada's most populous – and profitable – air-travel sector, which was not our charter market anyway.

After more than a decade of asking, we could now carry freight in the belly of our passenger aircraft, and the topping-off provisions that I had asked for on the international side were not only allowed, but extended to the home market. That is, up to one third of the seats on any given flight could be sold right up to the day of departure, as long as we charged more for them.

When the rules were promulgated, I told a press conference that they had "saved our souls," and that, without them, we would have been out of business within a few months.

Five days later, the Conservatives lost the general election, we had Pierre Elliott Trudeau for Prime Minister again, and the philosophy of government took an abrupt lurch backwards. However, from one point of view, it was too late; the entire industrial world had gone to a more deregulated environment, and the new rules, once in place, were not going to be removed (although I worried that they might be, and indeed a presentation was made by a scheduled carrier, calling on the new Liberal Minister of Transport to reverse the order-in-council).

Had the minister not pressed as vigorously as he did, and had his personal staff not been as diligent as they were, I have no doubt that the bureaucracy would have rung up yet another victory. It is interesting and significant that, when a journalist went after a spokesman for the CTC to get that agency's official response to the changes, he could get no comment whatever.

I was sorry to see the Tories go, but I believed that under the new and more open skies that Don Mazankowski had given us, we could hold our own, despite the best efforts of the CTC.

Once again, I was wrong.

CHAPTER 20

▼

The Crunch

We pitched into the domestic charter business just in time to run head on into an economic downturn, recession, readjustment – call it what you will – which represented the worst setback the nation had seen since the days of the Great Depression of the 1930s. The sharp rise in interest rates in 1980 and 1981 played havoc with our financing, since we had a lot of loans out on floating rates; and, at the same time, customers stayed home in droves.

We came through those years because Wardair continued to be the most efficient airline, person for person, pound for pound, dollar for dollar, mile for mile, in the country, as study after study has shown.

We were still confined to charter flights. The Air Canada customer could go whenever he or she chose; ours had to pre-book weeks in advance. The Air Canada customer could return when he or she wanted, and change his or her mind about it; ours were informed, by government regulation, as to when they could return. To add insult to injury, the rules said that the customer had to buy a round-trip ticket from us – we could sell no other kind – and I could never understand why Canadians did not rise up in their wrath against this obvious infringement of their freedom to choose. The truth is, I guess, that Canadians had either become so used to being told what to do by their governments that the spirit had gone out of them, or they had actually bought the line that it was in the public interest to pay high fares to travel with the government-designated scheduled airlines. We were still assigned the poorest gates at airports, were afraid to go into the largest national computer-reservations system (because our display would be relegated to the most insignificant spot), and were shut out of the federal government's central travel service, the largest single pool of air-travel funds in the nation.

Nevertheless, we were still operating the finest service available, with little touches that caused *Air International Magazine* to note, in its January 1984 issue, that "Wardair has earned a reputation that airlines many times its size might envy."

The magazine went on (this is the sort of thing that made some of the knocks worth bearing):

> Passengers receive a standard of service greatly superior to that commonly encountered in the economy-class cabins of long-haul scheduled carriers. Such things as a 34-in (86 cm) seat pitch, free headphones for in-flight music programmes, free bar service throughout most of the flight, and meals that always include a top quality steak cooked on board to passengers' preference and served on Royal Doulton porcelain, with linen-covered trays and stainless steel cutlery, all made it difficult to remember that all this was being provided at fares well below standard economy-class levels.

Old friends talk about old times. I'm in the cockpit of the reproduction of my Fox Moth, chatting with Phil Garratt. The occasion was the delivery of the first 747, named for Phil, in 1973. (Photo by George Hunter)

When we moved into Dash 7s, we lined up the Fox Moth in front of one, to show something of the changes wrought by four decades of aircraft design. That's the de Havilland hangar in Toronto in the background. (Photo by Terry Wildman, with permission of de Havilland Aircraft)

This is the Dash 7 hard at work, during the Lorex expedition in 1979, when it made nineteen trips – I guess you could call them "Dashes" – to the North Pole. (Photo by George Hunter)

My son Kim loves flying almost as much as I do, and here he is atop our Bristol Freighter in 1979. The moustache has gone since, but not his love of flying. (Photo by Rod Dyck)

We flew thousands of Vietnamese refugees to Canada, and here, the Hoang Chiminh family are welcomed aboard at Hong Kong by Captain Doug Nicholson. Hoang Chiminh was our 10,000th refugee passenger.

You are looking at $28 million worth of hangar and buildings at the Wardair complex on the Toronto International Airport (Lester B. Pearson Airport). The office building is in the foreground and just behind it is our hangar, with the largest welded steel plate clear span in Canada. I get a kick out of comparing this with the pictures of our early Yellowknife operation. (Photo by George Hunter)

BOARD OF DIRECTORS
WARDAIR CANADA

Maxwell Ward
1953–1989

Tom Spalding
1970–1989

George Curley
1975–1989

Marjorie Ward
1953–1989

Norman Hyland
1979–1988

Kim Ward
1985–1989

Stan Milner
1987–1989

Tom Brown
1968–1982

Lillian Nicholls
1953–1970

Les Duncan
1983–1989

Michael Brown
1984–1989

Portraits by Carl Durban

My old friend George Curley and I in our Toronto offices in 1987. He was President of Wardair and I was Chairman and Chief Executive Officer at this time. I can't remember what we were smiling about – I guess we didn't know what was going to hit us in the next year.

Three of the fourteen Airbus A-310-300s, which we ordered in hopes of rising to the top of the scheduled carriers, are lined up outside the hangar in Toulouse, France. (Photo by Airbus)

Five of our seven grandchildren were all able to crawl into one of the power-plants for the Airbus A-310-300. The power-plant is called a General Electric CF6-80C2; the children are called (I am going to give you their ages when this picture was taken, in 1987, as certified by their grandmother, Marjorie): Jordan Wilkie, seven (left), Meredith Ward, eighteen months (in front), Darcy Ward, seven (behind Meredith), Chelsey Ward, four-and-a-half (right), and Brennan Wilkie, eleven. (Missing: Brett and Reid Bastin.)

Here I am swinging the prop for the last flight of the Fox Moth, from Toronto to Ottawa. George Neal is the pilot of this reproduction of my original aircraft, and you can see Doug Weaver in the passenger cabin. The Fox Moth was on its way to the National Aviation Museum on May 10, 1989. (Photo by "Caz" Caswell)

I was in good company when I received an honorary degree at Trent University in Peterborough, Ontario, in 1983. That's Maureen Forrester, who was then President of the Canada Council, beside me, and Donald Chant of the Ontario Waste Management Corporation. I should have asked him about government waste! (Photo by Trent University)

The two most important things in my life have been Marjorie and flying, so it was natural that when I bought a Challenger jet in mid-1991, I would give it my favourite nickname for my wife, Marjorie Morningstar. She was pleased, as you can see, although she told me that the book – which I have never read – was pretty racy! Never mind, I just like the name.

We went to endless trouble to keep up the quality of our meals. The steaks, for example, were bought from the same in-flight caterers the other airlines used, but we paid more and demanded a higher quality. In Canada, we were fortunate enough to have Gunter Otto of Cara take a personal interest in maintaining our high catering standards, together with Mike Kozac, who was Wardair's director of catering services for many years. Our steaks were always cut from centre-cut, non-frozen tenderloin; they were seared for forty-five seconds, then chilled, and cooked in convection ovens during the flight. I like coffee, and I hate to have it cold, but most airline coffee seems to be made by scraping the bark off some dark tree, steeping it in cool water, and then serving it. In many cases, it is instant coffee. A solution to the problem of providing hot, good coffee was difficult to achieve, but in the end we found coffee-makers that would work in aircraft and produce excellent percolated coffee. We installed them at fifteen thousand dollars per unit, a fact that made our accountants groan and our customers purr.

When we bought a new aircraft, our galleys cost an average of an extra million dollars or more for special amenities tailored to our special cabin services. The average airline customer has no idea, when he or she looks around the interior of a 747, for example, that, on any given overseas flight, between ten and eleven thousand items of dry goods and commissary supplies have to be checked, loaded, and accounted for. The comfort of the passenger is directly dependent on the degree of care that is brought to such details.

Looking after the passenger was what it was all about, and from Day One we emphasized that, not only was the customer always correct, but if he wanted something reasonable on the aircraft that we couldn't provide, we would make sure it was there on the next trip.

I must say, we sometimes got more than we bargained for from groups who chose us because of our reputation for providing good service. We took one charter down to Houston, for a group of vegetarians going to visit some Texan guru. On their leader's instructions, we removed all alcoholic beverages from the aircraft. We also provided vegetarian meals, and they were so delicious that everything on the plane was eaten by the time we got to Texas. However, the passengers, once they were fed, seemed to spend all their time in the lavatories. Could it be that there was something wrong with the food? Well, no, actually; the flight attendants noted that every time the lavatory doors opened, a puff of strange-smelling smoke emerged.

If we were told that someone scheduled on one of our flights was going to have a birthday, or that we had a honeymooning couple aboard, we endeavoured to produce a birthday cake or a bottle of champagne as required, and that was a lot of fun for everybody.

The fact that we served our meals on china, with good cutlery, was nice for the passengers, but some of them liked the stuff so much that they walked off with it. We lost thousands and thousands of dollars every year, in cutlery, dishes, even blankets, but we hoped the advertising was positive.

Almost as important to our operation as flight safety-checks was the complaints department, run by Doreen Rouse, my private secretary, and Jeff Shaffer. They had a large and competent staff, second to none. They worked from the premise that if a passenger wasn't satisfied, and had any grounds whatsoever for the complaint, he or she was entitled to some compensation, or even an entire trip, or whatever seemed reasonable in the circumstances. I always left this to Doreen and Jeff, and they kept meticulous files on every complaint or compliment. We had a few chronic, professional complainers, those who try to take advantage by grousing about something perfectly unreasonable. They would find that they were on file, and that they might get away with something once, but, I believe, seldom more than once. Doreen wrote wonderful letters to disgruntled customers. The Air Transport Board once told me "your letters are the best we ever see." She was terrific on the phone, too, polite and kind. Doreen wrote the manual on office procedures. She was with me more than twenty-seven years, a total perfectionist in every way and truly a person who understood what service to the public should be.

It is fitting here to mention our Board of Directors. They were always a tremendous help to us, and we depended on them more than most companies do, I believe. Often, the board is just a rubber stamp for decisions already taken; ours was an active source of advice. An airline is an incredibly complex business: whenever you speak of money, it is usually in millions of dollars, so the board has to be alert. Our meetings were hard work; they went on all day, with a working lunch of sandwiches at noon. At their close, I always had a feeling of stability, knowing that all corporate matters were being well and competently handled. We in management made mistakes, but our shareholders could be certain that their money had been productively employed. While we didn't pay any of the company-associated directors, as Wardair grew and took on outside directors, they did receive a stipend; however, it was minuscule in comparison to that of other directorships.

Our Toronto boardroom was attractively decorated and many-windowed, with the usual long boardroom table and leather chairs. On the walls hung two Maurice Haycock pictures of Port Radium and Coppermine, as they were in the early days when I first knew them.

However fine we thought our boardroom to be, our directors suggested now and then that it would be nice to meet instead in Hawaii or some other exotic spot, but it never happened. Truthfully, we never had the extra time it would take for the unnecessary travel.

Our meetings were often attended by some of our executives, usually financial people like Tom Currie, Neil Driscoll, Jim Ormiston, or Marilyn Day-Linton, or by someone from Marketing or Maintenance. Our Corporate Secretary was Ian Wilkie, Vice-President of our corporate legal department.

After Wardair was sold, we realized that we had never, ever taken a picture of our board. Marjorie had to phone all of them to request head-and-shoulders pictures so that we could have a grouping made up.

In the 1960s, as soon as we had been allowed to run inclusive tours, providing our own package holidays, I dreamt of putting together a complete holiday service to the traveller, to include both transportation and accommodation.

I finally appeared to be on the way to achieving this objective when we leased the Trelawney Beach Hotel in Jamaica through a friend, Moses Matalon. Being a hotelier was both exciting and enlightening. Although I did not achieve the degree of excellence that I was looking for, our tours turned out to be very popular. The hotel was completely booked for the first winter period, and we had planned to operate charters from the United Kingdom and Europe during the summer season, which, although they would not fill the hotel, would at least cover operating costs. Unfortunately, we did not have the aircraft capacity to operate these flights ourselves, and so had intended to charter a Boeing 707 from a U.K. operator. To our consternation, the Jamaican government told us that we had to operate the charters ourselves, or place the passengers on Air Jamaica flights from Europe and pay their much higher fares. This rendered the whole operation, including the hotel, uneconomic. In total frustration, we finally gave up the hotel and abandoned a most successful concept.

Our ingenious Vice-President of Sales and Marketing at this time, Brian Walker, then leased a Greek cruise ship, *The Jupiter*, to provide an air-and-sea package in the Caribbean. *The Jupiter* turned out to be somewhat less than a luxury ship, however, and our disenchantment became total after the air-conditioning broke down in the hot climate. People literally had to sleep on deck, and we ended up giving most of the people their money back, getting them back to land, and providing them with accommodation there, only to be advised by the Greek shipping line that failure of the air-conditioning was "an act of God." Or, to put it another way, we were not going to get a penny back from them.

In Marine law, if the reader is familiar with it, the hopes of successfully suing an international shipping line are roughly equivalent to a snowball's chance in hell.

Never mind, we would try again. George Curley was also enthusiastic about becoming a shipping magnate. So he and I went over to Portugal, where we had heard there was a shipping company that owned a hull that would be ideal for conversion into a high-quality cruise ship. We went so far as to inspect the hull with the shipping company and to begin preliminary discussions on a purchase price. We also brought in a ship's architect to start the process of redesigning this hull to make a first-class cruise ship.

By this time, I knew what we wanted for our customer aboard the ship. I had investigated where it would be rebuilt and how the project could be financed. We were going to have space for the passengers of one Boeing 747-load, and we had made arrangements with the government of the Barbados for the duty-free basing of the ship in the Barbados. Just when everything seemed to be fitting into place, we were informed by the shipping company that the government of Portugal had other plans for the ship, so somebody else got our beautiful hull and the project died. Too bad; I always wanted to be a Sea Lord.

One of our most interesting jobs grew out of flying the Queen around Alberta in the Dash 7 early in 1979. About nine months later, Brian Robertson, one of our northern employees who had been in charge of that tour, got a phone call from Lieutenant-Colonel Terry Thompson, who had handled the military aspects of the tour. He told Brian that the Canadian Armed Forces were having great difficulty keeping up with the flood of refugees then coming out of Vietnam and Cambodia. He wondered if Wardair could help. Of course we could. Soon after, Brian went to Ottawa to arrange the first of three trips between Kuala Lumpur in Malaysia and Edmonton and Montreal aboard our DC-10s. There were five more trips during November and December and, on one of these, when the refugees arrived in Edmonton, the ground was covered with snow. The captain ran down and brought up handfuls of snow for the refugee children, who touched it and drew back in shock. They had never seen snow before.

We were asked, while this was under way, to submit a plan to Ottawa for weekly trips during 1980, using 747 aircraft, with all our costs. We did so, as did Air Canada, and we were actually awarded the contract!

Our planes would leave Toronto on Wednesday afternoon, stop off in Edmonton, and change crews. That crew would take the aircraft to a joint United States–Japan airbase just south of Tokyo, which became the base of operations. We would fly down empty to Singapore, Kuala Lumpur, or Bangkok to pick up the refugees, return to Tokyo, and then fly on to Canada. We brought our passengers to two main camps, in Edmonton and Montreal, and most of them went from the camps on to Vancouver.

Most of the refugees were destitute, but there was one elderly gentleman who got off in Edmonton and suddenly remembered he had forgotten something. He went back into the plane, panic-stricken, to get it and emerged triumphant. It was a paper package containing eleven kilos of gold.

We carried 32,000 of the 50,000 refugees that came to Canada during that time. One of our flights was made more lively – a little too lively – when it turned out that one of the women was about to give birth, although she hadn't said anything about that to the immigration people in Bangkok. The pilot was about to divert to Hong Kong, when it turned out that there was a doctor among the refugees, who delivered the baby in mid-air without difficulty. The baby was entitled to become either Vietnamese or Canadian, and, of course, her mother chose Canada. We hope Wardair is included in the child's name. (We flew into Barbados for so many years, and were so well known there, that one mother did in fact name a child Wardair.)

We had been told that there might be a lot of damage to the aircraft during these flights, but there was none; in fact, I don't think we lost so much as a spoon during them all. We later learned that the American airlines who handled similar flights served meals on paper plates, with everything disposable, but we gave the refugees the full Wardair service, and they loved it.

We were proud of the role we played in helping the refugees, and proud of our country's role. One of those who shared our enthusiasm was Cardinal Léger, who expressed an interest in going out to visit the refugee camps. We were happy to oblige. As word of what was happening got around, a number of organizations banded together to collect medical supplies to fly out to the refugees and, once again, we were happy to deliver the materials collected in Canada for people half a world away.

One of the stranger incidents that occurred during these flights took place during a routine flight to the Thai capital. At Bangkok airport, we loaded the refugees from a tin shed at the back of the airport. On one flight, the captain had to apply some extra power to get up the ramp going away from this building; the blast caught the building and it went down with a crash. We felt badly about it, but when our representative went to the airport manager to make his apologies and pay for any damage, the manager said, "Don't worry about it, you did us a big favour. We didn't have the money to take that old building down!"

There was really only one problem about those flights: the union for the cabin attendants wanted our people to be paid overtime because they would be flying an extra two hours beyond the duty day when they went from Tokyo down to Singapore and Kuala Lumpur, even though they would be on an empty aircraft, and would not be working. This part of the flight was entirely outside Canada – and thus outside the jurisdiction of the union that insisted on this demand – so we refused. In the end, we readily hired qualified cabin crews in Thailand who were delighted to have the work. Then our crews would take over for the trip back to Canada. I know a lot of our attendants were disappointed, because they had looked forward to seeing some of those exotic places, but they couldn't go against the union.

We were not in a position to turn down any business that came our way, and we got a good deal of pleasure out of some of these off-beat contracts. For example, we had contracts for a number of years to fly some of the hadj trips operating between Libya and Saudi Arabia. The hadj is the pilgrimage every adult Muslim tries to make during his or her life, to visit the birthplace of Mohammed at Mecca. (Following the pilgrimage, one is allowed to use the title "Hadj" after one's name.) Every year, two million people from seventy or more nations descend on Mecca, a city outlawed to anyone who is not a Muslim. We would fly a 747 from Tripoli to Jedda, on the Red Sea coast, and the pilgrims would go overland to Mecca from there.

We were paid for these flights well ahead of time. However, at one point pre-payments from Libya began to slow down, and, being concerned, I had a telegram sent to our crew in Tripoli that said, "Be prepared to depart Libya on short notice unless the money for the balance of the trip is received within the next forty-eight hours."

Unbeknownst to us, every message going into the Libyan capital went through the communications office of the dictator, Colonel Muammar Qaddafi. We discovered this when some of our diplomatic friends told us the Colonel was very ticked off with us for the implied insult. Just the same, he paid up, right smartly.

We did the hadj flights on behalf of Egypt Air, and the Egyptians were always astonished when one of our flights arrived ahead of time. They had heard of planes arriving late, but they had apparently never even contemplated the notion of one arriving early.

Those kinds of contracts came to us, I believe, because we had competent people who cared enough to make things work.

While these exciting developments were taking place overseas, we were moving ahead at home, too – or at least, we seemed to be. One May 8, 1980, we commenced operating with our newly acquired authority to conduct charter flights within Canada. Our first flight was from Toronto to Vancouver.

Domestic operating authority launched us into a whole new market. In order to operate efficiently, we required short- and medium-haul aircraft, rather than the long-haul, international fleet that had fitted our total requirements up to this time. We now considered we were one step closer to scheduled services, which also require various sizes of aircraft to meet demands on various routes. Our fleet of 747s and DC-10s would continue to serve on the North Atlantic and winter-holiday runs, but they were much too large for regular, scheduled domestic service. (We had sold our two 707s in 1978, and did well on them; one went to Kuwait, the other to Austria.)

I had heard a good deal about the Airbus, built by an international consortium – mainly British, West German, and French – out of Toulouse, France. The first generation, the Airbus 300, had done well since its introduction in 1972, and Eastern Airlines were operating them up and down the east coast from Florida.

Somehow, I didn't have the impression that the Europeans were experienced enough at building a good commercial airliner; maybe I was being brainwashed. However, after I heard how well the Eastern Airbuses were doing, my curiosity was aroused. On a trip to Ottawa, I went to talk to some of the Eastern Airline personnel on the ramp at the airport-servicing area, who actually had to deal with these aircraft, and they were very positive. Apparently, they had had some concern about what would happen when the Ottawa cold closed in, but the machine had no trouble overnighting in the coldest temperatures Ottawa could throw at it. Morning departures were normally on time, with very few incidents of "unserviceability."

I decided that George Curley and I had better go over to Toulouse to check the Airbus out. On a plant tour, we were very impressed by the high quality of the workmanship.

The aircraft we were really interested in was the A-310, the successor to the A-300. The performance figures of both were very good indeed. The A-310 is smaller than the A-300, which suited us, and it was a state-of-the-art aircraft.

Before we left the plant we had made up our minds, and we started negotiating for six of them. In the end, we made a deal not only to buy the six, but to take an option for six more. The first two were to be delivered in October and November 1983, and four more were to follow in 1984 and 1985.

We would be the first airline in North America to operate the A-310s, the most advanced version of the Airbus, and that made us proud. However, we would be committed to a minimum outlay of $430 million, and that made me nervous. It was very shortly after the purchase was announced, on March 25, 1981, that interest rates soared out of sight. Between October 1, 1980, and September 4, 1981, the bank's prime rate went from 12.75 per cent to 22.75 per cent, and we were plunged into a recession. Most air travel of the kind we were supplying – that is, for vacations – is discretionary, and, as soon as hard times hit, sales drop. The crowds we needed to expand with were nowhere to be seen, and what appeared to be a shrewd market move to stay ahead of the crowd now began to look like a wild gamble.

Two weeks after the prime hit 22.75 per cent, we received delivery of the first of two DC-10s we had bought from Singapore Airlines, for the expansion, we thought, of our charter business overseas. These were second-hand aircraft, and I normally didn't buy second-hand machines, but they had low hours – they were practically new – and an attractive price, so we went ahead with the arrangements. This involved committing another $65 million, with the additional complication that aircraft prices are normally given in U.S. funds.

The U.S. dollar held up better than the Canadian during the recession, so we had high exchange-rate differentials to pay, on top of everything else.

Just before the world began to come apart in my hands, I had launched an extensive building program. We had to have better hangar facilities, and office space as well, in Toronto. Marjorie and I had already bought a condominium on the Toronto waterfront, and we spent most of our time there rather than in our home in Edmonton. We built a $14-million hangar at Malton, in 1980, contracted by F. J. Reinders and Associates. It had the largest span of any hangar in Canada and would house two Jumbo Jets at the same time. There were doors in both ends, for ready access to the aircraft, and a million-gallon underground reservoir for the fire-fighting system. Contrary to the norm in most hangars, which have very few windows, ours had as many as we could put in, to provide as much natural light as possible. I delighted in watching the new hangar's progress as it went up. It was a long road from my first aircraft shelter, a tent frame on Back Bay in Yellowknife! My admiration grew daily for the skilled, cheerful Italian-Canadian workmen on whom so much of the building depended.

Danny McNiven, Vice-President, Maintenance, at that time, was often on the scene to share my enthusiasm for this much-needed facility. Dan always had ten irons in the fire at once, and his influence was felt in many areas of the company besides Maintenance. But Maintenance was his first love, and it thrived under his crews and his guidance. Succeeding Dan was Terry Nord, another extremely competent and innovative man. Wardair's maintenance was always of the highest quality, thanks to the continuous, meticulous care of our own engineers and mechanics. They always kept the hangar spotlessly clean and organized, and I loved to go in there and "kick the tires."

Next to the hangar and connected to it, we built, for another $14 million, a new office building. The centre core contained an atrium with skylights, so that there was an aura of openness and space and natural light. On the ground floor was a cafeteria, managed by Noreen Tully and run at cost for our staff, many of whom had their main meal of the day there, at noon. The aroma of cinnamon buns and six-inch-wide cookies could raise the spirits in a flash! Because of the economic turndown in 1980–81, we never did have this cafeteria as adequately furnished and decorated as we would have wished.

Wardair had outgrown this building long before 1989, and many of our services were once more lodged elsewhere, so we had planned to repeat the building, doubling our space. Among other things, we planned to have a day-care centre and a display area for the rebuilt Fox Moth.

Some of my business associates, particularly Freddie Laker, used to kid me about the excellent office and maintenance facilities we had, with everything in its place, clean and organized. But this established an order within the company that was vital to us, and to everyone associated with us.

All of these activities left us tremendously exposed, and within a few months, as the recession hit, we were in trouble. By the fall of 1982, we were running out of cash. We trimmed every cost we could and offered DC-10s or 747s for sale, but the problem was that no one else had any money, either, so there were no takers. Finally, Tom Spalding, Wardair's Executive Vice-President, went back to Singapore Airlines and asked them to let us out of the second DC-10 contract, which, on payment of a penalty, they were willing to do. The one we did buy was financed on what was called a "samurai lease," a form of Japanese conditional sales contract, and I often wondered what would happen to me if we missed a payment.

The bulk of the financing for the 747s and DC-10s we were then operating was covered by a group of Canadian banks in Toronto, led by the Canadian Imperial Bank of Commerce. We had a cash-flow requirement for $21 million, and after long-protracted negotiations primarily led by the Toronto-Dominion bank, the group of banks agreed to extend us the cash. Having extended us a $21-million line of credit, they were somewhat nervous, but not as nervous as I was. After all, since planes go up in value rather than down, the manufacturers had given us a back-up agreement that they would repurchase the aircraft in case of need, to secure the bank position, which would enable them to realize on the assets.

I, myself, was not so lucky. On the second 747 purchase, in 1974, the financial institutions wanted more equity, and the only way we could get the money was for me to take out a personal loan from the Alberta Treasury Branch. My position would be subordinated to all other corporate debt. I gave the money to the company and got in return preferred shares. The dividends on the shares would pay off the loan, at the prevailing rate of interest. However, when the company began to bleed, there were no dividend payments, and the bank payments, plus the accruing interest, became overdue. We were under personal threat of losing everything, our corporation, our home, everything but the clothes we stood in. I couldn't sleep at night for worrying, and every day was an agony to drag through.

We had prepaid $16 million on the A-310s, so I had to get out of the deal and get that money back. The consortium of banks was sure we could not, but Tom Spalding went back to Airbus Industrie, and they returned the entire down payment – minus $300,000 per aircraft. I doubt if there is another aircraft manufacturer in the world that would have treated us so well, and I will never forget it.

The worst of the nightmare was over but we were still in trouble. That was the most frightening period of my life, and it went on for months and months. The Industrial Development Bank, whose name had been changed to the Canadian Development Bank, was very supportive but, as a government bank, didn't have the terms of reference to be able to help us at this time. We really credit a friend at the Bank of Montreal, Hart MacDougall, now Chairman of the Royal Trust Group of Companies, and Merle Chriss at the Toronto-Dominion Bank for keeping us afloat during that period.

During 1982, when we trembled on the brink of disaster, we were flying with 94 per cent of our seats filled on each trip, and we had a service that linked Toronto, Montreal, Vancouver, Edmonton, Calgary, Halifax, and Saskatoon. But we were flying the wrong airplanes, and, without a scheduled service to assure a steady source of funds, it appeared that we would never break out of the circle of financial and regulatory constraints in which we found ourselves. In point of fact, we improved both our passenger loads and passenger-miles in 1982, but, because passenger-mile yields were not enough to make up for the increases in our interest costs, we lost $14 million that year.

We had trimmed our staff to what we considered the bare bones; all our people knew the crunch was on, and it was a frightening time for them, too. My presence seemed to reassure them, so I made a point of being very visible, especially in the Toronto office, which was now the heart of our organization. On the weekends, I always flew on a return flight somewhere for the wordless support this seemed to give staff and crews.

That time is a blur of endless work and worry in my mind and I hate to think about it. When the crisis eased as the economy began, slowly, to recover during 1983, the airline stock began to recover, too, and I was able to sell enough to pay off my note to the Alberta Treasury Branch. That eased the personal burden from Marjorie's shoulders and my own, but we were a long way from solving the airline's problems.

However, we had a new Minister of Transport, Lloyd Axworthy, from Winnipeg, so in early 1984, I went to pay him a courtesy call during a trip to Ottawa. Under his predecessor, Jean-Luc Pepin, we had gone back to the familiar pattern of harassment, threats, show-cause orders, and other tortures dreamt up for our chastisement by the various layers of bureaucracy. There were even signs that the government was going to tighten up regulations on charter flights all over again. I was therefore pretty apprehensive when I went into the minister's office in the House of Commons.

I told him that we were unable to compete with the scheduled airlines, because they could cream money off their monopoly routes to finance the undercutting of prices on the domestic charters, and I laid out some of the background for him. I pussyfooted around the regulations imposed on us, to sound him out, and the conversation swung onto the subject of operating authority – the scheduled airlines could do what they wanted, but we couldn't do anything without a long hassle. To my absolute astonishment he asked, "Why can't all you carriers compete on the same basis?"

I took a quick look around the room and said, "Am I in the office of a Liberal government minister?" Canada was now about six years behind the United States when it came to deregulation, and about three or four years behind most other modern nations; Axworthy seemed to recognize this and to realize that action would have to be taken. I came away from his office with a much better feeling than I had had for some time about the future of aviation policy.

My optimism was justified when, on May 10, 1984, he announced a new Canadian Air Policy, as the first step towards full-scale deregulation. The new policy applied only to domestic flights, but it would give us, for the first time, the right to sell our seats to *all* comers, for one-way or return travel, right up to the moment of departure. The dreaded ABCs were scotched, if not yet slain, at least on the domestic routes.

Six weeks later, on June 29, 1984, we got our first scheduled route. We had been flying between Toronto and Montreal and San Juan, Puerto Rico, since 1978, and our record of service on the route was impressive enough that, when a scheduled service was negotiated by the government, we were given the nod. A small chink had opened in the armour of protectionism. Puerto Rico was not a major destination, but it was a start, and we were grateful.

The minister wanted further changes to follow, but the civil service dragged its feet and not much happened until the Tories came back to power. On September 4, under a new leader, Brian Mulroney, the Conservatives won 211 of the 282 seats then available, and Don Mazankowski was back in Transport (he would later become Deputy Prime Minister).

On October 29, 1984, the Advanced Booking Charter requirements were abolished on flights to the United States.

On May 10, 1985, Wardair was officially designated as a scheduled carrier to the United Kingdom – the first time a Canadian airline other than Air Canada or CP Air had ever been licensed for scheduled service over either the Atlantic or the Pacific. The licence came into effect on September 9, 1985, but we would not be ready to go with promotion of our new fare structure and schedules until May 4, 1986.

In July 1985, Don Mazankowski had produced a discussion paper called *Freedom to Move*, setting out proposals for what was being called, in the kind of buzz-phrase beloved of Ottawa, Economic Regulatory Reform. The necessary amendments to the National Transportation Act were delayed in the Senate and didn't receive final approval until August 7, 1987, but the CTC (which would shortly become, instead, the National Transportation Agency and be shorn of much of its power) was instructed to follow the new policies forthwith, and it did.

The most significant change was in a clause permitting entry into any class of domestic commercial air service on the basis of a requirement that the applying airline be "fit, willing and able" to perform the "service." Previously, as we had reason to know, the CTC was to license a newcomer only if it was convinced that "public convenience and necessity" required it. Public convenience and necessity, for decades, had been equated with the convenience of Air Canada and the necessity to protect it. Public convenience and necessity were nowhere defined in law, so there was no way to attack decisions made on this basis. All that was gone in one stroke. Henceforth, any company could vie for any route in Canada, so long as the company had valid certificates attesting to the fact that it was equipped and able to conduct a safe operation and had liability insurance.

On March 20, 1986, we were granted a Class 1 Licence to conduct scheduled service within Canada, and we soon launched our first scheduled flights in the Canadian market, starting in Toronto, Vancouver, Calgary, and Edmonton.

Our financial picture was soon greatly improved. After losing money in 1981 and 1982, we made a modest profit in 1983, did better in 1984, and at the end of 1985, we had carried more passengers than ever before – 1,567,000 – and had gross revenues of $473.8 million. Although our profit was a comparatively modest $24 million, it looked mighty good to us.

Our friends over at *Air International* magazine reported in September 1986 that the year was "already marked as the year in which Wardair achieved the status of a fully scheduled long-haul international airline, in line with the service standards it had already been demonstrating for many years."

The trouble with rushing merrily headlong down a hill, after a steep climb to the summit, is that you are then in a position to fall over a cliff. This we now proceeded to do.

CHAPTER 21

Be Careful What You Wish For – You Might Get It

It is easy now to see that the changes had come too late for us. I had been saying, for years, that unless action were taken immediately, we would not be able to compete in the new world of global aviation. There is not much comfort, when all is said and done, in being right about predictions of impending disaster. Had Canada moved to deregulation at the same time as the Americans, in 1978, or soon after, I believe we would not only have survived, but come to triumph in the industry.

Deregulation in the United States had been in place for over a decade. It was resisted all those years in this country, in the name of protecting the scheduled carriers, and it then arrived full-blown when the changes discussed in the last chapter were made in 1988. There was very little time to adjust.

I had spent a lot of my time in aviation trying to guess what would happen next, so as to prepare for it, and I hadn't done badly. What I could see now, as I looked ahead, was the true globalization of airlines, with perhaps a score of giant, multi-national firms carrying the bulk of passengers.

We were moving into the age of hypersonic aircraft, rather than mere supersonic craft such as the Concorde, and, indeed, the American government was already spending large sums of money to master the technology for these planes, which will be capable of travelling at many times the speed of sound. The genius of the aircraft, as I have already noted, is found not in the plane itself, but in the power-plant. It is the modern jet power-plant that can lift and hurl a million pounds of people, airframe, and fuel through the sky for seven or eight thousand miles non-stop. With the arrival of the hypersonic airliner, technology will need to be just as sophisticated as the power-plant technology. In the next stage, early in the next century, the planes will be larger, much faster, and much more expensive. If companies are now paying $150 million U.S. for a single airplane, just think what they will be paying for a much more sophisticated machine like the hypersonic airliner.

These will be aircraft as different from the ones we know today as the modern jet is from my old Fox Moth; they will operate out of much larger, hub airports, and they will be almost fully automated.

If these planes have pilots, it will only be for monitoring. In a well-designed automated aircraft, the only crew really needed aboard will be the cabin attendants. When I mentioned this to a journalist friend of mine, he said he would never fly in a pilotless plane; he just didn't trust machines that much.

"Would you ride in an automatic elevator?" I asked him. There was a time when the thought of an elevator running itself was considered not only novel but dangerous, but custom and common sense have carried the day, and the same will apply to the automated aircraft of the future. If I were a young man today going into the airline business, I would work on the assumption that twenty-five years from now – and twenty-five years is a reasonable planning time-frame for these matters – the manufacturers will be an integral part of the airline operation: not outside suppliers, but a part of the economic unit, because the costs of the machines will be so high. As a matter of fact, the manufacturers are funding airlines today.

Even without such mental leaps into the future, it didn't take very much imagination for me in 1984 or 1985 to look forward and see that the squeeze of the purchase price of new aircraft and the inherently high airline running costs were going to force the amalgamation of airlines. It was a process already well under way. In the United States, deregulation had brought mergers in its wake, until there were eight major carriers dominating the industry. One out of every five air passengers flew on United, the largest domestic airline in the United States; American Airlines moved 18 per cent of the customers, and Delta, 15 per cent.

In Canada, over the previous decade, CP Air had acquired Eastern Provincial Airways and control of Nordair. Air Canada and Pacific Western (which had been taken over by the government of Alberta in 1974, and then sold back to the public under its president, a brisk young accountant named Rhys Eyton) joined together to buy 49 per cent of Air Ontario; Time Air bought Southern Frontier Airlines, and then PWA bought 40 per cent of Time Air. City Wings bought Air Atonabee and became City Express. It was like watching one of those cartoons where the small fish is gobbled up by a large one, then a larger one comes along and swallows that one, and so on. Then PWA turned around in 1986 and bought CP Air from Canadian Pacific Limited – a small fish swallowing a very much larger one.

None of this was unexpected or illogical; it was so logical, in fact, that the other party trying to bid for Canadian Pacific Air Lines in 1986 was Wardair. We were too late. If the United States, with a population of 241 million, had been reduced to eight major airlines, which in turn will probably shrink to four or five, and if Britain really only had one carrier, and it was already making deals with other national carriers for joint operation, where did that leave us? Could the Canadian marketplace support even two major carriers?

We had not come so far, worked so hard, risked so much, to become a feeder line to someone else's company, so it was obvious our only hope was to turn ourselves into an instant scheduled airline so that we could compete fairly for survival. The scheduled-carrier operation demands a somewhat different philosophy, technical arrangement, and fleet than a charter operation. Could we expand fast enough to create the necessary route structure?

I charged ahead. Regardless of the problems that loomed, I felt that with all I had now got from Don Mazankowski, I had to justify the faith that had been shown in me, I had to see it through. It reminded me of the old saying, "Be careful what you wish for – you might get it." In this case, Mazankowski's success in bringing about massive change in the regulatory climate meant, among other things, that we would have to acquire an instant fleet, for scheduled airline service. Fortunately, this process was already under way.

As early as 1985 – in fact, as soon as we had recovered from our almost fatal financial disaster of 1982 – I had begun studying the latest aircraft technology to see where we should go next. I already knew something of the capabilities of the Airbus – its long range and high productivity – so we started to scramble at once to acquire some on a second-hand basis. The waiting time for new aircraft was extensive. We had a line on some aircraft that Varig, the Brazilian flag-carrier, had for sale, but Continental Airlines stepped in at the last minute with a better offer, and we lost out. Then we tracked down three A-300s – the slightly larger, older version of the Airbus – that South African Airways was willing to let go on a day-lease basis. We sold one of the 747s, for more than we had paid for it, and with the gain we phased the A-300s into our fleet. The first of these went into service on August 22, 1986.

When we got our first domestic schedule approval two months later, we really went on a buying spree. We ordered twelve A-310s for delivery between November 1987 and December 1988. The cost: $650 million U.S., with parts and spares (our first dozen, cancelled during the recession, would have cost two-thirds of that). The first two Airbus A-310s were turned over to us on November 27, 1987, and the rest came through, right on time, during the next twelve months.

To finance this deal, Tom Currie, our Chief Financial Officer, worked out a unique new arrangement. Ordinarily, the airline industry funds its purchases in U.S. dollars, but the trouble with that, for a company like ours, which didn't earn its funds in the American currency, is that you can get blind-sided by fluctuations in the exchange rate and end up paying far more than you bargained for. Tom arranged to raise most of the needed money in Canadian dollars by using fixed-rate bonds on the Canadian debt market. For his innovative thinking, Tom won the "Deal of the Year" award from *Airfinance Journal*.

To go with the Deal of the Year, we staged the Party of the Year, in Toulouse, to celebrate delivery of the first two Airbuses. We filled one aircraft full of guests in Canada, and another came down from Paris. Nina Ricci had designed new uniforms for our cabin attendants, and these were shown as part of a fashion show. (These lovely uniforms, alas, went into the discard when Wardair disappeared.) We named the first A-310 for Z. Lewis Leigh, a pioneer pilot – the first ever hired by Trans-Canada Airlines, in 1937 – and the second for Don Braun. After the party, and a tour of the Airbus plant, all the Canadian guests flew home in our new planes.

To the shock of Bay Street, we signed up deals to purchase sixteen McDonnell–Douglas MD-88s for delivery beginning in 1989. The first eight cost $300 million, and we were committed to that, with an option on the rest. These are twin-engine jets that carry up to 118 passengers, and they would serve on short- and medium-haul lines within Canada and across the U.S. border. We also agreed to buy twenty-four Fokker 100 aircraft, hundred-seat airplanes, for short hauls, to give us the capacity to operate feeder lines to the major terminals. We were, in effect, trading in our wide-bodied fleet for a whole new fleet, and it was still the profits we made on the sale of our 747s and DC-10s that kept us going.

But, as I have mentioned before, the barriers to entry into the scheduled airline business were many: network and schedule, pricing, agent commission structure, computer-reservations systems (CRS), consumer-incentive plans such as frequent-flyer programs and secretaries' clubs, interline agreements, terminal facilities, consumer habits, gates and landing slots, airline image, supplier relationships, licences, entrenched competition, and numerous others.

At the outset, we needed to structure a competitive flight schedule to tie together both domestic and international routes. This allows the airline to create a mass flow of passengers. We had sufficient aircraft by the fall of 1988 to serve scheduled routes Canada to London and Canada to Paris, plus competitive frequencies between Toronto and Edmonton, Calgary, and Vancouver. We had marketing agreements in place with Air France and Thai International and were negotiating other agreements to build our network – that was phase one. A very critical problem occurred in phase two of our expansion with the MD-88s. These narrow-body aircraft were needed to provide frequent flights between Toronto and Montreal, Ottawa and Winnipeg. In addition, we wanted to add Halifax and other smaller markets to our route structure. The first MD-88s, due in May 1989, were delayed by problems in manufacturing until the end of that year. The delay would prevent us from getting the traffic we needed for our trunk and international routes.

The lack of short-haul feeder carriers also affected our traffic volumes. Certainly Air Canada and CAIL were not about to let their commuters feed us. This meant that our markets were restricted to major city pairs with no ability to carry passengers into or out of outlying communities. (Ironic, in view of our beginnings.)

Another major challenge was to displace the market entrenchment and strength of our two primary competitors. Air Canada, long a protected child, had a powerful route infrastructure, and it was the airline most Canadians knew best. Canadian Airlines International was also a formidable and aggressive competitor. Together they attracted most of the "must-travel," high-yield business travellers. Despite its monumental inefficiency, Air Canada was able to earn just over fifteen cents per revenue-mile in the first nine months of 1988, and CAIL earned just over fourteen cents. Wardair, as a new entrant with a charter background, earned only nine cents. Vacation passengers knew and liked us, but at this time it seldom occurred to these same passengers to give us a try when travelling on business.

But the most serious barrier we encountered was the distribution system – travel-agent commissions, computer-reservations systems, secretaries' clubs. Travel agents earn a base commission of about 8 per cent on every ticket they sell, but if a particular agent or agency chain hits certain dollar-sales volumes, they receive an override cheque, which raises their commission to, say, 9 per cent, right back to the first seat they sold for that airline that year. Keep hitting the next level, and up the override goes, all the way to 12 or 13 per cent or more. The next year, each airline raises the hurdles to try to squeeze more business out of each agent. Even more damaging to us were the long-term market-share agreements which Air Canada and Canadian had put into place in 1987. Along comes a new entrant like Wardair – the agent promises support – after all, "our customers love Wardair!" But obviously, with such a strong monetary incentive in place, there was no way they could support another airline entry. So much for doing what's best for the client!

The President of J. Walter Thompson, our own advertising agency, got into a battle with the travel agency his company used, which kept sending over Air Canada tickets when he had specifically ordered Wardair. On one flight, his own travel department told him Wardair was showing "Closed Out" for the flight he wanted. Air Canada tickets arrived on his desk. He phoned Wardair directly and booked the flight. There were lots of seats available. He sent the Air Canada tickets back and asked for Wardair tickets. The Air Canada tickets came back with some other excuse. He sent them back and demanded Wardair. He had to insist that if the travel agent didn't book JWT employees on Wardair he would get another travel agent – which he very nearly did. How many travellers are going to be loyal enough to go through that?

Then there were the secretaries' clubs. If you were a secretary who booked a fair amount of travel for your boss, you could join a secretaries' club with Air Canada, Canadian, or both. The more travel booked with a given airline, the more free travel received from that airline. Just think of the bonanza for those working in an in-house travel bureau, booking for the whole company! Enter Wardair – if the executives travelled Wardair, then the secretary did not add to her already-established free travel with one of the other airlines. Quite a disincentive to allow change; quite an incentive to find always that Wardair had no seats free at the time the executive wanted to travel. As a result, Wardair was often just "not available."

A striking example is the case where our Vice-President of Marketing made a deal with the President of a large Vancouver company to fly Wardair. Somehow, the travel department couldn't quite bring the President's command into action. When we looked into it, we quickly discovered a travel department employee who said, "I fly home to Nova Scotia every summer on a free ticket. If I book Wardair, I might not get my free ticket next year."

There is some irony in the fact that it is Wardair who brought down the prices of airplane tickets and allowed a lot of people, including many of those secretaries and people in travel departments, to fly for the first time.

What a strange business is air transportation! We spend billions of dollars on aircraft, facilities, training, complete with huge world-wide infrastructures. And yet the marketing of our product is in the hands of others. This is a throwback to the old International Air Transport Association (IATA) cartel and the artificial forces inherent in government interference in the marketplace. As the airline industry is dominated by fewer and fewer carriers, I wonder what will eventually happen to the role of the travel agent.

A seemingly insurmountable distribution problem was the computer-reservations system (CRS). The key to airline reservations is a screen in the travel agent's office that is connected to a network of computers containing information on flight schedules around the world. Initially every airline set up its own computer system, but inefficiencies and technical difficulties led to a gradual tendency for one or two systems to dominate. In Canada, the dominant systems were Reservac (Air Canada) and Pegasus (CP Air) – which were amalgamated to become Gemini – and Sabre (American Airlines).

Our system was independent but would communicate with Gemini, so travel agents could book Wardair through Gemini. For this, Wardair paid a fee, which was fair enough. However, there were biases in the system to discriminate against carriers other than the host – which owned the system. As a result, if the agent wanted to book Wardair's flight from Vancouver to Montreal, he or she might have to go through two or three screens of information before finding the flight. Too much trouble. Why not just book the first flight that shows available – which was almost always Air Canada or CAIL! Of course, the Competition Bureau had been dealing with this for years, but the airlines were always one step ahead of them, and the biases were still there.

Another bias lay in the "default" mechanism, which is, in brief, the quickest route for the computer to take when looking for a flight. If you told your agent you wanted to travel to London from Ottawa, for example, the agent might type in YOW (the Ottawa call sign), then LON (the commonly used London call sign), and the date of the requested flight. The system would default to London's Heathrow Airport (LHR), Air Canada's airport, and would not show London Gatwick (LGW), which was Wardair's airport. The computer would route passengers from Ottawa to Toronto or Montreal, where they would have to change aircraft to carry on to London. The joke was, Wardair had a good non-stop schedule out of Ottawa to London, but it wouldn't show on the screen.

We tried to get the system modified so that, when the agent punched in LON, both airports would show. We were told it was very complicated and would cost thirty-eight thousand dollars. "Fine," we said, "we will pay." Suddenly, it was technically impossible. Not surprisingly, that programming was already in place with most other reservations systems that were not owned by our competitors.

We had another computer-reservations problem. Somehow, our flights just weren't appearing properly in the system, or they were incorrectly showing sold out months in advance. This was especially true in the lucrative business class. We thought at first that we were making mistakes. We had a person assigned full time to check this, but problems kept popping up. On one occasion, a businessman phoned to say that he wanted to show his boss the new Wardair business-class service from Toronto to London, but he had been informed by his travel agent that Wardair was sold out two months in advance. We checked: there were only three seats sold in business class. It seemed odd that we kept having all these problems, so we asked the Competition Bureau to investigate, but before they could get very far in their inquiries, the airline was sold.

Never underestimate the impact of consumer habits. A party travelling to Vancouver and accustomed to flying Air Canada knows where to check in, where the gate and the business-class lounge are. The secretary knows the schedule, the travel agent supports Air Canada and is used to booking them – what could be easier, it's like falling off a log, by rote – the customer, secretary, and travel agent book Air Canada.

Then there were the frequent-flyer programs. Business travellers, particularly those that fly hundreds of thousands of miles each year, were locked into established carrier programs. The really frequent flyers were members of both Air Canada and Canadian programs and flew one or the other. We just couldn't get them on our flights because they were busy building up points for that free trip – first class.

They preferred one carrier but used the other if their favourite wasn't available – and Wardair was left out of the calculation. This meant that when we did finally get a frequent-flyer program in the fall of 1988, we had to make it so rich that we would virtually dynamite our way into the lives of those who travelled extensively – we offered them four times normal mileage. That is, for every mile flown, they got credit for four. We were matched by Air Canada, then Canadian; and we raised the ante to six times mileage – they matched again – they couldn't afford to let their best customers travel Wardair or even try the service.

It is the business passenger flying at full fare who keeps the airlines alive, and we were pushing a mighty rock up a long hill, even with our superior service and lower fares, to get and keep that business passenger.

There was also an interline agreement dispute. Surprisingly, CAIL would not sign an agreement with Wardair to handle each other's baggage on connecting flights, or to allow a single ticket to have both Wardair and Canadian flights on it. You could not fly Wardair from Toronto to Vancouver and Canadian on to Australia without having a separate ticket made up for the Wardair portion of the journey to Australia – and you can transfer your own bag, bud! The international system for handling flight coupons (called the Bank Settlement Plan) doesn't contemplate one scheduled carrier not dealing with another, so travel agents could book someone jointly on Wardair and Canadian, and often as not everything would go fine. Sometimes, however, the passenger would get caught in the middle and end up inconvenienced.

Let me deal briefly with our terminal facilities. In airports across Canada, Wardair was unable to procure good facilities – because of our history as a charter carrier, second in class to the scheduled carriers. Our facilities in Toronto and Montreal were particularly bad. Terminal One in Toronto was hated by virtually all business travellers; our passengers used to say that even if they could find the check-in desk, they had to walk halfway to downtown Toronto to get to the boarding gate. In Montreal our check-in desk was hidden at the back of the terminal. The passengers in Montreal had to walk outside through the rain or ice and snow to get on the aircraft. When we did finally get jetways to the aircraft, they were still a long way from the check-in desk – more hassles. It's not that there weren't other gates we could have used, which would have meant less walking and would have been more "environmentally friendly," but other carriers protected them. We were told by one man, who worked for a ground handling firm at Dorval Airport, that Air Canada aircraft used to be towed to certain gates so as to meet Transport Canada minimum-usage criteria – and to keep Wardair off.

Who needs it? The only way we could get customers onto our aircraft was to buy our way in. To do this, we started Premium Pass 2000, with discounts of 30 per cent or more, often going past the travel agents, travel departments, secretaries, even the traveller, directly to the person most interested in the bottom line – the VP Finance or the President. That did the trick. By Fall 1988, we were increasing our share of business traffic at unprecedented rates, but not fast enough, and we knew it. Time was running out.

The issue is not whether our competitors or government policies were playing dirty pool. The issue is, in fact, whether we were able to "grow" the airline into scheduled operations over a long period of time and thus adjust to marketing techniques as they were developed. Had we been permitted to compete in scheduled services when the computer-reservations system came into being, we would have had the necessary strength in place in that area. Had we been able to build a scheduled airline step by step we would have had public awareness of our service; we would have had a secure base to work upon, because we had by far the best productivity and the dedication to provide a good service. Airlines are major and complicated businesses that cannot be built overnight.

All of these pressures came to a head in the fall of 1988. We now had a long-term debt of $300 million, which was about to go up. That was because a projected loss of $50 million for the year – not unreasonable in the scramble to launch scheduled services – now looked more like $100 million. We were not meeting our projections. The discount war was still raging, conditions at the airports were not improving, and we couldn't persuade the Canadian traveller, who had been so loyal to us on the charter flights, to switch to us on the scheduled flights until we could get our act together. I must say I was a little disappointed at this, but I guess it was foolish to think that business travellers and bureaucrats would give us the support we so badly needed during the rocky early years of our scheduling. However it came about, I could no longer kid myself: if we didn't take action of some sort, soon, we would be faced with having to acquire more funds somewhere; we needed another $200 million at least.

I telephoned Rhys Eyton, President of PWA Corporation, the holding company that owns CAIL, to see if we could come to an agreement. He expressed immediate interest, and we met in a hotel out at the airport in Calgary. No one on my side knew about this meeting except Marjorie and George Curley. This was at a very exploratory stage, but we agreed to meet again, and did so in Toronto, later in the fall.

When Rhys suggested a further meeting in Toronto, on January 18, 1989, I agreed. I took it seriously enough to say that I would bring along my bankers, First Boston, just in case anything transpired. J. R. Ryan, Vice-President of Corporate Finance, and W. C. Sharpstone, Vice-President, Mergers and Acquisitions, came up from New York.

The results of that meeting are given in Chapter One. With everything that had happened, all the good times and the bad, I nonetheless came away with an underlying certainty that I was doing the right thing in selling. So, Wardair was sold, for $17.25 a share, a total of just under $250 million. The offer was conditional on the financial statements being as I had given them, which they were, and the deal would close on April 14.

Of course, it was not as simple as that; the regulators were not through with us. The deal had to be approved by the Bureau of Competition Policy in Ottawa, as well as by the National Transportation Agency, the new and slimmer version of the CTC. The NTA gave its approval very quickly, but the Bureau of Competition waited until a week before the offer was to be closed and then directed me to seek other buyers. This led to a certain amount of excitement in the press and to speculation that American buyers, led by American Airlines, might step in, all of which was complete nonsense. American had no intention whatever of buying into our company, and the press created a situation that was stupid. No offers were received, and the agreement went ahead. It was bizarre that a government that had fought for so many years to put us out of business was now fighting hard to keep us there!

By May 2, it was all done. I was Honorary Chairman of Wardair, with George Curley as Chairman and Kevin J. Jenkins as President and Chief Operating Officer. I was also given a seat on the CAIL board. Rhys had committed to the continuance of the Wardair name and the operation of the company as a separate entity under the PWA wing. I hoped that was possible, but two overheads don't make sense, and, in the end, Wardair disappeared entirely.

As it turned out, CAIL did not take up the option on the twenty-four Fokker 100s, because they have a fleet of 737s of their own for short-haul, but the options on the other planes we had committed to were quickly resold for a clear profit of more than $30 million U.S., which eased the pain of losses that continued after the takeover. For its money, CAIL not only rid itself of a competitor, but gained access to the international routes we had built. We carried about one third of all the Canadian passengers to Britain every year, a market we had served for twenty-six years, and we had rights in two French cities – Paris and one more to be decided – where CAIL did not. Finally, our fleet of eighteen up-to-the-minute jets represented the youngest fleet in the Canadian industry, and CAIL was transformed into an equal of Air Canada, with almost as many planes (101 compared to 111), slightly lower revenue ($2.2 billion for the first nine months of 1988, compared to Air Canada's $2.6 billion), higher passenger-miles (13.1 million to 12.3 million for the same period), and higher productivity (18,000 employees to 22,000).

We tried to keep as many of our people in their places as possible, but it was inevitable that the amalgamation would cost jobs, and it did, to my sorrow. It made perfect sense to collapse our reservations system, for example, and expand CAIL's, but many of Wardair's people lost out. One of our greatest assets lay in the remarkable abilities of our employees – engineers, ramp and baggage people, catering and marketing staff, reservationists, accountants, air operations, security personnel, office staff, telephone operators, management, people in the complaints department, cabin crews, pilots, cleaning staff, record-keepers – the list is endless. It took team work from every corner of the company to make it all go. Wardair people developed a great pride in, and enthusiasm for, their airline. They made themselves the best, and in so doing, they made Wardair what it became. It is sad that many of these dedicated, experienced people have been lost to the industry as fewer and fewer airlines survive.

So, the Wardair saga was finished. Being on the CAIL board has kept me in the aviation picture, yet I finally have time to do all the things I have wanted to do for so many years. I have a wonderful workshop in Edmonton, where I pre-fabricate structures and other oddments for our wilderness camp on the Coppermine River, my favourite spot. I've gone full circle from my bush-flying days – from the bush back to the bush – by thumping around the Arctic in my Twin Otter. But I will not pretend it is the same as running a world-class airline.

I have had a lot of time, in recent months, to think about what happened to me and my airline, and not all my thoughts are pleasant ones. It is clear that what defeated me, in the long run, was the persistent obstructiveness of the air-transport authorities from the day I opened the door for business in 1946. The obstructionism Wardair faced was applied – as I think I have shown in these pages – crudely, unfairly, belligerently, and sometimes, I suspect, with malice aforethought.

At the time of selling, I realized, however unwillingly, that the Canadian market was not large enough for three carriers, and I suspected that it was not large enough for two. But little did I think that the globalization of the airline industry and the probability of an "open skies" policy could mean that the market might not sustain even one Canadian carrier.

The question I am asked most frequently is: "Why did you want to get out of the charter business?" Well, take a look at what has happened in the charter market today. They are all in trouble. Even the scheduled carriers are in trouble.

When Wardair bought its first Boeing 747 in 1973, it cost $24 million U.S. Our second Boeing 747, one and a half years later, cost $45 million U.S. Today (1991) a Boeing 747-400 costs in the vicinity of $130 million U.S. ($152 million Canadian), plus another $20 million for spares.

The costs, which are more than five times as great in 1991 as they were seventeen years ago, have far outdistanced the yields. Inflation has escalated the costs of labour and equipment to a point where the economics don't, and haven't, worked.

It is just not possible to operate today's modern airplane on charter revenue per passenger-mile yields. We couldn't have done it years ago but for our ability to buy and sell airplanes.

Air transportation is, of necessity, pricing itself out of the mass market, even while the world is relying more and more on air travel.

I wonder where the airline industry in Canada would be today had it been left to its own devices on a free-enterprise basis. I cannot help but believe that it would have been much more capable of facing today's global challenges.

Government doesn't create anything, and if we are to compete in the world market, the entrepreneur must be permitted to build commerce unhampered, in order for this country to survive as an independent nation. Deregulation, free trade, and other swiftly moving events are forcing us to become competitive in the international community, and unless we move to meet the challenges they bring us, we will face a bleak future indeed.

On the heels of half a century of total protection, how can an organization such as Air Canada, completely devoid of the free-enterprise philosophy, possibly think of the competitive environment inherent in today's and tomorrow's air-transportation industry?

It is interesting and unfortunate that even today, as I write this in the spring of 1991, the Bay Street boys and the press chew up free-enterprise CAIL, while supporting what was the former national airline. I guess after fifty-odd years of brainwashing, that is to be expected.

After all my pain and agony, and the dedication of hundreds of civil servants to the pursuit of a government air-transport policy, it is not gratifying to be confirmed in my belief that their policy was wrong from the outset, and may now lead to the destruction of what they strove to protect.

CHRONOLOGY

November 22, 1921	Maxwell William Ward born in Edmonton.
November 2, 1941	I get my wings.
June 28, 1944	Marjorie and I are married.
June 1945	I leave the air force.
April 15, 1946	Birth of Gai, our first daughter.
Late April 1946	I join Jack Moar, flying out of Yellowknife.
June 1946	Polaris Charter Company Limited, my first company, formed in Alberta.
July 1946	I buy my first aircraft, a Fox Moth, and fly it back to Yellowknife, with a crash on the way.
September 1946	Polaris and I begin flying in Yellowknife.
October 1946	Stranded at Spud Arsenault Lake.
Late May 1947	I am told I must have a licence to charter.
June 1947	Polaris Charter folds. I join George Pigeon in Yellowknife Airways.
August 8, 1947	Marjorie and Gai join me in Yellowknife.
June 2, 1948	Our second daughter, Blythe, born.
September 1948	Our Yellowknife house burns down.
January 22, 1949	Grant Ford crashes the Fox Moth.

June 1949	I join Associated Airways.
October 1949	We move to Lethbridge, and I go into house-building.
May 1951	I go back to Yellowknife, for Associated Airways.
November 22, 1951	The flight to Bathurst Inlet.
November 27, 1951	Rescue.
May 1952	I am fired from Associated Airways.
July 1952	I apply to Air Transport Board for a charter licence.
May 1953	I get unofficial word that the ATB finally approves Class 4B charter licence.
June 1, 1953	I pick up my first Otter at de Havilland.
June 3, 1953	Official approval of my licence, under Wardair name.
June 6, 1953	I arrive back in Yellowknife with the Otter.
July 22, 1953	Wardair Limited officially incorporated.
September 21, 1953	Kim Maxwell Ward, our first son, born.
March 1954	The "Starving Eskimo Dog" Saga.
June 5, 1954	I buy my first de Havilland Beaver.
August 1954	The Dove Saga. The Adventure of the Flying Muskoxen.
June 11, 1955	I buy a second single-engine Otter.
July 1955	The Gold Brick Affair.
November 1955	Crash with the Beaver.
December 17, 1955	We buy a new Beaver.
February 10, 1956	We buy another Otter.
June 3, 1956	Our second son, Blake William Ward, is born.

June 1956	Begin applications for Bristol Freighter.
April 1, 1957	ATB finally approves licence for Bristol Freighter.
April 1957	I take delivery of the Bristol Freighter.
June 1958	We buy another Otter.
February 16, 1961	ATB turns down our application for a charter licence out of Edmonton.
May 1961	ATB grants licence to fly charters, but grants it to us in Yellowknife, population 4,000.
June 22, 1961	Company name officially changed to Wardair Canada Ltd.
January 1962	Douglas DC-6A leased from CP Air.
March 16, 1962	First Arctic charter for DC-6.
May 10, 1962	Our first charter passenger flight in the South, taking Alberta School Patrol Band from Calgary to Ottawa and back.
June 1962	Our licence is suspended by ATB because of a misunderstanding about flying passengers free. Licence restored a week later as ATB accepts explanation.
June 22, 1962	Our first overseas charter, Edmonton to Copenhagen.
December 1962	I return the DC-6 to CP Air: loss, $350,000.
March 1963	We buy a DC-6B from KLM in Amsterdam.
May 23, 1963	We apply to serve Pine Point from Yellowknife. Refused.
January 1964	We fly the magnetic survey for the

	Dominion Observatory, charting 2.5 million square miles of the Arctic.
February 1964	We begin charters to Hawaii.
April 28, 1966	We take delivery of our first jet, a 727, christened the *Cy Becker*.
February 9, 1967	Legislation to establish Canadian Transport Commission passed.
April 21, 1967	We buy our first Twin Otter.
1967	We buy four more Bristol Freighters for the Northern operation.
May 5, 1967	Don Braun lands the Bristol Freighter at the geographic North Pole, first wheel-equipped aircraft there.
September 18, 1967	Wardair goes public, and Jack Pickersgill takes over Canadian Transport Commission.
October 1967	Split charters and inclusive-tour flights approved.
December 1967	U.S. Civil Aeronautics Board gives us a permit to fly inclusive tours in the United States; our winter package program to Hawaii, the Bahamas, and the Caribbean begins.
March 4, 1968	ATB order suspends Wardair for nineteen days, threatens to close airline down permanently.
March 25, 1968	ATB lays new regulations about verifying that all charter passengers on Wardair have been bona fide members of clubs for six months,

	but regulations do not apply to scheduled airlines.
May 10, 1968	We buy another, and larger, jet, a Boeing 707, christened the *C. H. "Punch" Dickins*.
May 11, 1968	ATB abruptly cancels flight scheduled for May 15 to Holland.
May 1968	Wardair expelled from Air Transport Association of Canada.
June 8, 1968	My balloon ride and Gai's wedding.
March 14, 1969	Second Boeing 707 delivery, the *W. R. "Wop" May*.
May 30, 1969	Another Twin Otter for Northern operations.
June 13, 1969	Third Twin Otter.
October 20, 1969	Affinity charter rules no longer apply to Air Canada. They do to us, though.
November 7, 1970	Wardair 727 establishes a record, flying 3,930 statute miles from Windsor, Ontario, to Gatwick.
January 5, 1971	We are ordered to cease booking charters, except to the U.S., as of February 15, because the CTC says, wrongly, that we are in violation of Trust Account rules.
January 12, 1971	Leaked story suggests – wrongly – that CTC inspectors caught us violating Trust Account rules six months earlier.
January 28, 1971	Air Transport Committee member of the CTC says he is "too busy" to receive proof that Wardair will not strand passengers overseas.

January 29, 1971	We get a meeting with the CTC, which accepts our proof of insurance and calls off suspension.
February 9, 1971	Supreme Court denies us permission to take CTC to court.
May 31, 1971	Bristol Freighter lost at Snowdrift.
September 1971	I get the Billy Mitchell Award.
January 18, 1972	A fourth Twin Otter.
September 8, 1972	Air Canada deal announced; it never comes off.
October 7, 1972	Wardair 707 makes first non-stop flight from Honolulu to London, 7,776 statute miles, a range record for the 707.
November 21, 1972	Intervac and Canada–U.K. Travel Centre incorporated.
January 1, 1973	Affinity charters finally abolished.
February 1973	Two more Twin Otters.
March 31, 1973	I am made a Companion in the Order of Icarus.
April 23, 1973	We get our first Boeing 747 Jumbo Jet, the *Phil Garratt*.
May 15, 1973	I am awarded the McKee Trophy.
July 13, 1973	ATC orders us to stop giving customers a bonus on package tours.
October 9, 1973	ATC threatens cancellation of flights because Elkin Tours, which we don't own or control, has put out brochures the committee doesn't approve of.
May 28, 1974	I am given Transportation Man of the Year Award for Alberta.
July 16, 1974	My induction into Aviation Hall of Fame.

October 31, 1974	Wardair ordered to make Skylark Holidays, which we don't own or control, stop advertising a free flight for "group leaders" on their tours.
December 12, 1974	Second 747 delivered, the *Romeo Vachon*.
July 1, 1975	I am appointed an Officer of the Order of Canada.
October 28, 1975	Official opening of Yellowknife hangar.
June 10, 1976	Company changed from Wardair Canada Ltd. to Wardair International Ltd.
November 20, 1977	David Dalling killed in Bristol Freighter crash at Hay River.
January 1, 1978	Deregulation comes into effect in U.S.
April 28, 1978	Wardair flight from Gatwick to Honolulu, longest westbound flight of a 747 on record.
May 23, 1978	We buy the first Dash 7 sold in Canada, christened the *Don Braun*.
June 9, 1978	A third 747, the *Herbert Hollick-Kenyon*.
August 4, 1978	I write Prime Minister Pierre Trudeau, in desperation. No response.
September 5, 1978	Transport Minister Otto Lang announces changes will be made to ease regulations. But nothing changes.
November 5, 1978	Our first Douglas DC-10.
December 15, 1978	Second Douglas DC-10.
December 19, 1978	Otto Lang replies to my letter to Trudeau.

April 26, 1979	Another 747.
May 16, 1979	ATC announces it will "consider" changes announced by Otto Lang the previous September.
May 22, 1979	Minority Progressive Conservative government, under Prime Minister Joe Clark.
May 29, 1979	Chicago crash of DC-10 leads to suspension of all DC-10 flights.
June 5, 1979	Second Dash 7 delivered.
June 30, 1979	DC-10 flights restored.
September 14, 1979	I am named 1979 recipient of the Gordon R. McGregor Memorial Trophy.
October 18, 1979	We close the northern operations.
November 1979	Refugee flights from the Far East begin.
November 3, 1979	ATC finally announces changes to Air Carrier Regulations, ignoring reform proposals.
November 5, 1979	Don Mazankowski, now Transport Minister, directs the CTC to solve cargo question, "without undue delay." Nothing happens.
December 5, 1979	CTC announces proposed changes in air regulations, with no reference to Don Mazankowski's order.
December 13, 1979	Tories lose House vote, election called.
December 21, 1979	CTC publishes final regulatory changes, ignoring Mazankowski's direction.
January 4, 1980	I write Mazankowski, warning that Wardair could fail.

February 1, 1980	Cabinet considers changes in regulations, but no decision taken.
February 4, 1980	Draft proposal from bureaucrats to Prime Minister effectively reverses policy changes.
February 5, 1980	Mazankowski finds out about draft proposal, demands restoration of original changes.
February 8, 1980	Cabinet meets, accepts Mazankowski's view, passes order-in-council to provide greater flexibility in charter regulations. Wardair gets domestic charter air services.
February 13, 1980	New regulations made public.
February 18, 1980	Liberals win election.
March 10, 1980	Wardair named Airline of the Year.
May 8, 1980	First domestic Advanced Booking Charter, Toronto to Vancouver.
November 9, 1980	New hangar completed.
March 25, 1981	Purchase of six A-310 Airbuses announced, with option for six more. We were unable to complete this deal when the 1982 recession hit.
April 23, 1981	Two Singapore Airlines' DC-10s purchased.
March 1, 1982	Workshop and support buildings completed.
May 1982	Office building completed.
May 10, 1984	New Canadian Air Policy announced by Lloyd Axworthy, with much greater liberalization of operating rights.

June 29, 1984	Wardair gets first scheduled operating authority, between Montreal/Toronto and San Juan, Puerto Rico.
September 4, 1984	Brian Mulroney's Conservatives win.
October 29, 1984	Canadian Transport Commission eases ABC regulations.
February 20, 1985	I become Chairman of Wardair, George Curley is President.
March 1985	Wardair named world's top chartered airline by *Holiday Which?* magazine.
May 10, 1985	Wardair gets international scheduled routes between Canada and the United Kingdom.
July 15, 1985	*Freedom to Move* paper, proposing airline deregulation, released by Don Mazankowski, now back as Transport Minister.
March 20, 1986	We get a licence to conduct a scheduled service within Canada.
March 1986	*Holiday Which?* magazine awards Wardair Golden Wings, as the world's finest scheduled carrier.
May 4, 1986	First Wardair scheduled service in Canada, begins with Toronto/Vancouver, Calgary, and Edmonton.
May 20, 1986	I am named "Marketing Statesman of the Year."
August 1986	Three Airbus A-300s obtained from South African Airways.
January 15, 1987	We announce purchase of 12 Airbuses, for $650 million U.S.

March 1987	*Holiday Which?* magazine awards Wardair Golden Wings as world's finest airline, again.
August 7, 1987	Deregulation legislation finally passes Senate.
November 26, 1987	National Transportation Agency replaces CTC.
April 12, 1988	We sign deal to purchase sixteen McDonnell – Douglas MD-88s, for $300 million.
May 17, 1988	We get schedule rights to France.
October 1988	First discussions with Rhys Eyton.
January 18, 1989	PWA offer of $17.25 a share for Wardair accepted.
January 19, 1989	Wardair sale proposal announced.
February 2, 1989	Competition Bureau tells us to seek other buyers.
March 1, 1989	Official offer to purchase made by PWA.
March 22, 1989	National Transportation Agency approves sale.
March 23, 1989	Competition Bureau again insists we seek another buyer.
May 2, 1989	Deal closes, Wardair is sold.

INDEX

DESTINATIONS

HAWAII

Reproduced with permission from
MapArt, 60 Advance Road,
Etobicoke, Ontario.
(416) 233 5033